Can My Petunia Be Saved?

Published by Cool Springs Press
101 Forrest Crossing Boulevard
Suite 100
Franklin, Tennessee 37064

Cataloging in Publication Data is available.
ISBN 1-59186-292-2

First Printing 2007
Printed in the United States of America
10 9 8 7 6 5 4 3 2 1

Managing Editor: Cindy Kershner
Cover and Book Design: Bill Kersey, Kersey Graphics
Illustrations: Bill Kersey, Kersey Graphics
Horticultural Editor: Troy Marden
Copyeditor: Michelle Adkerson
Proofreader: Sally Graham
Production Design: S.E. Anderson

Can My Petunia Be Saved?

Practical Prescriptions for a Healthy, Happy Garden

Tamson Yeh, Ph.D.

COOL SPRINGS PRESS

Acknowledgements

Thanks and Appreciation
The author would like to offer her profound thanks to Hank McBride for being kind enough to think of me for this project and to Cindy Kershner for being so easy to work with. I would like to also express my appreciation to Kathie Wegman, Mike DiRusso, and Marie Camenares for their help and encouragement, and a special thanks to Rosa and Philip Yeh, offspring extraordinaire!

Photography Credits
176B, 177B—Kathie Wegman
124—Marie Camenares
All other photographs—Tamson Yeh

Bibliography
Color Atlas of Pests of Ornamental Trees, Shrubs, and Flowers by David V. Alford

Cornell Guide for Planting and Maintaining Trees and Shrubs by George L. Good and Richard Weir

Cultural Practice Problems of Trees and Shrubs in the Landscape and Nursery by Robert D. Childs, Deborah C. Swanson, and Ronald F. Kujawski

Diseases of Annuals and Perennials: Identification and Control by A.R. Chase, Margery Daughtrey, and Gary W. Simone

Diseases of Trees and Shrubs by Wayne A. Sinclair, Howard H. Lyon, and Warren T. Johnson

Garden Insects of North America by Whitney Cranshaw

How to Recognize Hazardous Defects in Trees USDA Pamphlet NA-FR-01-96

Insects That Feed on Trees and Shrubs by Warren T. Johnson and Howard H. Lyon

Liveable Landscape Design by John Collins and Marvin I. Adleman

Pruning: An Illustrated Guide to Pruning Ornamental Trees and Shrubs by Donald A.Rakow and Richard Weir

Soil Biology Primer published by the Soil and Water Conservation Society (www.swcs.org)

Turfgrass Problems: Picture Clues and Management Options by Eva Gussack and Frank S. Rossi*Urban Soils: Applications and Practices* by Philip J. Craul

Weeds of the Northeast by Richard H. Uva, Joseph C. Neal, and Joseph M. Ditomaso

Contents

Saving Your Petunia Without Blowing Your Budget

Introduction

This might surprise you, but **the most common garden pest could be Panic.** Instead of thinking through why the problems are there, many people just react and do what they think will help. The result is a "solution" that costs time and money but doesn't help the plants.

The antidote to Panic is wheelbarrows full of information—and that's just what this book offers: Advice on how to make your landscape look its best without a bunch of useless products and information jumping in the way of getting the job done!

I want to give you control over the problems found in your landscape so it will give you the most pleasure. Problems are usually not from one isolated cause; they are usually from multiple sources. All too often, we tend to spray first and ask questions later, so the underlying cause is not discovered. Significant contributions you can easily make for the health of your plants—planting the right plant in the right place and giving it the correct amount of fertilizer and water—are overlooked due to the pressure to treat your landscape quickly.

How to Use This Book

You can journey through this text in the same way that you stroll through your garden, stopping as you wish to examine your handiwork. The first stop is to learn how to assess your site for potential problems; another is for those vital cultural controls, such as how much and how often to water; and a third offers information on the proper planting techniques that help ensure the health of your plants. Visit the chapters that describe many of the common diseases and insects to learn which ones are actually beneficial. Then meander along further to examine the habits of a few pesky vertebrates and invertebrates in the garden; investigate the most common problems of some very popular plants; and make a sojourn into the wonderful world of evergreens and the not-so-wonderful world of their problems. At the end of the book, you should be able to stroll through your garden and view it while clutching only your sweetheart—and not your chest!

I also hope you smile a bit, and maybe even chuckle, as you travel through this book to learn more about caring for your property—little is accomplished without a sense of humor. **And do keep in mind that the best tools for any job are restraint and common sense!**

If you journey with me on this virtual trip through your landscape, you may never have to act as your own SWAT team again. So put on your garden clogs, grab your ailing petunia, and let's tour your property before those pests get comfy.

Pulling the Wool Off Your Eyes

The Site Assessment

So you've had one too many snide comments from Ms. Uppity-Perkity next door about the sad, sad condition of your yard. Meanwhile she's prancing around clipping posies for her bridge club meeting and pausing for photographs in front of her prize-winning peonies. Your blood is boiling, and so is that limp scrap of would-be lawn in front of the dingy twin junipers guarding your front door. You've had it, haven't you?

Throwing caution and back problems to the wind, you go to the local nursery, buy one of every plant and shrub, order a load of mulch, a pallet of stone, six dozen pansies, four rose bushes, a pond kit, a do-it-yourself sprinkler system, and a bird house. Because you are now a loyal customer, you get a free petunia.

Where to Start

But where you really need to start is with a **physical**! (Not for you—although if you haven't been to the doctor for a while and plan to do strenuous garden projects, that might be a good idea.) **Your yard needs the physical, better known as the site assessment.**

What are your yard's strengths and weaknesses? Will the plants you want be healthy and strong under those conditions? Without a solid foundation (soil and roots) for your plants, the whole structure (the plant) will fall.

Of course, your site assessment may cause a little pinch near your wallet, especially if you realize that every single thing you purchased and planted (even the free petunia) is located in the wrong place, planted incorrectly, or just plain incompatible with your site.

Climate or Hardiness Zones

So first, figure out where you are: What is your climate zone? You'll find several climate zone or cold hardiness zone maps to choose from, each of which differs slightly from the other. Some of the zones are even split into "a" and "b" parts. But let's use the simplest format, which splits the country into eleven zones. Regionally, we are most interested in zones 3 to 8, which encompass most of our gardening needs.

The Climate Zones

The climate zones are based on the worst-case scenario for winter temperatures; in other words, the coldest it is likely to be in that zone. While zone maps don't take into account that your plant may be heat sensitive, drought sensitive, or light sensitive, they are a great place to start.

Zone 3: -40 to -30 degrees F.

Zone 4: -30 to -20 degrees F.

Zone 5: -20 to -10 degrees F.

Zone 6: -10 to 0 degrees F.

Zone 7: 0 to 10 degrees F.

Zone 8: 10 to 20 degrees F.

Microclimates

Once you know your hardiness zone, assess your yard for microclimates. **A microclimate is a small space in your landscape where temperature, light, wind, soil type, drainage, soil acidity, or a number of other factors differ significantly from the rest of your landscape.** A microclimate usually occurs because of a change in the physical structure of the site (a hill, a dip, a boulder) or due to a large man-made structure like a fence, hedge, or building.

Once you know what to look for, you can make good use of your microclimates—although those benefits often have a catch. For example, soil that is higher than the surrounding ground (in raised beds or on a slope) and faces the sun warms more quickly in the spring, but that soil is also likely to be drier and hotter earlier in the year. The same benefit results from a south-facing wall, which has an added bonus: The large structure absorbs the heat and reradiates it around your tender purchases, keeping them toasty for improved flowering, fruiting, and survival. (No wall? Stick your chilly divas next to a warm foundation wall or in a sunny corner where warmth will reradiate from the foundation of your house.)

A microclimate is like those friends or neighbors you don't quite trust. Whenever they show up, you know they want something from you. So while the existence of a microclimate opens up wonderful possibilities, the end is usually the same. You can sometimes take advantage of a microclimate to nurse along for several seasons those plants that are only marginally hardy or not hardy for your climate, but finally Old Man Winter will get good and cranky. Then those Popsicle sticks that marked the plants should be put to better use.

Microclimates and Wind

As you assess your yard for microclimates, look for signs of excessive wind, which in winter can fry your evergreens to a crisp and toasty ever*brown*— and cost you money. (See Chapter 9 for more on evergreens.) Evergreens lose water all winter long through leaves and needles that stay attached to the tree or shrub. When wind blows across them, the water evaporates more quickly and the roots can't pull water from frozen soil to replace what is lost; this results in desiccation (drying) and "burn."

Signs of extreme windiness at a site include trees and shrubs all leaning in one direction, stunted growth on the side of the plants facing the prevailing wind, and perhaps even some twisting. Think "bonsai" shapes, which are often clipped to approximate the form of a wind-tortured tree. If you want to reduce wind burn during winter, you can erect a burlap windbreak by driving in two stakes and stapling a piece of burlap to them as a screen for your plant. Windbreaks may be unsightly, but for the most part, they work.

Microclimates and Soil Moisture

Excessive overhangs from your roof can create a "rain shadow" that excludes valuable moisture from foundation plants. If the sun hits these water-deprived plants for a good portion of the day, this can make the problem even worse and lead to mite and lace bug populations, which thrive in hot, dry conditions. The same rain shadow effect can occur under the bonnet of a large, densely leaved tree. While moisture will take longer to evaporate from soil in the shade of such a plant, rainfall will be shed from the top of the plant and slide to the ground along the perimeter of the tips of the branches (the "drip line"). Anything planted under the drip line will have a hard time getting enough water.

Sun and Shade

How do you rate the amount of sun your plants get? It's simple: **Full sun means six or more hours of direct sunlight.** (That's right—the fifteen minutes your plant gets at 4:45 in the afternoon isn't enough!)

Keep in mind that sun and shade patterns change during the winter because of the angle of the sun and the lack of foliage. So think "big picture" when you plant in the winter and early spring. Rather than live with a constant cycle of

The Different Levels of Shade

* **Light shade** is an area that is in shade no more than four hours per day. A high thin canopy of leaves can create this effect.
* **Medium shade** is an area in shade for four to six hours per day. (You'll get more flowers on *Rhododendron* and azaleas planted with this amount of light, and growth will be more compact.)
* **Full shade** is an area shaded all day. Any area that faces north, like my backyard, will be in constant shade. Again, *Rhododendron* and *Hydrangea* will do well in this setting because there is still some indirect light.
* **Dense shade** is found under evergreens, under porches and decks, and in other dark corners where mosquitoes love to rest. It's especially difficult to plant in the dense shade under trees with shallow root systems.
* **Dappled shade** pertains to areas where the canopy is thin enough so patches of sunlight can find their way in. Ferns particularly like dappled shade, so get out houseplant ferns or create the ideal woodland garden.

spindly plants and poor performance followed by death and replacement (isn't that a novel by Leo Tolstoy?), you need to prune, get out, or give up. I suggest the last—give up planting the sun lovers in favor of those plants that absolutely thrive in shade. They are beautiful, they make good designs, and they are useful: You just have to accept that they won't be the plants every Tom, Dick, and Harriet down the street owns.

How's Your Drainage?

No one wants to acknowledge they have drainage problems. It's whispered about at family gatherings, hinted at before marriage, and remains a point of contention at readings of wills, where there's plenty of digging going on

Assessing Drainage

As you dig, judge your drainage by these indications:

❊ **Good drainage** may have a high proportion of sand or gravel. This soil will not have distinct layers but will show a gradual color change from dark to light at a 3-foot depth. You should see no free water during excavation.

❊ **Bad drainage** is revealed through abrupt color changes in soil. Mottling within 3 feet of the surface indicates a restrictive soil layer that inhibits the downward movement of water. The soil will look densely packed. If you bore a hole under 3 feet deep during the wet season and free water accumulates, you have bad drainage. Without supplementary drainage, deep-rooted ornamentals will grow but not thrive in these soils. Shallow-rooted ornamentals and turf generally do fine without extra drainage.

❊ **Really bad drainage** often stinks like an overflowing septic system. Dark surface soil that, 6 to 8 inches down, abruptly changes to light gray or brown mottling indicates long-term saturation at or near the surface. Usually you see this in natural depressions or in flat areas or areas with seepage or runoff from higher elevations. A great clue to bad drainage is the presence of large populations of sedges, willows, alders, and red maples. If you dig a test hole in one of these areas during the wet season, the hole rapidly fills with water and may not dry until late summer. The good news? This is where you should install your pond or wildlife marsh.

anyway. If you suspect you've got bad drainage, you need to be absolutely sure before you plant. Some plants can handle worse drainage than others, but planting elsewhere may be the better solution.

Late fall through early spring is the best time to assess drainage. You will see the worst drainage and erosion problems from November to April, so select a planting site and water control system based on this wet season. Dig a 2-foot-deep hole where you plan to put that prize tree, fill it with water, and then when the water drains away, fill it again. Come back forty-eight hours later. If there is still water in the hole, you have a drainage problem and you need to find out how far the problem extends. If it's only in one small area, drain tiles or a soil auger and some organic matter might help. But if the problem is widespread, use raised beds or plant somewhere else.

Another problem that can impact your drainage is bedrock close to the surface. Bedrock below 8 to 10 feet generally causes no problems, but bedrock at less than 18 inches is likely to cause the soil profile to dry out rapidly, making it hard to maintain turf and other ornamentals. Look at the cuts in nearby roads to show you the local depth of bedrock.

Compaction

Do you suffer from the heartbreak of . . . compaction? There's an easy way to find out. At random points during your site inspection, try shoving a large screwdriver into the soil. Do this on an average day, not just after rain, irrigation, or a prolonged drought. If you cannot penetrate more than a couple of inches, honey, you're compacted! (If you want to bother the neighbor who's always peeking at you, coat the screwdriver with ketchup, don a dollar-store shower cap, and pump the soundtrack from *Psycho* as an accompaniment.)

As with most forms of compaction, the remedy is fiber, in the form of organic matter. **Organic matter is the mesh that keeps the soil pores open so that air and water can be exchanged.** Sure, clay can help your soil hold onto water, and sand drains well, but if you start messing around by adding different soil components (sand, silt, or clay) to your existing soil, you can foul drainage and increase the compaction potential of the soil. The soil components pack around each other, leaving no room for pockets of air and water; traffic only makes this mess compact more solidly.

Don't believe me? Mix sugar, salt, and baby powder (sand, silt, and clay) together in a piece of gauze. Add water. Squeeze thoroughly. The little brick of wanna-be concrete you just made is what happens when you start mixing soil types. As for buying topsoil to take care of your problems, forget it. There is no standard, and what you get for a high price will likely be of little value. So if you have compaction, add organic matter.

Soil Testing

To determine your soil type (and then buy plants that enjoy growing there!), you need to examine your soil a bit further. So carefully extract half a handful of soil from your yard, and put it in the plastic bag in your coat pocket. (Anybody watching? After all that stuff with the screwdriver, and the sugar, salt, and baby powder, you have the neighbors really worried.) Now try these, er, manipulations.

1. Place 2 teaspoons of the soil in your palm and drip water onto it, kneading until it forms a ball.
2. Does the soil remain in a ball when squeezed? If not, you have mostly sand.
3. If a ball forms, squeeze it between your thumb and forefinger into a ribbon of sorts.
   - **Loam** forms a weak ribbon less than 1 inch before breaking. If the ribbon holds together and appears to be "ruffled" or has cracks it, you probably have a **silty loam.**
   - **Clay loam** forms a medium ribbon 1 to 2 inches before breaking.
   - **Clay** forms a strong ribbon 2 inches or longer before breaking, which could explain some of the drainage problems you have been having.

Now wash your hands and make yourself a bracing cup of tea because you are not finished tampering with the evidence yet.

Soil pH

It's time to determine a simple but critical portion of your site assessment: the pH of your soil. **To determine pH, you do not need a Ph.D.** You need a simple chemical test where a small, composite soil sample is split between two shallow wells in a testing plate. A few drops of reagent are added to each side, and the color change that occurs is compared to a color chart, thereby determining the pH. This shouldn't cost an arm and a leg; in fact, the best place to have a pH test run is at your local agricultural extension agency.

Are there other methods? Sure, but consider this: The homeowner-type pH meters that are poked in the ground like a thermometer in a free turkey are not terribly accurate, while the scientific pH meters are prohibitively expensive and more than you need for a home landscape.

People seem terrified of the concept of pH yet so eager to pour lime on their poor plants that you'd think there was a free prize in every bag. Yes, limestone *may* be your answer, but establish your baseline pH before you run off to add lime because you might not even need it, and if you do, you might not be adding the correct amount. Different soil types with the same pH require different amounts of lime to attain the desired correction.

Lime ENV

So what if you *do* need lime? There is a difference in how effective limestone will be at changing your pH. This is another of those easy calculations that can actually save you a lot of money! Basically, a pound of limestone will have varying ability to increase the pH of soil, so look on the label for the Effective Neutralizing Value (ENV).

For example, 100/ENV = the true number of pounds you need to apply for each pound of lime recommended by the soil test. Say lime No. 1 has an effective neutralizing value of 70. 100 divided by 70 = 1.42. For every pound of lime your soil test recommends that you add, you actually have to put down almost a pound and a half! Now lime No. 2 has an effective neutralizing power of 89.7, and 100 divided by 89.7 equals 1.11. Less lime down means less cost! For those of you buying many pounds of lime, that can add up very quickly.

That's right, my dears. The plant isn't the one requiring the lime; it's the soil. Lime is a kind of password to the bank teller of the soil's nutrient account. If the soil is too acid (low pH, not enough lime, sour), then it will not be able to release certain nutrients or there may be too many of some others. If the soil is too basic (high pH, too much lime, sweet), then it will not be able to release some nutrients while others may be too much in evidence.

A lot of our pH problems have to do with natural geology—what rocks underlie our soils, what was hacked up by glaciers, what plants have spent centuries contributing their leaf litter (some are acidic like oaks and evergreens, some basic like maples). In our suburban world, much of the problem comes from concrete, masonry, hardscaping, and other lime-based construction materials that leach into the soil, driving up the pH.

The solution is to **not** plant ornamentals with different pH requirements together in one bed (although this seems to be a universal practice). It's easy to find out the preferred pH of almost any plant and avoid making this kind of mistake.

Keep in mind that using plants suited to the natural pH of your site is far better than trying to amend the soil. Lime takes forever to incorporate itself into the soil. (A better bet is to incorporate it during the renovation or establishment of an entire bed when it can be dug in rather than top-dressed.)

The soil will always revert over time to the pH of the surrounding area. If you are trying to grow "lime-loving" plants that need a high pH, put them in containers where it is easier to control the soil conditions. For those of you in high-pH settings who wish to grow acid-loving plants, create a "peat-bed" where an area is blocked out with peat bricks and the soil within is enriched with peat moss, pine needles, and other acidic media. The peat brick barrier helps to maintain the lower pH over a longer time.

Compost and pH

Adding organic matter in the form of compost to improve soil is a recommendation we often hear. But compost with a high pH can negatively affect your soil. Compost that has not completely finished breaking down can also adversely affect your pH. If you are container gardening, you may need to add phosphorous since highly organic soil can't hold on to this element as well as other kinds of soil. You can get a tremendous decrease in a container planting's pH level over a two-year period. This phenomenon happens in heavy compost, as well. The pH of soil very high in organic matter should be 1 pH unit less than a "regular" soil. To balance all these variables, you have to know your pH before you begin to garden!

Once you know your specific pH, you need to be able to recognize true deficiencies versus conditions that mimic deficiencies or deficiencies that are due to root impairment (such as rot, you excess-water hound!).

Considerable organic matter or clay in your soil means any changes you try to introduce to the pH of your soil will occur much more slowly. It takes two to three times more lime to change a fine-textured soil than a sandy one. In fact, lime may move down only as little as 1 inch per year! That means it could take five years to get a pH change from 6.5 to 5.5. And it's much more difficult to correct a high soil pH than a low one.

The Root of the Problem

While you are probing around (and avoiding Fifi the poodle's calling cards), take note of excessive surface rooting, which indicates poor soil conditions, terrible compaction, or bedrock close to the surface. Also look for visible roots that seem to curl around the trunk. Far from caressing the trunk with a motherly touch, it's more like the kind of grip you'd like to put on your spouse when you find out he or she has weedwhacked the flower bed. In other words, a girdling root is just that: It is throttling your tree.

Girdling roots often arise due to excess soil being piled over the tree's root system or because the tree that was planted had been kept in a pot so long that circling roots had developed but weren't cut and removed before planting.

If you want to know about rotting roots, here's a weird, strange root ritual called "the panty hose test." In fact, if you have a plant in trouble, one of the things you check first is the status of the roots; the panty hose test is how you figure that out. Dig up a few roots and try slipping back the outer covering from the center of the root like pushing a pair of pantyhose down your leg. If you can do this easily, you have root rot and that plant is a goner.

Smile for the cameras, the neighbors have finally called the police.

The Silly Things People Do That Kill Their Plants

Because I like you, I'm going to share a couple of hints that could save you a lot of grief in the long run. We inflict on ourselves a number of plant problems. If you can avoid them, your plants will thank you! (And so will your pocketbook.)

Too Much Soil Over Roots

Here's a problem that "builds up" quite often. You see that tree with the 2-foot-high flower bed around it right up to the trunk? Well, you are going to have to choose the tree or the flower bed around it because all that soil piled over the roots is going to kill that tree. Don't believe me? Focus your attention on that branch up there, the one with premature fall coloration, which indicates that the tree is already in decline. Don't stand under it, okay?

Construction Damage

When you dig down next to the tree with the retaining wall around it (looks more like a straitjacket than a retaining wall to me), you'll see that the color of the soil is a lot lighter on top. That means someone either spread subsoil (inferior for plant growth) that was left over and then threw turf seed or sod over it, or they bought topsoil that was actually subsoil.

If you can't get the screwdriver in more than a couple of inches, your soil profile is completely light colored, and the turf is thin and pops right off the top like a bad toupee, yep, the construction vehicles drove across repeatedly after they scraped off all the topsoil.

So let's have a look at that tree in the straitjacket and others around the construction access. **Leaf color is always a valuable indicator of tree stress.**

Soil layering can contribute to plant failure.

Just like the doctor uses the color of your fingernails to ascertain certain conditions, a light green in the leaf tissue with dark green veins can indicate an iron or magnesium deficiency, which is often a pH issue.

Remember, too, that insects and disease are often the last straw, moving in after other predisposing factors stress the tree to the point where it begins to put out panic chemicals, which unfortunately attract insects, or after it develops cracks or other breaches that are good homes for fungi.

So make sure you exercise sensible precautions, and remember that construction may have been as massive as building an addition to a house or as minor as dragging a heavy pergola by truck across a backyard to its final destination. For soil, it doesn't matter whether the construction was done many years ago or yesterday. In fact, it can take up to five years for a severely compacted site to begin to die off; by that time, the contractor is far, far away.

Stockpiling topsoil during construction will not be the complete solution since compaction of the subsoil can also affect plantings. Consult a landscape architect or an arborist before construction begins, since it may be necessary to actually move valuable specimens elsewhere. And bear in mind that about 75 percent of all tree problems are root related. As I have said before, without a decent foundation (soil and roots), the whole structure (the plant) will fall down.

Mowing Damage

You are not finished yet, no matter how much you want to hoist your aching feet onto your patio ottoman. It's time to check trunks for wounds (better known by the medical terms *weedwhackeritis* and *moweropathy*); trunk wounds can girdle a young plant or lead to rot or insect invasion.

Trunk wounds are less likely to occur when the plants have been placed at their proper depth, so check this, especially if you have just purchased your house. Many times the seller will install a large number of plants during the marketing of the property to increase curb appeal. This often consists of substandard plants at incorrect planting depths or improper plant sites. A little attention to detail can save the lives of these mediocrities and can save you the irritation of replacement.

Trees

Trees are the most expensive part of your landscape, so pay attention to them.

Grab a branch, and take a look. At the end of the branch is a terminal bud, which is the growing tip of the tree. That tip should be intact. If you trace backwards with your fingers, you'll find the scar or bud scale scar from last year where this growing tip originated. The vigor of your plant corresponds to the distance between scar and growing tip. A distance of less than 2 inches is considered poor, 2 to 6 inches is moderate growth, and more than 6 inches per year is considered vigorous growth. You can also use this scale to assess a plant before purchase.

For trees, new growth of 12 to 18 inches per year is good, 6 to 8 inches is minimally acceptable, and less than that is cause to get out the hankies and mourning brooches. These standards change for trees that are quite old, when one expects less growth.

If the plant is newly transplanted, expect to see growth reductions for two to three years, with the first years being the worst. During these initial periods of adjustment, expect to see small leaf areas and extremely low annual growth, perhaps 0 to 1 inch, but as long as the plant keeps its leaves, it's likely to survive. A handy rule of thumb is that for each inch of diameter, you should expect to have one year's worth of adjustment after planting. Therefore, planting bigger specimens is not necessarily better—the larger, the longer it takes to adjust!

When a tree sends out suckers, it is probably dying.

Suckering Trees

Now you know and I know all about the process of suckering. That's when the dog sidles up to us during dinner and is a good dog, a suffering dog, a definitely-starving-but-saying-nothing dog. You slip the dog a piece of steak. Clearly there is suckering going on here, but it is not a life-threatening process.

If a plant is suckering, however, it can mean it's dying. Suckering—the process of producing many, small, thin, whiplike shoots from the base of the main trunk—is often a last-ditch effort of the plant to save itself because the main portion is either dead or dying.

A few plants normally produce suckers, but most do not, so look for other stress-producing events impacting the health of the plant. Dieback from stress usually starts at the tips rather than from the inside out. This causes inappropriate suckering because of the removal of apical dominance. That's a fancy way of the plant's saying, "The tip died, for goodness' sake, so get out some more branches and leaves!"

The Plant Died at Noon

Recipes for Cultural Disasters

Have you ever noticed that the word "mental" is in the word "ornamental"? That's the condition most people whip themselves into when they are struggling to understand why a plant is failing in the garden. People are likely to blame diseases and insects for their plant problems, but if the cultural conditions—the nonliving conditions such as the appropriate soil, sun and shade, water, and nutrients—aren't right for that plant, it will keep the plant from thriving, as well as make it easier for those living pests to get going.

When you have a problem with your plants, it is always more likely to be a disease than an insect, but all too often, a cultural problem has led to conditions that allow disease and insects to attack your plant. If you can use the right growing conditions to make your plants comfortable while making the pests uncomfortable, your plants will thank you.

Goldilocks

Remember the story of Goldilocks and the three bears? Everyone is always screaming about Goldilocks being so rude, sampling the food, breaking the chair, sleeping in the bed, yada yada yada.

Well, Goldilocks was framed. The bears left the door open for the pest, they left food and drink on the table for the pest, and they made not one, but two shelters for the pest. Then they went off for a nice little walk in the woods and were not even around to monitor for the pest. When they come back, they act all shocked and offended when they find out that a pest has come to call!

You have every opportunity to avoid being a bear when it comes to cultural factors in the garden. Cultural controls are those things that you do to make the plant as comfortable as possible while at the same time making the situation inhospitable for the pest. But how do you know where to start?

Turn your attention to some of those cultural tasks that can protect your soil without ever touching a crumb of it.

Volcanic mulching can kill plants.

Mulching

Mulching is the number one way to reduce weeds, to protect soil surfaces from compaction and erosion, and to maintain soil temperature and moisture.

Any kind of mulch. But not 3 feet of mulch!

Move over Aetna and Vesuvius. Volcanic mounds of mulch are worse than no mulch at all. Let me describe it to you this way: You're peacefully lying in bed, when your spouse plumps a pillow over your face and holds it there—for the next five years. Why? It looks "cool."

This is the effect that those mulch volcanoes have on roots: no oxygen. No oxygen means dead roots; low oxygen means microbes producing alcohol and toxic microbial byproducts. Toxic microbial byproducts mean more dead roots.

How to Choose Mulch

How do you choose mulch when there is such a bewildering variety of textures, colors, and types to choose from? Consider how long the mulch will last and whether it will add organic matter to the soil, pull nitrogen from the soil as it decomposes, or blow or float away. Be sure it's free of weed seeds and herbicides. Also consider whether it will change the pH over time. Research has shown that a fine mulch need be no deeper than 2 inches and a bulky one 4 inches to eliminate the light that weed seeds need to germinate. More than that and you risk smothering plant feeder roots.

There is a difference between winter mulch and an all-season mulch. Winter mulches are meant to act as an insulating blanket against extremes in soil temperatures and frost heaving during the winter. They are designed to be placed on the plants after the first hard freeze and to be removed as soon as temperatures warm sufficiently to prevent frost damage. Regular mulches keep the ground from warming in the spring, so if you are a first-time mulcher, apply mulch after the soil warms up a bit so that the greatest effect

Compost Compared to Mulch

So what is the difference between compost and mulch? Compost is organic matter rich in humus, formed from decomposed plant remains and other organic matter that is incorporated into soil. Mulch is a material applied in a layer to the soil surface to suppress weeds, conserve moisture, and maintain cool, uniform root temperatures. In fact, mulch may reduce soil surface temperatures by as much as 30 degrees F.

Additionally, mulch reduces erosion, provides insulation, acts as a buffer for a variety of environmental conditions, improves soil structure, and preserves soil texture by preventing crust formation. Mulch slows the flow of rainwater and therefore reduces runoff. Mulch reduces weed removal time by about two-thirds.

comes from insulating plant roots from very hot temperatures in midsummer. If you are using mulch primarily for weed control, apply it before weed seeds germinate in early spring, but remember that it will also slow anything else coming up, as well. Winter mulches should be applied just before frost, or before windy rains, to prevent erosion and frost heaving. Roots continue to grow in the fall until soil water is unavailable due to freezing, so mulch will enhance fall root growth. Nitrifying bacteria are also more active under mulch.

Of course, nothing is perfect. In addition to all the good it does, mulch also makes a great overwintering spot for insects, disease, and rodents. You have to watch water retention characteristics because if the mulch dries up thoroughly, it may become water repellent, especially if the mulch layer is too thick.

Don't spread mulch right up to the house foundation: Leave 6 to 8 inches of bare soil there, or you may find termites, millipedes, ants, earwigs, and other undesirables joining you inside.

Kinds of Mulch

Here are some guidelines to help you choose a mulch:

- Peat moss is good for mulching evergreens or other plants that like acidic soil because it will decrease pH. It can keep the promise of the three basic functions of mulch (reduce weeds, protect soil surfaces from compaction and erosion, and maintain soil temperature and moisture) for a year or two, depending on the depth applied. Pine needles and oak leaves also decrease pH when used as mulch. But if you feel compelled to use peat moss, wet it down first and keep it damp to avoid having the material blow around.
- Hardwood shredded bark mulch is dark and will decompose nicely. Unfortunately, it makes a great home for artillery and other undesirable fungi, but these can be combated simply by raking the mulch lightly once a month.
- Pine or cypress bark mulch decays more slowly than shredded bark, making it the popular choice for areas that need to look picture perfect, like near the front door.
- Straw is a winter mulch or a summer fruit-and-veggie mulch to reduce weeds. Straw is also flammable, as those of you who remember the movie *The Bad Seed* already know.
- Marble chips, maple leaves, and elm leaves will all increase the pH, which makes them fine for plants that love lime.
- Sawdust deters slugs but may cake and create low oxygen situations in the soil beneath. It may also pull nitrogen from the soil as it decomposes.

How Much Mulch?

This formula should help you figure out how much mulch you need:

Area to be mulched (number of square feet) x depth of mulch (number of inches x 0.08) = cubic feet of mulch ÷ 12

For example, you have a bed with an area of 112 square feet. You want a mulch of wood chips 3 inches deep. Multiply the inches by 0.08 (3 x 0.08 = 0.24). Multiply 112 by 0.24; then divide your answer by 12 to get the cubic feet of mulch you need to order. Cubic feet are converted to cubic yards by dividing by 27. Easy as *pi*, tee-hee!

- Never mulch with elm chips because these can spread Dutch elm disease.
- Cocoa hulls have large amounts of potash, which is very bad for young maples, lilacs, tomatoes, and ericaceous plants (such as azalea and *Rhododendron*). Cocoa hulls are also attractive to dogs; unfortunately, the hulls have a higher concentration of the component in chocolate that is poisonous for dogs so it is more toxic than the average box of bon-bons and definitely not good for dogs to eat.
- Hops mulch has too many drawbacks: Hops are stinky, attract pigeons and rodents, and may heat up to the point that they kill young shoots.
- Grass clippings are great for mulch, but you must mow three times after treatment with herbicide before the clippings are safe to use for mulch.

Slimy, Moldy Mulch

Although we spend a great deal of time reaping the benefits of mulch, it can make a stink or make your beds look like the ingredients for witches' stew—slime molds, stinkhorns, and other fungi make October and November mulch rather unpleasant. These nasties aren't harmful to the landscape plantings or to you (unless you eat them!), but they can be distressing.

Another sneaky little visitor is artillery fungus, so called because it discharges its spores with a force that defies the imagination. Dark brown spores sit on top of specialized cup-shaped cells that accumulate an artillery of water and cellular contents. When the pressure has built high enough, the cups invert, causing the spores covered with a very sticky substance to be propelled nearly 20 feet, where they adhere to whatever is in their path.

The spores end up as tiny dark brown spots on houses, cars, and plants. The spots are often mistaken for scales. The fungi most commonly colonize on dung or other organic matter, such as wood mulch, wood benches, or wood sheds.

Artillery fungus shrapnel are apt to appear as yellow-brown or darker disk-shaped spots 0.04 to 0.08 inches in diameter. The fungi are light sensitive and orient toward bright areas. This means that new snow-white paint job on the fence and the cream-colored car are in for it. No structural damage occurs, but the spots are nearly impossible to remove. Cleaning is often more damaging than the spots because tools or soaps damage the surfaces to which the stubborn spores cling.

To reduce the incidence of sneaky, slimy molds, use gravel, stone, pea gravel, and black plastic near buildings instead of wood products. If you are using wood products, adding about an inch of fresh mulch to cover the old each year may also reduce the likelihood of trouble. Use of bark products rather than wood will help to retard fungal spread. Lightly raking mulched areas once each week, especially in spring and fall, will also retard growth.

Sour Mulch

Under certain conditions, mulch such as stockpiled bark, wood chips, and sawdust can produce volatile organic acids. This occurs most often when mulch is piled so high that compaction occurs, with resulting high temperatures. In turn, you lose oxygen, so fermentation and its byproducts result.

A buildup of these fermentation products results in "sour mulch," with pH values dropping to as low as 2.6 in bark piles of 20 feet or more. Chips or bark in piles higher than 10 feet are also prone to this kind of fermentation.

When sour mulch is applied to plants, a rapid response takes place, including wilting and yellowing—it looks almost like a herbicide contamination problem. So, take mulching products only from windrows piled less than 10 feet high (preferably 4 feet high or less to be on the safe side). If you are producing your own mulch, turn the piles frequently to help keep air incorporated.

If the mulch is already sour, correct the problem by spreading it out in a thin layer on a tarp and watering heavily to leach out the problem compounds. You can also add large amounts of limestone to neutralize acidity, thus making the mulch useable again.

If you've already spread the sour mulch, rake it back off the plants and drench the area around the plants with water. The plants usually recover if this is done promptly.

Water and Your Plants

You know how it is when you ask kids if they've washed their hands. They think dog spit is sufficient. Unfortunately, we carry that concept into watering plants. People have very little idea how water actually affects their plants.

Water has to travel through the pores of the soil to reach the roots—all of the roots. But if you keep watering and that water sits around those roots and drives all the oxygen out of the soil pores, the roots will suffocate just like you would under water.

Note: **The symptoms of overwatering and underwatering are almost identical.** The plant wilts because in either case the roots can't perform their function. There's either too little water for them to suck it out of the soil or so much water that the oxygen-deprived root dies and the plant wilts.

An extremely common cause of overwatering is incorrect irrigation zoning. If trees, turf, flowers, and shrubs are on the same system—and they usually are—your shrubs get too much, your flowers get too little, and the trees end up with trunk damage.

Overhead watering is another culprit in leaf spot diseases on shrubs. When that irrigation head splatters the shrub late in the afternoon and water remains on the leaves overnight, a perfect environment exists for leaf spot.

How Much Water?

One of the most confusing things about plant care is water and how much plants really need. Research shows that plants transpire (give off moisture) 1 inch a week when well watered; that means the landscape needs about 16 inches between April and July. This doesn't mean that you need to have rainfall of an inch per week—in fact, that's rare. Instead, plants use water stored in soil pores. Six inches of productive soil stores about 1 inch of water. But not all soil has the same storage capacity, especially not sandy or compacted soil. And even if water is stored, it may not be available to the plant unless there is enough water to overcome the bond of that water to soil particles; only then can the plant roots suck it off.

So the rule of thumb is 1 to 1$\frac{1}{2}$ inch of water applied or received from natural precipitation. **A rain gauge is absolutely essential and dirt-cheap.** Set up at least two on your property—one in the sun and one in the shade. This way you know when to cut back or water more.

That same screwdriver that provided a cheap compaction test in Chapter 1 also offers cheap moisture analysis. Plunge it into the upper 6 inches of the soil, and then pull it back out to check for soil moisture. A barrel that comes out smeared tells you the soil is too wet; if the barrel is powdery or dry, so is the soil. But a barrel that is covered with grainy crumbly soil and feels moist to the touch is just right.

Drought

Given a very droughty summer, watering may need to continue late into the fall. A single heavy rainfall, particularly if it happens quickly, is often insufficient to restore soil moisture or to do any good for plants suffering from drought. A far better solution is to provide slow, deep watering on a consistent basis, since symptoms of drought damage may not be evident for up to two years after the drought event has occurred. Trees and shrubs, like turf, need about 1 inch of water each week to a depth of 12 to 18 inches.

Drought may predispose plantings to attack from diseases or insects that specialize in weakened individuals. Environmental pollutants such as salt and airborne chemicals will also seriously affect drought-stressed plants. Dogwoods, elms, white pines, and hemlocks are some of the trees most seriously affected by drought, and many of these are currently battling other plant demons, as well.

Drought stress may also largely be a function of the right-plant/right-place principle, which is too often ignored in favor of aesthetic sensibilities. Planting practices, improper preparation of rootballs, improper planting depth, or mulch so thick that water cannot penetrate properly all make drought worse for the plant. Even if a selection is touted as drought tolerant, you can't stick it into the ground and go away, or the plant will too.

Also be aware of re-reflected heat and the increased water stress that results. Buildings are the most likely culprits.

Desiccation

Winter desiccation (drying) is an indirect function of cold. Evergreens give off moisture (transpire) through the winter, but often the soil is frozen or may have been dry before cold weather set in so that roots cannot replenish the water that plants lose through transpiration. A plant positioned in a warm sunny spot or a windy area tends to lose even more water. Symptoms on broad-leaf evergreens include leaves with yellow scorched areas around the margin and on the tips. Narrow-leaf evergreens suffering from desiccation are likely to have needles that are entirely brown or brown extending from the tip rather than the base. The terminal buds are brown and twigs snap easily when bent.

The best winter watering strategy is to hand water with 1 to 2 gallons per plant right at the roots before the soil freezes. Spray irrigation is not as efficient as drip. Overwatering will lead to root rot and root injury if water freezes around the roots. (Irrigation systems should be a controlled substance!)

Use of antitranspirants to reduce winter desiccation is a hotly debated topic. Many people advocate them, especially on newly planted conifers in windy sites. Scientific studies, however, have seldom shown any benefit to their use. A better bet is to water plants when the ground thaws during an especially dry winter or to build the old-fashioned burlap "flag," where burlap is stretched between two poles to form a wall near the plantings to break the wind.

Fertilizing Your Plants

By now it should be obvious to you all that I have no life. So in keeping with my no-life theme, I lie around and think about fertilization—er, plant fertilization, that is.

Fertilizers are chic, and in some cases, essential, but remember that an excess of fertilizer can lead to all sorts of insect and disease problems!

N-P-K Ratio

Let's start with a review of the basics of fertilizing. The fertilizer bag is labeled with three numbers, which are the N-P-K ratio—for example, 20-10-10. Nitrogen (N) is always represented by the first number, phosphorous (P) is the second, and potassium (K) is the third. The numbers represent the percentage of each of those elements in the package.

Is Your Fertilizer Slow or Fast?

Here's how to calculate whether you're dealing with slow- or fast-release fertilizer:

1. Locate the W.I.N. (Water Insoluble Nitrogen) number on the fertilizer bag. (For example, the W.I.N. on our bag is 4.)
2. Divide the W.I.N. number by the nitrogen number from the N-P-K ratio. (If our N-P-K is 20-10-10, we divide 4 by 20 to get 0.2.)
3. An answer above 0.29 indicates a slow-release product; 0.29 to 0.15 is a medium-release product; a number smaller than 0.15 is a fast-release product. (In our example—0.2, we're using a medium-release product.)

The lower your N number, the more fertilizer you need to get up to the recommended amount of actual nitrogen per 1000 square feet. Many of the all-natural organic products have very low nitrogen numbers, so you'll need lots to achieve your goal. This is not necessarily a bad thing because slow-release fertilizer has less of a tendency to burn the plants, push growth too quickly, or wash or evaporate away. Plus you'll have to fertilize less often since it sticks around for a long time. However, the response may be too slow during periods of cool soil temperatures or low soil moisture.

Why Overfertilizing Is a Problem

The basis of the plant immune system is chemical—the plant manufactures chemicals to defend itself. It uses compounds such as tannins, caffeine (oh, yeah!), nicotine, phenol compounds, flavenoids, and cocaine (you didn't know you had a yard full of addicts!). When the bug pest in question bites into a leaf loaded with these and other defense compounds, the compounds are released and then change form in the enzymes of the insect's gut, becoming unusable protein and therefore poor nutrition for the pest! When we overfertilize our plants, we stimulate lush green growth, but the nutrition that would normally go into the manufacture of defense compounds now must go into the production of growth instead. Yes, we end up with more lush and succulent growth, but the plants have fewer defense compounds. That means greater susceptibility on two fronts—lowered defense and yummy taste. So excessive plant feeding isn't such a good idea. That's why it's important that you do all those preplanting soil nutrient tests.

Fertilizing Trees

Trees are your biggest plant investment, and an overfed tree has as many health risks as Aunt Hester's hand-fed pug. Overfed trees attract insects, like aphids, because of the larger quantity of tender leaves bearing larger loads of sugars and other nutrients. Foliar and twig diseases like powdery mildew are also at their best in this kind of environment. The faster the tree grows, the less resistance the woody parts have to fungal decay and mechanical stress, as well. The tree simply cannot keep up with its own growth rate, in terms of deploying protective and strengthening self-produced chemicals. An overfed tree, then, is essentially a weak tree. The risk doubles for high-hazard species such as willows, cottonwoods, poplars, black locusts, tree of heaven, and silver maples. In fact, if these species are situated near occupied structures, don't ever feed them!

If the trees are in a suitable site, they actually don't need to be fertilized at all, particularly if twigs and leaves are allowed to compost around the tree naturally. In urban environments, however, anything natural is highly unusual. If you aerate around the tree, the roots have a far better chance to get what they need than if you fertilize.

For a very sandy site, an annual application of organic mulch made of composted leaves and twigs is the kindest preservation of water and nutrients that you can provide for your plantings. Small amounts of additional nitrogen will, however, help young, deciduous trees. Applying low-nitrogen (such as 10-6-4), slow-release fertilizer in early fall or spring will give young trees a little boost during establishment. Using this fertilizer on older trees every few years is an okay practice, along with using it after tree damage has occurred. However, it is unnecessary to fertilize most conifers at all.

Removing the grass from around the drip line and mulching the area or planting ground covers will provide much better nutrient maintenance. Surface application of fertilizer is the easiest and cheapest route and does not provide significantly different benefits from root feeding, which may appear to be better due to the benefits of aeration.

Nutritional Deficiencies: Mug Shots and M.O.s

Nutritional deficiencies can affect your plants. Here's a list of some of the most common.

Potassium deficiency is the most likely scenario. Symptoms include leaf scorch, where the margins of elderly leaves turn brown and then die; curled leaves with dead areas on the undersides (in rosaceous plantings); reduced shoot growth and leaf size. If you apply too much potassium to compensate, you run the risk of causing a magnesium or calcium deficiency, or possibly even yellowing—especially in white oak, pin oak, and red maple. Potassium deficiency is defined as less than 350 pounds per acre by soil test.

Phosphorus deficiency (most commonly found in heavy clay soils in the Deep South) results in very dark green (almost black), reddish brown, or purple over the entire leaf surface, with red or purple tones most prominent on the undersides of leaves. (Remember that certain plants are bred to look like this, so check the variety!) A true deficiency is less than 20 pounds per acre by soil test.

Iron deficiency is caused by high soil pH. It shows up as yellowing between veins occurring first in new tissue and, as the iron levels drop, moving into older tissue. Soils close to concrete or other hardscape materials may have a high pH due to leaching of components. If you have basic soil because of limestone or chalk deposits in the soil, use incorporated amendments rather than soil-acidifying agents such as ammonia fertilizers or elemental sulfur compounds.

Manganese deficiency symptoms include necrotic (dead) spots on the upper leaf surface, or possibly marginal necrosis. Leaves are also apt to be small and have a "blurred" shape.

Zinc and copper deficiency can result not only in yellow leaves with green veins but also stunted plant growth and, with deficient zinc in rosaceous plants, the formation of weird little rosettes at the ends of shoots. This happens because the current year's growth of twigs is reduced, so all the leaves pile up on each other.

Magnesium deficiency causes yellowing between the veins, but the veins stay green. Magnesium will usually be deficient only in soils that are below pH 5.8 and in soils not formed from limestone. Preplanting preparation of acidic soil should include incorporating dolomitic (rather than calcitic) limestone. Dolomitic lime sources provide magnesium because low pH can bring on magnesium deficiency, particularly when coupled with drought-prone soil. Magnesium should be 5.8 to 23 pounds per 1000 square feet.

Calcium deficiency causes root tips that turn brown and die, while leaves curl, turn brown on the edges, and die. Newly expanding leaves may stick together and then shred as they pull apart. Calcium should be 46 to 138 pounds per 1000 square feet.

Nitrogen deficiency is always in a state of flux. In fact, landscape plantings tend to end up with more nitrogen and phosphorous than they should have due to overfertilization of turf grasses. More often, nitrogen deficiency is actually due to poor root health or soil drainage (or both). If for some strange reason your plants do develop a true nitrogen deficiency, look for light green or pale yellow leaves, or smaller than normal leaves (but these symptoms occur for other reasons, so watch your step!). Excess nitrogen leads to drought and frost damage, especially with late freezes in early spring.

More on Healthy Soil

We spend an awful lot of time trying to figure out what the heck is going wrong with our landscape plants, but I have to say again (and yes, it seems like the millionth time to me, too): It is all in the soil! We waste a lot of time (and money) on sprays and gadgets to do this and that, but little consideration is given to the soil quality indicators that really tell us what is going on with the soil and how it affects the plants on a site.

Here are a few more cultural considerations that can make or break plants.

Soil Indicators

Soil is air, water, minerals, organic matter, and the pores between these materials. The percentage of pores filled with air or water is controlled by the percentages of sand, silt, and clay that make up the aggregates, or soil crumbles. These components combine to form aggregates that stick together by virtue of clay that swells and shrinks with the addition of water or by sticky stuff produced by soil microbes and organic matter. Soil will form these aggregates only if clay and organic matter are present. Aggregates without organic matter are not water stable. It's like leaving adobe out in the rain: It melts.

Aggregates of sand, silt, and clay have a negative charge, the extent of which is based mainly on the amount of clay in the aggregate and on organic matter. This negative charge is the soil's cation exchange capacity (CEC). If you have little clay in your soil, the brunt of the CEC must come from organic matter. We care about this because the CEC holds nutrients, such as calcium, potassium, magnesium, copper, manganese, zinc, and iron, and prevents them from being leached. (Earlier in this chapter, we discussed these nutrients and the symptoms of deficiency.) The CEC also holds the nutrients in a form that makes them available to the plants.

Gypsum, a popular soil amendment, only works to recondition sodic (high sodium) soils. It does so by displacing sodium with calcium, which allows the soil aggregates to reform. But only a small percentage of soils are sodic, so gypsum is of value only for very low calcium levels or sodic soils (which we tend to see in the West).

The negative charge responsible for the CEC properties has a second function: to hold on to water. Water has both a positive charge and a negative one (the original bipolar relationship!). The positive end bonds with the negative charge on soil aggregates. The free positive end of that water molecule bonds with another water molecule in the open space between aggregates (pore space), and so on. Nutrients are dissolved in the water of that pore space so that plants can take them up through their roots. The accessibility of environmental water, and thus the nutrients dissolved in that water, is controlled by the soil structure and the biological community.

Soil aggregates are different sizes, with different percentages of clay and organic matter, and therefore different adhesive potential for the positive charge of water. In small pores, the cohesive force is stronger than in large pores because water molecules are in closer contact both with each other and with water molecules adhesively bound with the aggregate. In large pores, water moves the same way, but gravity is more of a strain on the water droplet bonds. As the soil becomes saturated with more and more water, the weight of bound water in large pores coupled with the pull of gravity becomes great enough that water rolls off and drains through the larger pores, taking with it any nutrients dissolved in that water—hence the potential for leaching with quick-release fertilizers, especially in sandy soils.

So the take-home message is this: Make sure your organic matter is up to snuff!

Testing Your Soil

When testing the soil for nutrients, pick one lab and stick with it since different labs use different tests and you really don't want to keep up with them (trust me).

If you are testing your topsoil for suitable physical properties, it should have about 2 percent by weight organic matter and no more than 6 percent organic matter (most soil is not topsoil). It should also have not less than 20 percent material passing through a No. 200 sieve and not be more than 15 percent clay. Topsoil should be free of stones over 1.5 inches, free of noxious weeds and trash, and less than 10 percent gravel by volume. Take the time to check! Also, soil containing more than 500 ppm (parts per million) soluble salts cannot be used.

Compost Can Help

How do you boost soil life? If you are trying to enhance microbial activity, compost gives the most consistently positive response. By keeping enough oxygen in the soil on a consistent basis, you enhance nitrogen-fixing on or around the roots, and this in turn boosts nutrient exchange between the root and the soil, as well as water absorption. But for there to be sufficient nutrients and water for these activities, there must be enough organic matter that the soil has the correct water-holding properties.

Bottom Line: For the best results, spare the root by spoiling the soil—it's not just one organism or one physical or chemical event that runs the show.

Winter Stresses

One of the things we forget about when we look for problems in the landscape is the very serious side effects that cold weather can have on our plantings. Our plants can't just get up and wander in for some hot cocoa and mittens when conditions get rough!

Winter stresses can show up in odd ways. Have you ever seen plants leaf out in the spring, flower, then suddenly die for no apparent reason? It could

Review Your Landscape in Winter

The winter landscape unclothed is actually a great time to spot potential problems and weaknesses, as well as to plan beautification projects for the spring. In fact, winter is the perfect time to think about how naughty you were (yes, you, Little Lord Drownem) last season and how nice the coming season will be.

be that a bizarre cold snap the previous fall or winter is the killer, especially if the snap occurred during an otherwise mild time so that the plants were not properly hardened off. So don't be lulled into a false sense of security and get lax about your watering and fertilizing schedules and regimens.

Damage that occurred during a cold snap last January will be very visible as trees start to leaf out. Look for things like tip burn, desiccation, and cracked bark. Mild autumns for the preceding several years can lull us into a false sense of security, and we push the planting season further and further into late November and even early December.

Situations that help add to the amount of winter damage are sudden cold snaps after abnormally warm periods, as well as variations in soil temperatures and the depth of frozen ground. So be aware of the problem, and before you apply a pesticide for an insect or a disease, make certain that the pest isn't just Old Man Winter loafing around in the warm spring air.

Winter injury may be subtle, manifested only as delayed bud development and slightly reduced growth, but in the worst-case scenario of severe desiccation, there will be dieback, the previous season's growth will be lost, and the stressed plant will become more susceptible to opportunistic pests.

Low-temperature injuries are most common where seasonal variations in temperature are the greatest. In spring we see wilting, blackening, and the death of tender twigs, blossoms, and leaves. On conifers, we see reddened needles and defoliation of the newest needles. If you have frost injury to the swollen buds, you end up having leaves with symmetrically placed holes. Plants in valleys or low areas have the worst damage, and that damage is located on the lowest branches. In early spring or late winter, you may have warm days that initiate premature growth. The worst scenario is when you have low-temperature injury on advanced growth.

Winter hardiness is influenced by drainage, location, natural protection, species, characteristics of the root system, and the weather. The trees with the root systems most susceptible to cold in poorly drained sites include maple, ash, elm, and, most of all, pine. In the case of winter damage to roots, you do not see the result until the next summer when the aboveground portion of the plant suddenly wilts and dies. The worst cold injury to roots occurs when there is low snow cover or bare soil. Container-grown specimens, of course, have a greater chance of cold damage to roots due to the lack of insulation.

Marginally adapted flowering trees may not bloom following extremely cold January conditions—that is, the flower buds, but not the trees, are killed.

Preventing winter injury can be as easy as selecting a well-drained site, aerating around trees, and protecting *Rhododendron* and laurels planted in quantity with windbreaks of conifers. A heavy mulch of oak leaves will decrease the potential for deep freezing of the soil, keep water in the root zone, and still provide the acidity needed by these plants. Soaking the soil around evergreens before freezing weather sets in can also help.

How do you care for winter-injured plants? Do not drastically prune them! If you must prune, wait until the buds open in spring so you can see which parts are dead. And then prune only moderately for most rapid recovery.

Moderate fertilization in the spring following winter injury may be warranted so that the plant can get through the summer better because the foliage can manufacture and store the materials needed for recovery.

Specific Winter Injuries

Black heart (sounds like one of those bodice buster books that are two for five dollars at the drugstore) manifests as dark, discolored internal tissue. While twigs, limbs, and root collars appear healthy, the plant often dies by midsummer. This is particularly visible in the water tubes of the smaller branches of trees and shrubs. Even if the plant doesn't die, you may still see poor growth, reduced flowering, and the death of some shoots.

Frost cracks (radial shakes) are long fissures that can extend radially all the way to the center of the tree and are likely to occur when there are serious temperature fluctuations. Frost cracks occur when water in wood cells near the outer surface of the trunk moves out and freezes, the wood dries down, and the center is still warm and moist. The shrinkage between the outer and inner layers of wood increases tension, the layers separate, and you get breakage along the grain of the wood. Frost cracks are seen primarily on the south and west sides where the sun's rays cause the greatest temperature differentials. The cracks tend to heal over and reopen every year, leaving the tree with masses of callus over the seam. Young trees and fruit trees are especially susceptible. Isolated trees have a greater chance of frost cracks than groups in the forest, and trees of 6 to 18 inches in diameter are the most susceptible size.

To prevent frost cracks, watch that weed whacker and lawn mower! Frost cracks most commonly occur along the sites of old trunk and root injuries that may have happened years previously. Mulching around the tree can prevent injuries that may lead to future frost cracks. The cracks can admit wood decaying fungi, too, so watch for trees with these cracks. A coat of white latex can reduce frost cracking by deflecting the sun's rays and keeping temperatures moderated.

Frost cankers or sunscald are localized areas of temperature-induced injury on the trunk, branches, or crotches, and are again most often seen on south and west exposures. They result from scalding by the sun and can be as deep as the layer containing the food and water tubes of the tree or shrub. You will see what appear to be long strips of discolored, dried-out bark on the southwest portions of the trunk that sink in as decay sets in. This condition is most likely to occur on shade-grown, thin-barked trees following sudden exposure to direct sun. Often exposure results after transplanting the tree from the close confines of a nursery into an open, windy site, or after construction clearing when there is sudden exposure to the hot sun. Providing shade on the southwest side and adequate water for the first few years of growth can sometimes mitigate this problem. Even sudden shading of the landscape by cloud can be enough to drop the temperature so that frost cankers occur.

Frost heaves occur in the soil, not in the plant, but they are particularly injurious because they break the roots and unearth the plant, exposing it to desiccation and the roots to cold temperatures. Mulch is critical, or you can simply wait till spring to install your plants. Keep in mind that plant parts just above the mulch layer may be damaged by enhanced temperature extremes. Cold damage to roots can be monitored from the surface by

Winter Protection?

People sometimes use burlap wraps to protect evergreens from salt or snow damage, leaving a hole in the top for winter growth, but this is a good way to get sun scald on the southwest side or to cause frost cracking. People tend to leave burlap on deciduous tree trunks year around, which not only invites pests, but also prevents the bark of certain species from photosynthesizing, which weakens the trees.

observing those plants whose new shoots and leaves wilt and die on the first warm days of spring.

Problems Caused by De-Icing Salts

One of the most common winter problems is the injudicious use of de-icing salts. Not only do these prove toxic to plantings near sidewalks or at the bottoms of slopes, but they also increase soil compaction by making the soils hang together in platelike clumps with changed chemical properties that affect nutrient and pH levels. Depending on state regulations, a single lane of high travel road may get 40 to 80 tons of salt per mile each year! Salt is insidious in that you may not see the result of salt damage until the following June or later, when you'll suddenly see browned leaf margins when the tree gets its first stress of the season. Salt-weakened plants are also more susceptible to insects, pathogens, and the environmental stresses of drought, wind, or ice.

Plants are damaged in two ways by salt: as airborne spray that kills dormant buds by penetration of leaf scars, and in the soil where it separates into its two components of sodium and chlorine, which each act differently to kill your plant.

Chlorine is taken up in early spring and enters into sap, concentrates in shoots, and prevents buds from opening. Snow cover on branches will somewhat mitigate this effect. Later, this nasty chemical is transported to actively growing leaf margins, causing leaf scorch, curling, and death. Sodium uses the same route as tree nutrients, blocking the road for magnesium and potassium uptake, both of which are necessary for chlorophyll manufacture. The most common result is a potassium deficiency that can inhibit disease and drought resistance. Salt can also cause a physiological drought, since the brine near tree roots is more concentrated than sap, which leads to the tree's not being able to take in water.

Salt damage in any form can occur in plants that are up to 50 feet away from heavily salted areas. Salt damage to conifers is most noticeable in spring and contributes to white pine decline. Branches experiencing road salt spray have yellow and brown needles that drop off. The color change starts from the tip of the needles, with salt uptake from the soil causing the needles to take on a blue-green cast. Deciduous trees may have witch's broom near the ends of branches in response to salt having killed terminal buds; flower buds that don't open; twig dieback; sparse, stunted, or yellow foliage; and the dead giveaway: leaf scorch. How do you tell the difference between fungal scorch and environmental or salt-induced leaf scorch? Fungal or bacterial scorches are often on the lower, more densely shaded parts of the tree, or there will be a history of sharpshooter leafhoppers in the vicinity. Environmental causes may predominate on the side that gets more sun, wind, or road spray.

As with everything (so it seems), the list of *don'ts* is long. The worst time to expose a tree to salt is in late October and early March. Dormant trees are less likely to take up salt and be damaged. If areas near trees are plowed, snow melt or runoff is a problem. Use snow fencing, mulch trees, or place them in a raised container. If worse comes to worst, shovel salty snow off the areas around susceptible trees.

The *do's* include improving drainage so that there are no underground pools of salty water that won't go away. To mitigate salt damage in spring, water, water, water to leach it all through. Do this not only for your trees but also for areas of Kentucky bluegrass and rye that may have received extra salt to offset salt stress that may lead to leaf spot disease. If drainage is good, you can irrigate thoroughly over a prolonged period and wash salt away from as much as the top 18 inches.

Young trees are more susceptible to salt damage because they have fewer roots than older ones. Plants that are intolerant of salt should be placed at least 30 feet away from a potentially salted surface. Trees that are particularly

Herbicide injury of leaves can mimic disease or insect damage.

sensitive to salt injury include hornbeam, hop hornbeam, Redmond basswood, Crimean and little leaf lindens, red maple, pin and swamp white oak, white pine, and tuliptree, *Liriodendron tulipifera*.

Another sneaky way that salt damage can occur is when snow is pushed up by a plow and then melts down. This more concentrated salt is then taken up by the plant. But no damage is seen until summer when a scorch appears.

Accidental Herbicide Injury

You, gentle garden reader, have just stumbled through the quagmire of bad things that happen to good plants, and I know you would like to rest. I must insist, however, that no discussion of cultural crudities would be complete without a mention of the accidental herbicide injury to a desirable plant.

If lots of different plants in a particular area all have deformed leaves on only one side but the rest of the plant seems normal enough, a chemical spray drift is a strong possibility.

Let's take this one step further. Find out how the products you were using work. External contact could show up as yellow leaf spots or dead leaf tissues, particularly between veins or along the edge of the leaf. Generally, fertilizers or herbicides are going to create this kind of havoc. The solution is to exercise great care when you use herbicides.

Pruning

Now picture this: It's a beautiful Monday following the first beautiful Saturday of spring. The air is crisp and clean, the buds are swelling, and so is your heart, with pride. You pull up a folding chair in front of your absolutely most favorite part of your property—and discover that, lo and behold, your beloved has decided to do a little pruning over the weekend. There isn't a shrub left alive.

Pruning is highly misunderstood. Think about it in terms of your own body, by chance also called your trunk. Extend your arm. This is your branch. If someone cuts off your arm to the elbow, it's a bad thing called a stub cut. The stub becomes a full-course meal for rot and canker. If someone cuts off your arm beyond your shoulder and into your trunk, the wound will never heal. This is called a flush cut, perhaps

A stub cut encourages rot and poor healing.

because you are about to flush all the money you spent on the tree down the drain. Have a look at your arm pit. Chances are you will see little wrinkles in the skin near your shoulder. Trees have these where the branch joins the trunk. This area is called the branch collar, and your pruning cut should be even with this wrinkled area without digging into it. This way the branch collar can grow around the pruning wound and seal off the area around a lost branch with a perfect doughnut of bark just like those formed when a tree sheds a branch naturally.

Everyone loves painting tree wounds because it makes them feel better about performing surgery on their plants. I object! Do not dress wounds! This is like sprinkling your feet with athlete's foot fungus and then sealing them up with black plastic bags for a week. You are trapping the bad

Flush cuts allow rot to proceed directly into the tree trunk.

organisms against the very thing that they want to infect—and protecting the pathogen in the meantime. Wound dressings do not stop rot, and they may encourage it!

Do not canopy-prune during a drought or during transplant to bring "roots and canopy into equilibrium." This is suggested in older texts and does nothing but further stress the tree. The tree needs all the leaves it has to help produce food to provide the roots with enough stamina to keep functioning during severe droughts.

Double stems that grow close together up from the point of their union have a greater chance of problems, since the likelihood of bark inclusions increases their chance for cracks or splits. Don't be tempted to buy them because you like the way they look.

If the tree has a crack between stems, assess the age and health of the tree, as well as the size of the crack. Large trees with deep cracks should be removed. A young tree could have one of the stems removed, or you could prune one stem more than the other so that the highly pruned portion will grow more slowly and encourage tissue growth of the stronger one around it.

Topping Trees

Okay, here's a good one for you: What has a trunk, no limbs, and a short time to live? No, it's not Freddy Krueger's latest victim; it's that sycamore down the road that somebody just decided was too large for its own good.

Major Reasons Not to Top Trees

* Topping removes so much of the crown that the crown-to-root ratio is messed up, and the ability to make food is temporarily interrupted. A similar scenario is seen when grass is cut too short. Topping also incites shock since the crown acts as a sunscreen. Bark exposed by topping may become scalded.
* The large stubs on a topped tree cannot effectively form callus or scabs to exclude disease and insects. Trees, like humans, don't heal well if they are damaged too greatly—not just a finger cut off, but a leg. The terminal location and the size of these amputations prevent the tree's chemically based immune system from working properly. Also, when you top an already diseased limb, you are opening the gates to the fungus World Series with free tickets for all.
* Topping results in the formation of smaller, weaker limbs at the stumps of the amputations. Moreover, if rot exists in the stump, the weight of the sprout is going to make matters worse.

Those who want to control the height and spread of a tree are not going to achieve this by topping it. Topping has the opposite effect. It causes the tree to produce a huge number of spindly twigs called water sprouts, which elongate so rapidly that the tree returns to its previous height in a short time with a much denser, weaker, and more dangerous crown.

Trees are topped—have all of their major limbs shortened by about half—for several reasons. These include aesthetic concerns (obstruction of view), growth into power lines, and the mistaken belief that it will improve the health of the tree. Sometimes homeowners think topping will prevent or reduce potential storm damage. While selective pruning is always a good option for those fears, topping actually weakens the tree and makes it more prone to storm damage and rot. Be aware of aliases for "topping": stubbing, heading, heading-back, stubbing off (that sounds rather nasty), tipping, hat racking, topping-off, dehorning, lopping, and roundover.

The Devil Made Me Do It

No-Excuse Planting and Aftercare

Many people are as anxious to blame the death of their beloved plants on insects and diseases as the people in Salem were to blame their sick cows on witchcraft. The sad truth is that improper planting coupled with bad plant choices for the location are actually far more blameworthy. Everything from the largest tree to the smallest bulb needs to have thought put into process before it gets put into the ground—but this is where we cut corners, often to the detriment of the plant's health and our wallets!

Before you go out shopping, **invest in an inexpensive gardening book that has the Latin and common name of the popular plants** you will probably encounter on an average trip to the nursery or garden center. Take this and a measuring tape with you so if you have trouble visualizing how big your plant will grow, you can lay it out in the parking lot. That way you know whether you even want to deal with the plant in its infancy, let alone its maturity. Be sure to look up whether the plant does better planted in fall or spring—for some plants, that can mean the difference between life and death!

Food for Thought

Think about the following list before making a purchase decision:

- **How tall will the plant grow?** Little plants have a bad habit of becoming big ones. Excellent examples from the tree world are fast-growing maples and spruces, which play cat's cradle with power and phone lines.
- **How wide will it grow?** Today's cute baby seedling may be reaching a branch through the window for a cup of coffee in a decade or two.
- **How much light does it need?** Plants that have evolved for full sun or shade are not forgiving in an environment with improper light. For example, flowering dogwoods are an understory tree and do not fare as well in full sun.
- **How cold hardy is it?** Unless you have fallen in love and have a spare microclimate, plant for one zone colder than the one you are in, just in case Old Man Winter gets rough.
- **Is the plant unusually susceptible to insects or disease?** Different cultivars of the same plant have improved insect and disease resistance. Do your homework!
- **Does the plant have serious structural problems?** Is it pruned poorly, or is it a natural hazard? You've seen those beautiful but brittle ornamental pears that are a hazard for pedestrians, buildings, and parked cars!
- **Can the plant withstand the soil pH or texture native to your site?** Many plants that love acidic soils will do poorly at a high pH.
- **Can the plant tolerate the average amount of ground water at the site chosen for it?** For example, certain pines do well on poor, dry soils and others in saturated ones, while hemlocks like rich, moist soils but succumb to insects. Although these trees may appear related, they cannot tolerate each other's growing conditions.
- **Is the plant invasive?** This may sound like a silly question, but plants such as purple loosestrife drop seeds at an alarming rate.
- **Will the plants exchange diseases with each other?** Douglas fir and Colorado blue spruce share diseases and insects and are often planted

Think Before You Plant Trees

* Large trees (60 feet high) should be at least 35 feet away from a building.
* A bed or a median area should be greater than 8 feet wide to allow for a large tree's root system, trunk diameter, and root flare.
* Medium trees (30 to 40 feet high) need an area 4 to 8 feet wide or a planting bed 8 feet square or larger.
* Low trees, shrubs, and plants (20 feet high or less) can handle narrow planting areas of 4 feet or less, containers, or areas surrounded by concrete.
* Conifer windbreaks should be 50 feet from buildings on the north or west side.
* Deciduous trees should be on the south or west side for cooling in summer and sun in winter.
* Trees need a minimum of 6 inches of topsoil for growth—10 to 15 inches are better.
* Know the proximity to heating/cooling units and dryer vents, setbacks, rights of way, neighbor's property (especially if there is the potential to overhang or shade a neighbor's pool), and signs that must be read while driving.
* Know where the utilities are!

within just a few feet of each other, while trees in the apple family and junipers share orange and slimy rust diseases.

The Root of the Matter

Roots in any transplanting situation are subject to drying and tearing, which can affect the life and health of the stock that you plant. Bare-root plants, for instance, do not have many of the nonwoody, absorbing roots necessary for easy establishment. So it is absolutely essential to choose stock whose roots have not dried out.

Balled-and-burlapped plants also have their share of problems since many roots are lost or damaged during the digging process—and this damage is hard for the buyer to see. If specimens have been manhandled (notice the phrase is not "womanhandled"), there may be tears and breaks to the roots, and the rootballs may dry out, killing the roots.

Never buy a specimen with a wrapped trunk; the wrapping may hide wounds or harbor insects. Do not wrap it yourself because wrapping a plant may also promote frost cracks. White paint (latex) is okay, but the best bet is to have your bark as natural as possible.

Plants should be thoroughly watered the day before being transported, and the covering during transport should always be something breathable like shade cloth or burlap.

When you are selecting stock to plant, make sure that there is good root attachment. This is easy to check in balled-and-burlapped specimens by wiggling the trunk. If the trunk moves independently of the ball, look elsewhere! **Always handle balled-and-burlapped stock by the ball and not by the trunk,** or roots that you cannot see will rip!

If you are not ready to install delivered plants, you must mulch and water them. Group them to shade each other. Remember that preplanting stress invites borers!

Root Girdling

How long has that plant (annual, perennial, shrub, or tree) been in that pot? The longer the plant has been in the container, the greater the likelihood that circling roots have formed, which can lead to girdling roots. **A girdling root wraps around the stem below the soil surface and kills all the other roots.** Trees or shrubs with a stem diameter that remains the same rather than increasing and

Girdling roots can strangle your plant.

with extensive branch dieback over several years may be suffering from a girdling root. When you examine the trunk at the soil line, you'll see signs of girdling beneath: There is no normal root flare, and one side of the trunk goes straight into the ground like a utility pole.

Planting the shrub or tree into too small a planting hole can create a girdling-root situation. Make sure the planting hole is not too deep, either, since a shrub or tree planted low enough to have stem tissue crossed by a root is a good candidate for strangulation. This is true of a deep hole that has been back filled with loose soil, because eventually the plant has to settle! Prune the offending roots off; if they are very large, do one each year so you don't compromise the anchorage of the planting.

If you are looking at containerized specimens, pull a few out and look for root circling. **Once the roots begin to circle, they never grow out of it.** If you are purchasing a few months before you are ready to install, make sure that the pots have been treated with copper compounds, which will prevent circling during the interim but will not permanently affect the plant. If you bought a plant with circling roots, tease out the roots with a weed scratcher, a dinner or cooking fork, or a spading fork to get them out of the circular pattern.

Planting the Specimen

Here are the brass tacks of installation itself:

The width of the planting hole should always be three times the diameter of the ball. If there is insufficient room between the curb and the sidewalk, don't do it! Even better, try to set aside **large** areas around your property for large groupings rather than solitary specimens in a line. This provides a greater area of open ground for roots to spread.

The hole should be just deep enough that the widened part of the plant base **just before** the root system starts will ultimately be even with the top of the soil. **Do not trust that the top of the rootball is this area!** Often the specimen is already too deep in the ball and it is your job to open the ball and excavate a bit of soil until you can see the widening or the flare of the plant's crown. Thin, hairlike roots above the widened area should be

carefully snipped off. These have formed in response to having soil piled too high above the flare.

For a group planting, select species wisely so that cultural requirements (pH, moisture, and sun) for different species will be somewhat similar.

When you purchase balled-and-burlapped stock, don't unwrap the ball till the specimen is in the planting hole and you are sure you won't need to remove it again. Remove synthetic burlap completely. Sometimes a piece of this will be wrapped

This plant has its root flare buried within the rootball and will die if it is not excavated.

loosely around the true ball and then covered by natural burlap as a kind of "diaper" to make sure the whole thing stays together. Only natural burlap can be left in place in the hole to rot away, but tuck the edges into the planting hole so they don't act as a wick for water to evaporate.

For trees in cages, the hole should be wide enough to accommodate your snipping the cage one-half to two-thirds of the way down from the surface of the hole. You don't have to remove the cage; simply cut the layer of wire in a couple of places.

Plants with greater root volume will establish more easily, so site preparation is critical. A good site will have consistent water movement. If the bed is more than 30 percent clay, the best option is to grow the specimen in a raised bed.

When you prepare the site, remember that most transplants have a greatly impaired root system. How well would you do if someone ripped out great handfuls of your veins and arteries? Pretty cranky, right? Disrupted root hormones (TREE-M-S instead of PMS?), less photosynthesis, and transplant shock lead to vastly reduced growth the year of transplantation.

Root pruning does essentially the same thing to the plant. When roots have been pruned, regrowth occurs **only** at the cut ends, and then mostly on thicker roots, which are not the ones doing most of the nutrient and water absorption. You end up with a witch's broom effect, just like when tree crowns are topped. After a few years, dominance is achieved by one of these root straws and the tree begins to recover.

No Need to Stake and Tie

Unless you live in a very windy area, staking and tying are really not necessary. Moreover, woody ornamentals **need to flex** with the wind; it's a kind of plant physical therapy. The other problem with ties is that they invariably remain on the tree too long and begin to cut into the trunk, effectively cutting the flow of nutrients and water and eventually killing or deforming the specimen.

Care After You Plant

Water the plant when one-third of the hole has been backfilled and is firm— but do not compact backfill. Then make sure that the trunk or stem remains at the original grade while you put in the remaining backfill.

Create a watering saucer by making a circular levee of soil around the newly planted ball so that water will not flow away from the point of application.

Specimen Planting No-No's

Don't prune back branches by a third to keep them "in balance with the roots," no matter what you have heard. When the roots are cut, the leaves stop growing anyway. What you must do is water the plants to compensate for loss of roots and transpiration by leaves. When pruning, only get rid of dead, diseased, or damaged branches.

Don't loosen the soil under the ball in the planting hole or **plants will sink**, causing the plant to be too deep and with soil piled too high over the flare.

Don't amend the planting hole with compost or other organic amendments; doing so may create a flowerpot effect where water either sits around your plant or is wicked off into the surrounding soil. Amending individual planting holes may also result in roots not spreading out into surrounding soil. But if you have a large planting **bed** with multiple tree and shrub installations, it is okay to amend the entire bed before planting.

Mulch is critical to reducing competition with turf, which will out-compete transplants for two to three years for water and nutrients. Mulch keeps temperature and soil moisture stable and increases microbial activity. It also keeps weed whackers away! Mulch 2 to 3 inches deep, and keep the layer in place at least three to four years during establishment (and preferably for the life of the plant). The best mulching material is coarsely shredded bark, which does not have to be composted if it is not to be incorporated into the soil. Make sure colored mulch comes from a reliable source because it may have been dyed to disguise contamination or other problems.

Watering

Newly planted trees and shrubs must be watered individually, leaving the hose in the saucer running slowly for ten to fifteen minutes at least twice a week. Better yet, install a drip irrigation system in the entire bed and operate it twice a week. Do not assume an overhead lawn irrigation system is going to properly water new or established ornamentals! Mulch beds with 2 to 3 inches (no more) of bark, chips, etc., for water retention.

Many of the container mixes in which purchased plants are grown are extremely light and fluffy, making the interface between the mix and the existing soil (if it has not been amended with organic matter) difficult for roots. To water containerized herbaceous plants thoroughly before planting, plunge the pot you are going to plant into a water-filled vessel one size larger and let the water displace the air until you see no more bubbles at the surface. This means moisture has been distributed evenly around the roots rather than having dry spots and dead zones left by top watering and finger flow (movement of water down the path of least resistance, like around the edge of your pot!).

Don't buy or install what you cannot water—especially you weekend gardeners at locations other than your main home. Drip irrigation does the best job on beds, since water goes directly underground. If you are wondering if your drip system is up to snuff, the rule of thumb is one 1-gallon emitter by each 2- to 4-foot plant, two 1-gallon emitters by each 4- to 6-foot plant, and four 1-gallon emitters by each 7- to 8-foot plant.

An excellent option for watering newly planted trees is green plastic bags called "treegators." These surround the woody ornamental, can be zipped

What About Drought?

Uh-Oh. You forgot to water and it didn't rain . . . now what?

Don't panic (easy for me to say, right?). Visual drooping is not a universal symptom, and leafdrop doesn't necessarily equal death. If you are not sure about a plant's status, peel back the bark on twigs. If you see a green layer beneath, the plant is still alive. The base of the buds is also green on a live plant. Drooping or curling of evergreens, especially spruce and pine, is a sign of severe water stress; evergreens can be green for several weeks even after they are completely dead.

Late-season drought does not usually cause wilting, but drought stress enhances *Botrysphaeria* canker and *Verticillium* diseases where one part of the plant will suddenly wilt and die—don't assume a plant like this simply needs more water. Root rots, although associated with wet, are also favored by hot, dry conditions on poorly drained sites and cause an off color to young perennials that are just being installed.

together to suit any size trunk, do not allow direct contact of water with the trunk, but do allow slow, deep watering. They also protect your specimens from weed whackers and can be stored easily for the winter. They should be used one season for normal transplants and two for hard-to-establish specimens or difficult areas.

Special Tips on Trees and Shrubs

One major reason your larger planting choice might not thrive is our desire for an instant "specimen" tree or shrub. This causes us to choose the largest thing we can possibly afford and *voilà!* We get instant shade, visual impact, curb appeal if we are selling the house, neighbor envy, and in a few years . . . firewood. Large transplants are statistically much more likely to fail. And older, larger transplants show particularly poor survivability in urban settings.

So always go with smaller, younger transplants. The physiological reason is relatively simple and ties into another reason most (but not all) plants do better when planted in the fall. For eight weeks after spring transplantation, transplanted specimens have negative midday water balances compared to those that remain undisturbed. Leaf canopy measured at the end of the season is only half as dense in transplanted specimens as in undisturbed ones, so the most notable effect of transplanting may be the inhibition of leaf expansion resulting from early spring water stress. This ultimately leads to an open canopy for the whole season following transplant—and a stressed plant. The poor things are in shock!

Now consider this: Root growth is essential to the success of any type of transplant, and it may take as much as ten years for a root system to recover from transplantation! So expect most large plants to look a wee bit pitiful for a time, appearing even less vigorous in the second season than the first. The reason for this is that nutrient reserves before transplant are used for the first season's growth but root loss at transplant reduces the ability to store these reserves for the next few years. **This means that although the specimen may look good the year of transplant, the second year will actually be the true test of the plant's ability to survive.**

What is the worst fallout from large transplants? It's the one-year warranty from the nursery (they know what they're doing.) The key is to educate yourself beforehand about why the vigor goes down the second year. Try to get a flexible guarantee from the nursery so that the ability of the tree to establish is actually tested by a second year's growth.

Root system diameter is much more important than the size of the top of the ball, so purchase plants with the largest root system possible. When purchasing a large specimen, look for any marginal burning around the edges of the leaves; this can be a sign of prolonged water stress. Large specimens receive special care in nurseries, so it is important to get the specimen into the ground as soon as possible after delivery. Chances are you won't be able to provide the same TLC. The sooner the specimen gets into the ground, the better, so that natural root growth and function can resume. Products containing mycorrhizae, fungi that help trees absorb water and nutrients, may be helpful for establishment.

Follow-up care of bigger specimens is once again critical to establishment. Irrigation and mulching are essential to reduce stress and competition from surrounding plants. Watch for stress-attracted pathogens and insects such as cankers and borers the year after transplant. Any foothold they get, as well as improper irrigation, could invalidate the warranty made by the nursery. That could lead to a nasty situation for your landscape and your wallet.

Potted Specimens That Will Remain Potted

If you are buying large plants that are already in pots, check for the presence of liverworts (sounds like something the witches from *Macbeth* would be selling at 99 cents per pound, doesn't it?). These flat, fleshy, weedy plants may indicate a potbound plant. If you find them, pull the plant out, scratch up the rootball, and repot in a larger vessel. Also look for proper planting depth in either prepotted purchased plants or in those that arrive as balled-and-burlapped or containerized specimens for you to pot up. **Make sure you can see the root flare.** Just like every other plant, potted specimens planted too deep are not long for your patio or this world.

Special Tips for (Almost) Perfect Perennials

Spring always leaves me with a strong desire to plant anything that doesn't get out of my way fast enough, including the kids, the dog, and my husband. Fortunately, they have learned to hide when they see my shovel. Many other people also get the same way during this season of renewal. Unfortunately, they satisfy their urge by going out to buy the largest, most expensive, most-likely-to-die plants they can find, and then spend the summer watching them slowly perish.

A much smarter solution for cramped space and spring planting is the perennial, a reliable, less expensive, and hardier plant that can be easily packed up should the family decide to move elsewhere. Perennials are the foot soldiers of the garden, and indeed we should always strive to install plants that will thrive even in the harshest "plant boot camp."

One word of warning: Often we kill perennials with kindness. For the most part, if you pay attention to the kind of environment they want before you plant, they can be planted and left alone. The following are tips for making the most of your perennial plantings while reducing the likelihood of pests and diseases at the same time:

Fertilizer. Go easy, especially on the newly planted. Several weeks **after** installation, or when the plants begin to grow, apply fertilizer (1 teaspoon **lightly** worked into the soil around the plants). A rule of thumb is that spring-installed plants should be four to five times their planting size by early summer, and even bigger by fall. But if they're not, don't immediately reach for the fertilizer (bear in mind it is very easy to burn new roots with fertilizers!). Instead check pH, drainage, and sun levels. Remember to avoid high-nitrogen fertilizers since they will promote leaf growth at the expense of flower growth.

Water. You should water containerized plants and their sites one day before planting. Plant each just below the soil line, and leave a levee of soil around the plant to act as a saucer for water, just as you did with the trees and shrubs. Water the area thoroughly again after planting to a depth of 8 to 10 inches (use your screwdriver test). Check your newbies every two days using the screwdriver to see whether additional water is necessary.

Drainage. This is an issue for perennials just like every other plant. Follow the twelve-hour rule: Dig some holes about 8 inches deep, fill them with water,

Unpotting Your Perennials

Never yank on the base of the stems of your perennials to pull them from their containers because you will crush the plant at its crown and invite disease. Instead, press the bottom of the container with your thumbs or tap the side of the container sharply to loosen the root mass. And for goodness' sake, trim any roots trailing out of the bottom of the pot so they will not rip others when you pull the rootball out! Ouch! You can also take a containerized plant and roll it gently on its side to loosen the root mass. Once it's out, use a dinner fork to tease out the sides, but don't then absentmindedly eat your lunch with that fork. (Been there and done that!)

and come back in twelve hours. If water is still in the holes, amend the soil or install subsurface drainage, or simply move your perennial garden elsewhere, and dig a pond, dude!

Hole size. Planting holes for perennials should be twice as wide as deep. If you have bought out the garden center and are up to your sweaty armpits in containerized plants, water them by placing the container into a slightly larger one filled with water just like we described under the tree section and watch for the bubbles at the top to stop forming. This means you have thoroughly saturated your plant so no more air pockets exist that could allow for the desiccation of roots.

New beds. If you have built a new bed, soil will settle 1 to 2 inches over the coming months, so plant slightly deeper than normal so roots and crowns (or bulbs) will not stick out of the soil once the soil settles. Otherwise, the squirrels will think you have **finally** realized they are the superior species and you are their willing serf!

Bare-root plantings. These are a slightly different animal (or plant, as the case may be!). Soak the bare-root plant in warm water for three hours before planting. Once again, holes should be twice the width of the rootball and deep enough to take the roots without kinking or coiling them. You can make a cone in the center of the hole to spread the roots over. Water thoroughly at planting.

Surgery. Before dividing perennials, use shears or scissors to clip the foliage back to a height of 6 to 9 inches. If you cut through diseased areas, disinfect the scissors in rubbing alcohol when you're finished.

Transplant recovery room. When you divide plants, make sure you take a generous soil ball to preserve root hairs at any time save early spring and late fall. Shade the tops of divided plants with an open box until new root hairs begin to grow, generally two to three days. Plants that are dead out in the center also badly need to be divided—ornamental grasses and sea pinks are two that will practically drag you in off the street for a division.

Special Tips to Keep Bulbs Healthy

Bulbs require most of the same conditions as trees and perennials, but they do have a few personal likes and dislikes.

Healthy choice. Bulbs deteriorate if kept dry too long, so make sure the bulbs you buy are healthy and firm, with no split tunics, damaged scales, or tiny sizes (which indicate they are offsets and will not flower the first year they are planted).

Destructive downspouts. Are bulbs planted around your house? Of course they are! Make sure the melt water from snow or rainfall coming from the roof, gutters, or downspouts doesn't pool over or stay in the soil around bulbs. Repeated flooding or continuous wet will kill most bulbs.

Dastardly drainage. Good drainage is vital—most bulbs rot while dormant if soil is wet and poorly aerated. Most like neutral to slightly alkaline conditions, so do a pH test before digging. If you are using manure as a dressing, always incorporate it **below** the level of planting to avoid problems (never more than 2 bushels per 100 square feet, please!). Planting bulbs in rock gardens requires coarse grit dug into the top 4 inches for good drainage. Clay soils may be the most difficult to grow bulbs in because of drainage issues— dig coarse sand or grit into the planting area at a rate of 1.5 to 2 buckets per square yard, and incorporate plenty of organic matter!

Pot-grown party poopers. Plant pot-grown bulbs as soon as they have finished flowering, and water occasionally until the foliage turns yellow. This will keep the bulbs from putting reserves into leaf tissue and allow them to strongly flower next season. Make a hole big enough to plant the whole mess without disturbing individual positions in the pot.

Foul flowering. Poor flowering is most often caused by overcrowding. Lift during dormancy (not necessarily winter!), and plant as suggested, interplanting with their offsets. If poorly flowering bulbs are not crowded, then inspect them for pests and disease. If that's not it, change the site, paying close attention to light and drainage. If you are planning to lift bulbs for winter storage, wait till the foliage has begun to yellow. Lift and lay them in a tray to dry, and then store them in **paper**, not plastic, bags.

Murdering munchkins. Never plant bulbs in pots or soil where they have previously disappeared. This could indicate vole or other rodent activity, or conditions conducive to rot. Mulching around bulbs with a light, well-draining mulch can help reduce weeds and prevent moisture loss but may also attract voles. Castor-oil-type products may provide some repellency. Daffodils and their relatives are toxic to voles, chipmunks, deer, and other pests and are a good option in areas where these creatures can be a problem. A fine mesh over beds can help prevent mice or squirrels from digging the bulbs out.

Time your plantings. October is the best month to plant all spring-flowering bulbs, and tulip planting time can be stretched out to December 15, although this is not ideal.

Use bulbs to map your bulbs. To create a living map of where you planted things, outline groups of bulbs with grape hyacinths, which will send up leaves in fall. Also, remember to remove seed pods if bulbs are to be left in the ground since leaving the seeds results in smaller bulbs, which in turn can reduce flowering the following season.

Special Tips for Happy Hedges

It seems everyone wants a fence or a hedge for a few simple reasons (it's cheaper than procuring a dragon to singe away those unwanted views and pesky children). Unfortunately, since hedges are used primarily as living fences, they are often all the same plant (monoculture) to maintain visual continuity. This fact should set off warning bells right away, since monocultures are quickly destroyed by insects and diseases.

Perhaps the first rule of good hedge-keeping is to start out by casing the neighborhood for healthy hedges, which indicate resistance to local disease and insect problems. Once the plant material from these healthy hedges has been identified, it is time to look at those plant materials in relation to the proposed site. For example, not all of you want a hedge that will totally block your view, so the height of the proposed hedge should fit with the growth habits of plants selected. This way you are not out there with the trimmers 24/7 (although I swear some retirees plan it that way). I don't necessarily mean you need to discard your selection if it has an incompatible height, but rather look for dwarf varieties of the same plant that will fit better into your hedging scheme.

Planting. Follow specific plant suggestions for spacing, remember to dig your holes two to three times wider than deep, and scratch up the rootballs like an angry cat. Be sure to install a little earth trough around the base of the plant to help retain water. Mulch is useful to retain moisture and keep down weeds, especially until the hedge plants attain sufficient size to shade out weeds and keep their own root runs cool with their shade. Water must also be carefully monitored for at least two years until the hedge is established.

Training. Training a new hedge may be the trickiest part of the whole operation. Plants should have each year's new growth cut back by one-third until plants reach the required height. The physiological reason for this is that by removing the growing point in this manner, you force the bushes to fill out to the sides, which closes the gaps between plants, you, and the Busybody family next door.

Pruning. Although square (or rectangular) cut hedges are immensely popular, it's not the best thing for the plant. Ideally, you should taper the plant so the top is narrower than the bottom, which allows light to reach the bottom. This way the growth of the hedge, as well as its thickness, remains uniform. A narrow top also allows the hedge to deflect wind better and reduces the amount of snow able to settle there, thus preventing some of the winter damage from snow loading.

A Whole Lotta Rotting

Plant Diseases

Now that we have established that I relish the pathognomic (expensive word meaning conditions that are easily confused with disease—try it next time you play Scrabble®), let's dally with the diseases, better known as fungi, bacteria, mycoplasmas, and viruses.

The Cast of the Pathogen Drama

We have in our plant pathology play Frank Fungus, Barry Bacteria, Maureen Mycoplasma, Violet Virus, and Nestor Nematode. The starring roles always seem to go to Barry and Frank. Nestor actually paves the way for disease rather than being one and directly causing problems, but he gets very put out unless you include him in the production. Go figure.

Silliness aside, most diseases are caused by bacteria and fungi. But the presence of either on your ailing plant is not enough to convict them. Their presence means one of three things: (1) You actually have the smoking gun, (2) They are innocent bystanders, or (3) They are zombies feasting on the dead flesh of your plant. No kidding—the name for an organism that survives by breaking down dead stuff is a saprophyte. Unfortunately, many fungal diseases both cause disease and eat dead plant flesh, so sometimes their primary motives are hard to interpret.

Plant CSI . . . I love it!

Disease, like a bad relationship, goes through three distinct stages of attack:
Inoculation refers to the transfer from infection source to susceptible host (falling in love).

Incubation is the period from contact with infectious agent to the first evidence of the disease. Protective fungicides are used to prevent completion of this stage (the seven-year itch—complicated prenuptial agreements are used to prevent completion of this stage).

Infection occurs when the organism irritates the plant until the plant produces symptoms characteristic of the irritation (the "wow, I didn't know my blood pressure could break the sound barrier" stage).

The whole process (disease attack or bad relationship) lasts several days to several years and may end with the death of the infected organ or the plant.

Disease Symptoms

The "symptoms" are the plant's reaction to disease. Think of what your body, and particularly your skin, does when it's under stress. Not a pretty sight.

Disease symptoms can be confined to definite areas (like leaf spots), have a generalized effect such as yellowing or off-color foliage, or affect only certain parts of a plant without spreading to others. Or disease attack can be systemic, spreading throughout the water and food tubes of the plant and generally affecting the whole dang thing.

Symptoms may occur on the plant at the point where the organism attacks or on other parts of the plant as a result of injury produced at the primary point of attack (for example, root disease produces secondary symptoms on leaves).

Leaf spots are caused by fungi and bacteria. They are localized lesions on host leaves consisting of dead and collapsed cells. Fungi produce leaf spots that are most often round and may appear to have concentric rings. Viruses can also cause leaf spots, but the spots often look very strange. Bacterial leaf spots produce water-soaked spots that are often angular rather than round and surrounded by a yellow halo; they eventually drop out, leaving holes in the affected leaves with a brown rim around them (holes eaten by insects have a green rim). Fungal leaf spots can also drop out in this manner and will also have a brown rim.

Anthracnose causes both spots and blotches (this has been my complexion for many years). Anthracnose also causes twig dieback, which other leaf spots do not.

Blights are caused by fungi and bacteria with general and extremely rapid browning of leaves, branches, twigs, and flowers, resulting in their death. Bacterial blight is often seen on forsythia, lilac, maples, and mountain ash, especially after a mild February followed by a cold, wet April. If your plant is in the rose family and its shoots, blossoms, or fruit appear scorched, chances are the problem is bacterial and fire blight is the culprit.

Cankers can result from bacteria or fungi. They are localized wounds or necrotic lesions, often sunken beneath the surface of the plant's stem. Cankers can be annual (must be renewed each year), or perennial (tissue is killed, heals over, and then the infection begins again the next growing season beyond the healed part, resulting in a bulls-eye appearance of concentric rings). Cankers can also cause drip fluid (bleeding cankers), or cause discolored branches, or branch dieback.

Root rot is the disintegration or decay of part or all of a plant's root system. Fungi or bacteria can cause the symptoms. You'll see wilting and dying of plants, with discolored roots. (We're going to talk with you irrigation sinners about root rot redemption in just a couple of pages. Stay tuned.)

Damping off is the rapid death and collapse of very young seedlings. It is caused by a fungus.

Basal stem rot can be caused by fungi or bacteria and is the disintegration of the lower part of the stem.

Soft rots and dry rots both lead to the maceration and disintegration of fruits, roots, bulbs, tubers, and fleshy leaves. Soft rots are usually caused by bacteria; fungi tend to cause dry rots.

Scabs are localized lesions on host fruit, leaves, tubers, etc., usually slightly raised or sunken and cracked, giving a scabby appearance. They are caused by fungi.

Galls, caused by fungi or bacteria, are strange growths that create enlarged portions of plants usually filled with fungal threads or bacteria. They are basically a plant tumor.

Witch's brooms are generally the result of mycoplasma infections but can also result from salt or bad pruning. Witch's brooms are profuse, upward branching of twigs.

Leaf curls usually result from fungi but can also be caused by mycoplasmas or viruses. Plants with leaf curls have distorted, thickened, and curled leaves.

Wilt is usually caused by bacteria or fungi but can be the result of other plant diseases or insects, or cultural problems like drought. Leaves or shoots lose their crispness like yesterday's graham crackers and droop because of a disturbance in the water and food tubes of the root or stem. Wilts are often accompanied by yellowing and dieback of foliage or dark streaks in the tissue beneath the bark.

Witch's brooms are often caused by mycoplasma.

And as a final blow to your gardening ego, bacteria can lie dormant for up to a year and fungi can hang out for two to twenty years, so a single year of crop rotation may not do the trick.

How Infections Start

The sources of disease are plant debris, soil, seed, tubers, corms, bulbs, weeds, alternate hosts, vectors (those miscreants that carry the diseases around), and disease reservoirs right on the plant called cankers. Diseases can be spread by wind, water, equipment, creatures accidentally tracking through, and vectors.

Steps in acquisition of a disease, if I may be so indelicate, are analogous to those on a baseball field. First base is landing or arrival, and, in fact, the disease may be attracted by chemicals the plant exudes. Second base is germination,

* How do you recognize the signs of irrigation abuse and, more importantly, subsequent root rot? Ask yourself these questions:

* Is your plant growth slow compared to others of the same kind?

* When you look at the terminal bud scars from recent years, are they closer together than on others of the same kind of plant?

Root rot can cause the outer covering of the root to easily slip off the inner core.

* Do leaves yellow, wilt, or fall prematurely?

* Do leaf margins die in summer?

* Are roots discolored and limp rather than crisp and white?

* Does the plant have only a few small side branches or have dead side branches, and only main branches are alive?

Shoestring rot, or Armillaria, *indicates serious root rot.*

* Are the roots dead? You can do the pantyhose test (see Chapter 1) by trying to slip off the outer covering of the root from its inner core. If you can slip it off, you're in deep trouble, my friend.

* Is the canopy asymmetric or misshapen because major branches are dead?

* During winter, has there been major cankering and dieback of small branches?

* On mature trees, can you see mushrooms sticking out of the trunk (shelf fungi) or from the base of the tree, especially in late summer and early autumn?

* When you remove a bit of bark just at the tree's base, is there a fungal sheath beneath or are there "shoestrings"?

All the factors above indicate root rot disease, which is usually linked to too much water either from nature or (more often) the gardener's hand.

which needs dew, rain, or a film of water. Third base is penetration either directly, through natural openings, or through wounds like those formed from bad pruning or weedwhackeritis. Bacteria usually enter only through wounds, while direct penetration through intact plant surfaces is the most common method for fungi. To get to home plate, you actually have to produce an active infection because a disease may penetrate then die if the host is not susceptible.

Symptoms appear in two to four days up to two to three years, but most appear in a few days to a few weeks.

Fungi

Threadlike filaments do all the dirty work, and fungi spread by bridging with these filaments from plant to plant or by making spores, which are microscopic cells that can be spread to other plants, germinate, and produce a new set of filaments. Fungi are spread by air, water, soil movement, insects, or animals. They don't need light, but do need moisture.

Fungal symptoms are easily confused with bacterial symptoms since both organisms can cause leaf spots, wilts, galls, cankers, and rots. Fungi are active, usually, at between 50 and 90 degrees Fahrenheit although there are turf diseases that occur at cooler temperatures. If your plant problem appears to have dry threads or specks, suspect fungus.

Botrytis. Let's start with the gray, hairy, elevated stuff on those strawberries you forgot in the back of the fridge. That's a fungal problem in your landscape too! *Botrytis* will give your flowers and fruit small, wet spots, which become that adorable fuzzy gray when the weather is humid.

Combat *Botrytis* by not wetting flowers or foliage when watering and by pruning or spacing for good air circulation. Remove blighted flowers or buds immediately, and never, ever push the season forward by tossing your bedding beauties into the ground too early in the season or crowding them. The cool, wet weather will bring *Botrytis* around and fast. Mitts off the overhead irrigation, boys and girls, mitts off.

You can screen for *Botrytis* by placing a suspect cutting on a wet paper towel in a plastic bag in the refrigerator for twenty-four hours and watch for the gray mold.

Botrytis **on dogwood.** One of the plants hardest hit by *Botrytis* is our old favorite the dogwood. The leaves of the dogwood appear gray-brown and water soaked, followed by the dreaded elevated gray mold. Leaves may have a reddish tinge to begin with, or "petals" may be stunted. You'll see more problems when humidity is high and excessive moisture is present. Leaf blight occurs when an infected "petal" falls on leaf parts. Remove infected

Humidity increases dogwood Botrytis *infection.*

parts promptly (bag up and discard), and avoid overhead watering. *Botrytis* is hard to control in many plants and is definitely promoted by excess shading.

Botrytis on peonies. This fungus also results in a well-known blight of peonies, forming masses of elevated gray-green dusty spores that appear different from the pepper dots of other fungi. New shoots are killed back, leaves and buds are spotted and blighted, and large portions of open flowers turn brown and naaaaasty. You can help by cutting stalks off at ground level in the fall and destroying them. Remove blighted shoots or buds as soon as you see them.

Botrytis on bulbs. You'll see resulting shepherd's crooks on daffodil foliage, but it also gets on gladiolas, hyacinths, lilies, ornamental onions, tulips, and rhizomatous *Iris*. Bulbs may fail to emerge altogether in spring as a result of *Botrytis* infection.

Bulb diseases caused by *Botrytis* can be divided into blight and basal rot called "fire." Daffodils actually get two forms called "smolder" and fire. Smolder is encouraged by cool, wet conditions; multiple-nosed bulbs; and leaving bulbs in the ground for more than a year. Newly emerged leaves turn red-brown and rot or form a shepherd's crook. The leaves form spores, which then infect injured leaves and flowers, or produce neck rot of the bulbs. Avoid low, wet areas for planting, and you'll help to avoid smolder. Fire is favored by warm, moist conditions and completely destroys foliage in two to three weeks. Fire starts with elongated tan spots, which progress to yellow streaks followed by premature death of foliage.

Tulip fire is the worst tulip disease, overwintering in soil and on bulbs. Leaves

Botrytis *infection of tulips is highly unattractive.*

emerge already infected and then spread their "joy" to other leaves. You'll see two kinds of spots: small water-soaked spots that turn tan or brown and larger tan-white-gray spots with water-soaked margins, which expand to produce additional spores. The flowers quickly get spots and are destroyed, while their falling petals help to spread the disease. You can somewhat reduce the impact of the disease by removing "fire heads," which are already infected emergent leaves.

Botrytis causes rhizome or crown rot on *Iris*, which unfortunately can appear healthy but still carry disease. Fire, leopard fire, and lily botrytis blight occur on Easter lilies, Asiatic lilies, and oriental lily hybrids. You'll get total foliage destruction in a short time with moist conditions and moderate temps of 50 to 65 degrees F. Once again, water-soaked or elliptical spots appear that turn brown or gray. Remove plant debris, remove flowers before petal fall, reduce planting density, and if you use a fungicide, get the undersides of leaves because that's where infection starts!

Anthracnose

Anthracnose is a catch-all term for a number of different fungi affecting a number of different hosts. The common theme is a combination of sharply defined leaf spots, blotches, and twig dieback. There is even a turf anthracnose. Anthracnose may get ugly, but it rarely kills trees. The fungus infects at temperatures of 50 to 55 degrees F. and is prevalent during cool, wet springs. You may need to prune out cankers. Even though the trees aren't killed, sanitation and good maintenance practices can help to minimize stress and infection. Remove fallen leaves and debris that may serve as a source of infection the following year.

Anthracnose on Japanese cut leaf maples. This fungus manifests as white spots and dying branches in the tops of the trees. Root system damage unrelated to anthracnose will also cause top dieback, so look for foliar symptoms to confirm a case of anthracnose in maples. You can compost anthracnose-infected leaves under several inches of soil.

Ash anthracnose. One of the primary symptoms is defoliation of the lower branches. Look for large, brown disfiguring patches on leaflets. This can also lead to distortion. No treatment is needed unless there is some other stressor. Most trees produce new leaflets. Both white and green ash can become infected. Again, cool, wet weather is the culprit.

Oak anthracnose. This shows up as red, bronzed, and scorched leaves. Don't confuse oak anthracnose with oak leaf spots, which are pinhole-sized spots seen in midsummer. Bilaterally symmetrical holes are not anthracnose either—they are caused by a fly leaf miner.

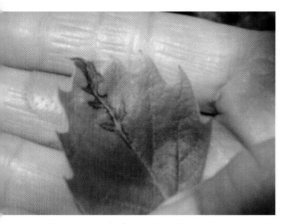

Sycamore anthracnose has the classic pattern of leaf injury along the veins and midrib.

Sycamore anthracnose. There are two kinds of anthracnose injury—early injury that kills young leaves and looks like frost injury, and secondary injury where you will see spots around the veins.

Dogwood anthracnose. This lethal anthracnose attacks leaves and twigs, causing crowns to thin so that water sprouts emerge. The sprouts then serve as a reservoir of anthracnose fungus. Repeated killing of new twigs by the anthracnose predisposes trees to insect invasion. Dogwood anthracnose is worse after a wet year with a cool, moist summer and in a densely planted site with low air circulation and high shade. To reduce dogwood anthracnose, prune dead branches promptly. Prune out dieback and water sprouts (twiggy growth growing straight up) in late winter, rake and destroy fallen leaves before spring, and minimize stress.

Dogwood anthracnose overwinters in twig and stem cankers.

For best results, plant dogwoods in sites with morning sun only and with afternoon shade; they like to be understory plants. Use Kousa variety dogwoods, which are somewhat resistant to anthracnose.

Apple Scab

If you have black or dark-

Dogwood anthracnose has decimated many dogwoods.

green circular lesions on leaves and fruits, especially those in the rose family (see Chapter 7 for more information on roses), chances are you have apple scab. Scab is something better managed by sanitation or resistant plantings rather than continual fungicide applications.

Apple scab is a yearly problem that attacks both leaves and fruit. The life-cycle of scab begins with overwintering fungus in fallen leaves and fruit. As the trees reach bud break, newly released spores from overwintered fungus land on the new leaves, and the primary infection cycle for the year begins. Mature spores from infections in new fruits and leaves are released six to eight weeks later, at the beginning of June, marking the start of the secondary infection cycle. Because new scabs will produce new spores, it is critical to control the infection process early in the season.

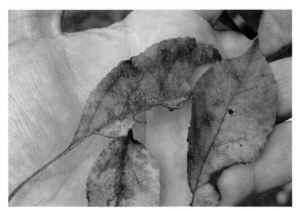

Apple scab is a very common disease in landscape plantings.

Scab management largely involves proper sanitation. Rake up fallen leaves and fruit, and in October remove any diseased fruit clinging to the tree. Proper pruning during the spring will also increase air circulation and drying potential for leaves. Full bloom to petal fall is the critical time for scab attack on trees. Cut down wild trees or susceptible plants within 100 yards to reduce potential for infection. Mowing around all susceptible plants will also speed up the decomposition of remaining diseased leaves. A judicious shot of fertilizer also seems to help the plants overcome disease attacks.

Sick crabapples often look like "plucked chickens" by early summer, while their resistant companions are still fully fledged. Olive apple scab spots lead to early July defoliation of apple, crabapple, hawthorn, and mountain ash. The defoliated trees will not die, but they certainly look a little odd for the rest of the season and provide the best source of reinfection in town. Unfortunately, having susceptible varieties around can cause resistant varieties to succumb! Apple scab spores will also survive in an average compost pile, so get rid of them!

Rusts

Common on many plants, rusts often flip flop between one host and another. It produces many small rusty-colored spots on leaves or stems and copious quantities of orange, powdery spores. Pustules on leaves and twigs that are bright orange or yellow are generally some kind of rust, but be aware that *Nectria* (that sounds very malevolent, doesn't it? Isn't she a Borgia countess?), a fungal canker, also produces what appear to be orange pustules, except that they are very hard. A quick squeeze should tell you the difference, with apologies to Mr. Whipple.

Cedar-apple rust. This most spectacular rust spreads itself between junipers, ornamental crabapples, pears, quinces, mountain ash, chokeberry, Juneberry, hawthorns, and apple trees. The galls on juniper look like bizarre, alien Christmas ornaments with dimples like golf balls. But those cute little dimples will break out in slimy orange tentacles covered with spores that blow to alternate, non-evergreen hosts where they will produce a truly spectacular leaf spot. The leaf spot will grow from the top surface of the leaf to the lower surface in order to produce spores, which will reinfect junipers. Despite the Sci-Fi Armageddon appearance, no serious harm usually occurs although eastern red cedar may be damaged with heavy infestation.

Crabapple varieties 'Ellwangerina', 'Henry Kohankie', 'Ormiston Roy', or 'Red Barron' are less susceptible to rust. Cockspur hawthorn is resistant.

Cedar-apple rust is a bizarre-looking fungus on juniper.

Simply removing galls in spring on junipers can reduce disease, or plant *Juniperus chinensis* 'Foemina', 'Keteleeri', or 'Sargentii' for resistant plantings. *J. communis* 'Aureospica', 'Depressa', 'Suecica', and 'Saxatillis' are resistant, as are *J. squamata* 'Fargesii' and *J. virginiana* 'Tripartita'.

Juniper-quince rust. The only evidence you'll see of this much more insidious and damaging rust is innocuous-looking cracks or roughened bark on the twigs—but they are filled with orange blobs (spores) just waiting for dispersal. On juniper, these early symptoms develop into cigar-shaped galls that can kill entire branches. Once the spores find their way to the alternate host (most commonly hawthorn), they raise further havoc by destroying fruits and causing infected twig tips to become swollen and distorted. At this stage, 1/4-inch-long whitish tubes protrude from the swollen cankers and orange spores are shed, causing the cycle to repeat itself when it goes back to the junipers. The best options for protection or prevention are to keep alternate hosts far apart. Physical removal of galls, although possible with cedar-apple rust, is impractical for the quince rust.

Rusts on herbaceous plants. They usually first appear as pale spots on upper leaf surfaces, followed by pustules on both leaf sides. There is a simple test for rust in herbaceous plants: Rub infected leaves on a sheet of white paper. If you get a colored spore streak, you've got rust! Rusts in herbaceous plantings may have an alternate host.

Common mallow, a turf and border weed, is an alternate host for rust in hollyhocks and garden mallows. If you eliminate the weed, you often eliminate the rust! Regardless, remove infected foliage to reduce overwintering disease. Remove severely infected plants totally, but bag them first—before you pull them out—to reduce the movement of spores around the garden!

Daylily rust causes infected leaves to turn yellow, die, and dry up. A yellow or orange streak can usually be found when suspect leaves are rubbed with a bit of tissue (or a clean white hankie if you are in a Gothic novella). Cultivars, including the popular 'Stella D'Oro', differ in their susceptibility to rust. All infected plants should be removed and destroyed in order to prevent rapid spread.

To reduce rust, water early in the morning rather than in the evening to reduce leaf wetness. Although most rusts don't do that much damage, rust on iris can be severe, campanula can be scorched and stunted by rust, and popular garden favorites like hollyhock, snapdragon, and dianthus may be rust prone.

Monolinia or Brown Rot of Stone Fruit Trees

Now let me ask you this: Do your plants have mono? No, I'm not talking about the "kissing" disease. I'm talking about *Monolinia*, a.k.a. brown rot of stone fruit trees. Think you don't take care of any stone fruit trees? How about all those flowering cherry, almonds, and plums out there? What about Japanese quince (and rarely apple or pear)? Flowering cherries are the ones getting absolutely clobbered with this fungal disease.

Several different forms of brown rot cause cankers, dieback, and fruit rot. The first symptom may be blossom blight (the sudden collapse and browning of blossoms, which may be overlooked during the natural die-off phase following peak bloom). Shoot and twig blight follows over the next three to four weeks as the fungus spreads from blighted blossoms into shoots and twigs, causing leaves to brown and fall off or leaves to fall off still green.

Brown rot is common during wet springs.

The fungus harms the twigs and shoots by cutting off the water supply and nutrients, causing blossom clusters and leafy shoots to wilt and die, resulting in a syndrome known as "wither tip" (my Auntie Mathilda may have succumbed to this if the family stories have it right). Cankers that do not girdle appear as small, dark, discolored areas from which gum may exude. These cankers may be invaded secondarily by fungi.

The final phase is fruit rot, resulting in a rapidly enlarging brown spot that spreads quickly from one fruit to another when there is close contact. Fruits that are ripe, or ripening, are the most susceptible. Dried fruits may shrivel, remain on the trees, and become "mummies," which can serve as a source of infection in successive seasons.

Tufts of tan to gray fungus will break through the surface of infected plant parts. Wounds are the usual portal of entry, but the fungus can also penetrate intact leaves and fruit through natural openings. With rain and wind, there are many mechanical abrasions that serve as perfect infection points with plenty of environmental moisture to sustain the infection. Fungi are spread by splashing water, air, or insects. The optimum temperature for infection is 75 degrees F. To prevent an outbreak again next year, clean up all fallen debris promptly.

To sum it all up, look for dark, sunken areas with a dead twig or fruit spur extending from the center surrounded by gummy exudates—and get rid of your mummies!

Verticillium Wilt

You'll see a lot of declining maples during a summer between a long, cool spring and a prolonged shortage of rainfall. These trees have prematurely red leaves during the summer months.

There are several possibilities for this decline, including planting procedures, *Verticillium* wilt, and insufficient water. *Verticillium* fungus lives in soil and forms resting structures that stay viable for years. These very tiny structures wait for roots, especially wounded roots. Once it comes into contact with the roots, wounded or otherwise, the fungus is stimulated, germinates, grows into the young root, and then into water-conducting tissue in the main stem. The tree tries to block the infection, but inadvertently blocks water and vascular tissue as well, resulting in wilt. *Verticillium* is more likely found in young transplants since these specimens are more likely to have wounded roots.

How do you manage a specimen with *Verticillium*? The fungus does not grow well into new growth rings, so if the tree has it and doesn't die outright, the best option is encourage a new ring of wood so the fungus will be trapped inside like an evil spirit. To facilitate a new growth ring,

Verticillium infects many, many different kinds of plants. To diagnose *Verticillium*, peel back the bark near the base of the plant. Because the fungus comes up from roots, you may see the discoloration in the area connecting the branch to the tree (the collar) rather than in wilted branches themselves.

accelerate tree growth through any means that will boost the tree's health. The good news is that *Verticillium* does **not** affect monocots, conifers, oaks, or *Ginkgo*. Goody!

Verticillium dormancy in the soil breaks because of the presence of root exudates from the host plant in response to wounding—in other words, when you dig up and move the plant from place to place or when you remove plants from soil each year for winter storage. This is why the most common time to see *Verticillium* is the first few years after transplant and the reason that *Dahlia* tend to get *Verticillium* infections so frequently.

Verticillium in Mimosa trees and Japanese maples. This disease is confirmed by the presence of brown streaks in the wood under the bark. There is no cure other than pruning out the infected portion. Make sure the plant has adequate water and nutrients since the fungus spreads more quickly in plants growing in less than optimal sites. *Verticillium* often shortens the life span of mimosas.

Verticillium in herbaceous plants. Many are affected, including monks-

Verticillium *wilt produces discoloration in vascular tissue.*

hood, *Aster*, *Chrysanthemum*, *Coreopsis*, *Dahlia*, *Delphinium*, *Dicentra*, *Impatiens*, peony, poppy, and *Phlox*. Plants can also be infected but not show symptoms until subjected to stress like high temperatures or drought. Again, remove affected plants for the best control.

Rots

Armillaria **and other shoestring rots** are everywhere in the soil, just waiting for an opportunity to make a good meal of something. The infective stage of these fungi grows through the soil from an existing host, looking for a new source of nourishment. These fungi live quite well from both dead material and live. Research has shown that the larger the stump you leave in the ground, the more likely the fungus will be healthy enough to infect the next tree down the line. Therefore, grinding out old stumps is important! And don't replant susceptible trees in infected areas.

How can you tell you have shoestring fungus? Look for honey-colored mushrooms at the base of the tree in the fall, or carefully remove a piece of bark at the base of an ailing tree and look for "shoestrings" clinging to the trunk beneath the bark.

Conk. Another major root rot is the beautiful conk. This sneaky little fungus infects healthy tree roots through lawnmower or trimmer injury, plugging up the vascular system and causing a rot right at the base of the tree. Conks are also seen farther up the tree where they are known collectively as shelf fungi. Shelf fungi decay the tree or shrub for years before they are visible to us as "shelves." Each ridge on a shelf fungus represents a year's growth of the fungus. The presence of shelf fungi could indicate a hazard tree, especially if the shelves are at the base of the trunk on the buttress roots. Shelf fungi usually attack wounds, so control your weedwhackers!

Mildew

Powdery mildew is probably the most common fungal disease you'll encounter over your entire landscape. It covers everything from *Monarda* (beebalm) to lilacs to maples with what looks like a fine coating of baby powder. Fortunately, it's usually not fatal unless it occurs in conjunction with other diseases or problems.

You are most likely to see powdery mildew in areas that are dry but have high humidity, especially where light intensity and air circulation are low. There is no need to ever treat large shade trees. On ninebark

Powdery mildew is one of the most common diseases of all plants.

(*Physocarpus*), you'll see witch's brooms induced by powdery mildew; these can be pruned off. Deal with powdery mildew bothering your *Monarda* by planting varieties with genetic resistance. The better varieties include 'Blue Stocking', 'Marshall's Delight', and 'Violet Queen'; less than 20 percent of the leaf surface is bothered on these. The worst varieties include Adam, Cambridge Scarlet, Croftway Pink, Purple Crown, and Souris. Seaweed fertilizers may help plants like peonies to grow out of powdery mildew.

Sometimes powdery mildew produces black fruiting structures that look like mites to the naked eye but are hard to dislodge. Don't be fooled! Leaves may also take on a reddish cast and become distorted, such as you would see with a nutrient deficiency or an aphid attack. Again, confirm what you are dealing with.

There are several indicator plants. You'll see it first on the older leaves of lilac and on new shoots and leaves of roses—leaves may curl or be stunted and twisted.

Baking-soda-based products can be used to treat powdery mildew, but remember that these can accumulate in the soil, so make sure you water the area surrounding your plants thoroughly after application.

Don't plant too densely, and do choose sunny sites. Overhead irrigation also promotes the disease, especially on very popular, very susceptible herbaceous plants such as *Aster*, *Coreopsis*, sweet pea, beebalm (*Monarda*), *Phlox*, rose, and *Rudbeckia*.

Downy mildews produce characteristic symptoms on the undersides of leaves, but you'll see pale green or

Downy mildew is easily mistaken for other diseases or problems.

yellow patches on the upper surface of leaves while fuzzy white, tan, or gray spores are produced on the undersides of leaves on the opposite side of the pale spots.

Older leaves are affected first by this fungus and often turn brown and dry. Closely related weeds may be the source of spores for infection. For example, *Geum* and *Potentilla* get their infection from Indian strawberry weed. Pansies and roses are hard hit by the disease. The main control is to remove infected plants. Spores persist for several years. Reduce leaf wetness time, and increase spacing, especially on susceptible plants like *Artemisia, Aster,* bachelor's button, geranium, *Geum,* lupine, *Nicotiana,* pansies, *Potentilla,* rose, *Rudbeckia,* snapdragon, *Veronica, Viola, Anemone,* carnations, goldenrod, *Gaura,* evening primrose, *Viburnum,* and *Clarkia.*

The interesting thing about downy mildew is that it appears in some years but not in others. It can mimic aphid damage or even other leaf spots since you may see reddish black spots on leaves, petals, and stems, especially on roses. Seeds can also be infected. The disease is most severe when days are warm with high relative humidity (85 percent or more) and nights are cool.

Nectria

Is your tree necking with *Nectria?* In the love fest between fungi and stressed trees, there is one story that poignantly calls attention to itself by producing concentric rolls of tissue on bark. This gives your tree more double chins than a Shar Pei has. This is target or *Nectria* canker, which is also called coral spot because of the orange or salmon dots on infected bark. *Nectria* particularly likes stressed trees. It gets in through wounds, colonizes only living bark, killing some of the food, water tubes, and wood. The fungus grows when the tree is dormant so that you get a ton of fancy callus formation.

Nectria will kill beech already attacked by scale, so beware. No others will be killed by the canker itself—but the disease poses a greater threat by providing an avenue for secondary invaders.

Dutch Elm Disease

One of the most well-known fungi, Dutch elm disease is vectored by a tiny insect called a bark beetle, which carries the disease organism under its wings. Bark beetles sense stressed trees by the chemicals the trees exude. The bark beetle samples the tree, and if the tree is suitable, the beetle itself exudes a chemical that calls all of its friends over for a nosh. The fungus gets into the hole that the beetle is boring, is sucked into the plant, and causes the initially fed-on branch to wilt (flag).

You must prune out that flag immediately; if you don't, a bit of the fungus is sucked all the way down to the base of the tree and then pushed back up through the pipes to infect the entire plant. Not only do you have no hope for this plant, but elms living in proximity to each other graft their roots together so the fungus can be sucked into a neighboring tree. If the tree's a goner, you must remove the tree and stump as soon as possible and remove the bark from the logs because this is where the reservoir of fungus lies.

Asiatic, Chinese, and Siberian elms are resistant to Dutch elm disease but can still get elm phloem necrosis. The Princeton variety of elm resists Dutch

If you are lucky enough to still have an American elm, remember that drought stress can enhance susceptibility to Dutch elm disease. Apply 2 inches of water per week to avoid drought stress in mature trees. In a typical landscape, 0.2 inches of water moistens soil to a depth of 1 inch; therefore, 2 inches of water should go down about 10 inches and get to the area where most of the tree's absorbing roots are located.

elm disease, as do the Valley Forge variety and New Harmony. There are eight hybrids between Asian and European elms.

Phytophthora

This soil-borne fungal horror attacks the roots and causes remote symptoms in the leaves. *Phytophthora* is a huge problem on many plants. In *Rhododendron*, leaves roll downward in a fashion similar to the effects of drought or cold. Leaves dieback near the stem of the leaf, and on the trunk, you'll find firm, red or brown dry rot or brown streaks beneath the bark when you peel a bit back with a pen knife near the base. Purplish foliage can also be a hallmark of

Phytophthora. You'll see it in heavy soil with nonacid pH, particularly in areas of high rainfall or irrigation.

Dull foliage, yellowing, and wilting may happen quickly or over several months. Symptoms often show on only one side of the plant. Prune out and remove the infected side. Most important to the diagnosis are brown, mushy, rotted roots. Use the pantyhose test from Chapter 1: Does the outer layer of the root slip back easily? If so and you have some of the other symptoms, chances are you have the

Wilting rhododendron with Phytophthora *infections are often seen in wet sites.*

Phytophthora fungus. Infection occurs when root tips are saturated over a long period, so don't plant shrubs under downspouts! Increase drainage and check for proper planting depth because a shrub planted too deep is a prime candidate for *Phytophthora*, as is a plant with too much mulch (over 3 inches). Increasing the acidity of the soil can also help to inhibit this fungus. Plants and their roots stressed by drought or flooding are most susceptible. If your plant is infected, cull it because fungicides are only going to delay the inevitable. Amending soil with shredded bark may help to reduce the incidence of disease.

Phytophthora in petunias. Petunia late blight is caused by the same *Phytophthora* that caused the Irish potato blight. Small spots on your petunias serve as a disease source for tomatoes planted nearby. The fungus can also cause a dry rot on one side of petunia plants or may at first only affect lateral branches. Later, the whole plant wilts. Sometimes you get petunia late blight with a secondary black soft rot of roots. A sick plant that lacks white mold may indicate *Phytophthora*. Once again, petunia *Phytophthora* infections are especially associated with heavy soils. Don't plant your petunias too deep!

This vinca is under attack from root and stem diseases.

Phytophthora in *Vinca minor*. A *Phytophthora*-induced root and stem rot can occur on the ground cover *Vinca minor*. Stems turn black, and entire patches of *Vinca* die. *Vinca* is also susceptible to a stem rot caused by the fungus *Phomopsis*. The disease causes the stems to (yep, here we go again) wilt, turn black, and die. Control involves removing the dead stems and possibly applying a fungicidal drench or changing to a ground cover that is not susceptible. Once the disease becomes established, it is difficult to eradicate.

Fungal Leaf Spots

Many fungi cause leaf spots, but many of them are inconsequential and can be completely ignored. Sometimes a leaf spot in conjunction with environmental factors can conspire against a plant to seriously sicken or kill it. Keep your eyes open for signs of decline!

Dealing with Leaf Spot

Dealing with leaf spots in general is a matter of common sense rather than reaching for a bottle of "stuff." Gather and destroy fallen leaves in autumn to reduce the amount of disease in the environment. A strong stream of water helps to remove dead foliage from dense evergreen shrubs like boxwood or arborvitae and can be used to flush the materials out from under a prickly shrub for disposal. This method also provides a necessary prewinter watering, which helps reduce winter desiccation (particularly for vulnerable plants like boxwoods!).

For conifers or other small-leaf plants where collection is not practical, try drying the conditions under the plant by installing fluffy oak leaf mulch. This reduces the chances of reinfecting the plant with leaf spot through alternate wetting and drying of dropped infected foliage and also conserves moisture to help reduce stress.

Make sure your plants are well spaced, and apply mulch to reduce grass and weeds that can provide moisture and humidity, which favor leaf spot activity. Prune lower branches so they won't touch the soil and so air will circulate freely.

Horse chestnut blotch is a very ugly fungal leaf spot that overwinters on fallen leaves. You'll encounter it starting in mid-July. Horse chestnut blotch defoliates the trees in about four weeks. Believe it or not, the disease is not significant to tree health because the defoliation occurs later in the season.

Botryosphaeria is a twin to apple scab, except that you get frog-eye leaf spots with brown margins and brown to tan centers (rather than olive spots). This fungus develops later in the spring than apple scab and causes a canker on redbud that may cause the tree to split. Clean up leaves to reduce the disease.

Sometimes *Botryosphaeria* can cause brown or black sunken areas or cankers on stems that actually girdle an area so the infected portion wilts. This is often the case on *Rhododendron* and azalea. The center part of infected twigs may be dark brown surrounded by lighter wood. You'll also see black dots on affected bark. If pruning cuts or wounds near the soil line are invaded, then large parts of the shrub may die. Prune back to at least 4 inches below a *Botryosphaeria* canker.

Privet decline is usually a combination of excess moisture coupled by leaf spots caused by *Cercospora* and *Alternaria* brought on by the stress of too

Volutella *blight is a typical disease of stressed pachysandra.*

much water. For the most part, fungicides are not effective; you must change the cultural practices that affect moisture.

Cercospora also produces a severe leaf spot on *Hydrangea* so that the poor plant is covered with small red spots sort of like the measles. Again, control is cultural because fungicides are not particularly effective. Infections are commonly seen starting in midsummer and through late fall. *Cercospora* may appear on nursery stock that has been held for several years. The spread of the fungus is wind and water driven. High humidity, low air circulation, and overhead irrigation hitting foliage all contribute to disease outbreaks.

Volutella (I swear I should have been named this) is a disease that primarily attacks either *Pachysandra* or boxwood in the landscape. It has a normal role in decay, but on stressed plants, you may see concentric rings similar to *Nectria* canker. You'll see it mostly on *Pachysandra* in full sun, on areas that have been exposed to excessive amounts of salt from walkway or street runoff, or on areas that have previously been in shade and are suddenly flooded with sun due to tree removal.

In all cases, *Volutella* is most likely to occur on plants that are stressed by winter injury, were grown in crowded conditions, or have been exposed to prolonged wetness. Improve air circulation and thin plants by pruning or mowing over. Keep *Pachysandra* in shade: Three to five hours of sun is enough to bring on the disease. Remember that high salts in soil will increase disease problems without any other evidence of salt injury.

Phyllosticta is a leaf spot seen in early summer on maples, but fortunately it is

Phyllosticta leaf spot is cosmetic.

cosmetic only. You'll get tan centers with purple to red borders. Later, you'll see black rings in the spots. It affects amur; Japanese, silver, and red maples; *Delphinium*; *Heuchera*; *Iris*; *Liatris*; *Monarda*; and *Rudbeckia*.

Septoria, a leaf spot similar to *Phyllosticta*, affects columbine, *Aster*, *Chrysanthemum*, *Coreopsis*, *Phlox*, and *Rudbeckia*. Another called **Colletotrichum** affects *Hosta*, *Bergenia*, and snapdragons, while one called **Didymellina** affects *Iris*. Do you need to remember the names? Nah . . . you just have to follow general leaf spot reduction protocols like reducing leaf wetness and increasing air circulation. You **would** need to know the difference if you were going to use a fungicide because not all fungicides work on all fungi. But for herbaceous plantings, using such a product is seldom justified because you'll just be rolling a stone uphill. Switch to more resistant plantings!

Root and Stem Rots

Root and stem rots are particularly common fungal diseases on annuals and perennials. An unhealthy root system usually produces symptoms of wilting, stunting, and nutrient deficiency. They are favored by cool, wet soils with poor drainage. The first symptom of a *Pythium* infection is yellowing of a plant's lower leaves. The infection starts at root tips, spreads rapidly, and turns roots brown, gray, or black. Salt excess from fertilizers, de-icing, or saltwater intrusion makes it worse. *Pythium* feeds on the outer core of roots, leaving a stringy center like soggy lettuce in a taco, so do the pantyhose test outlined in Chapter 1. *Phytophthora* usually moves up into the stem to cause a canker at the plant's base. *Phytophthora* can also cause black and bleeding cankers on such diverse plants as *Prunus*, yews, *Euphorbia*, lavender, and andromeda.

Do not overfertilize, especially with a quick-release product, or you'll get high salts around roots, which increases the potential for root rot.

Keep drainage in good form because roots injured by low oxygen in the soil attract root rot organisms! The more acidic the soil (low pH), the worse the root rot problem because there is no microbial activity to break down accumulated root toxins. Two major exceptions are *Phytophthora* and *Thelaviopsis* (black root rot), which are both antagonized by low soil pH.

Plants can be girdled at the soil line (damping off), or you can get shriveling and browning of the stem just at the soil surface during hot summer months. *Fusarium* is the major player in root or stem rots of annuals (basil growers, beware!), while *Verticillium* is the major player in perennials. *Fusarium* contaminates the soil, so susceptible plants will have to be grown elsewhere for at least five years. **Use kelp or seaweed amendments to reduce all root rots, and keep drainage as good as possible.** Once again, leaf yellowing, wilting, and main and feeder root dieback are the primary symptoms.

Damping Off and Seedling Disease

To reduce damping off and other seedling diseases, you can microwave your planting mix to sterilize it or you can treat seeds with a solution of 1 part bleach to 5 parts water for fifteen to thirty minutes to kill spores on the outside of the seed (but since seeds may be sensitive, do only a few and then try to sprout them just to make sure the surface sterilization isn't doing more harm than good). When watering seedlings, avoid splashing and don't use a hose nozzle that drops or drags on the ground.

Overhead watering can cause outbreaks of root and crown rot on drought-tolerant ground covers, usually manifesting as dry, tan to brown, sunken stems. The feeder roots and main roots become soft and mushy. Try using composted bark chips as a mulch to combat the situation, which can occur even with good drainage. You'll also see the worst disease with low calcium, nitrogen, and potassium levels, so a soil nutrient test can give you good information on ways to reduce your disease problem.

Black root rot (*Thelaviopsis*) is primarily seen on weakened plants, which respond by yellowing or stunting or wilting. Root cankers are discolored black or gray areas, and there are characteristic black stem lesions near the soil line. The disease is worst at pH levels below 5.6 and in heavy, cold soil with high organic matter levels. Hollies and inkberries are very badly affected. You'll have to avoid replanting with susceptible stock for two years.

Canker can affect even resistant plants like this kerria.

Canker of Annuals and Perennials

Cankers are brown or black areas that shrink with time as adjacent tissues continue to grow. Stressed plants will develop more extensive cankers than nonstressed ones. Prune out cankers when plant surfaces are dry. Cut below the cankered area, just above a node at a slight slant to minimize stubs. Stubs frequently die back and are a perfect place for new cankers to form.

Bacterial Diseases

Bacteria multiply rapidly: One cell can produce 17 million within an hour (which I find frightening). They need moisture and prefer warmth. They may produce toxins or enzymes, or simply clog up the plant's food and water tubes like they clog up your sinuses. They spread by water, insects, animals, and the movement of infected plants. Bacteria need wounds to infect, like those at the base of a cutting, pruning, insect feeding, or egg laying site, or from storm or mechanical damage.

Bacterial disease symptoms include spots with a yellow halo; soft rot of roots, bulbs, or corms; and especially galls or other bizarre growths, wilts, or cankers. If the plant problem is oozing, slimy, and stinky, chances are you have bacteria! You'll see more bacterial disease with a wet June.

Many bacteria come in after other infections or problems. A vector (often an insect) may transport bacteria from one susceptible plant to another. Bacteria may also persist in cankers.

Bacteria tend to produce lots of sticky slime, which helps it spread, so sanitation is very important. Be sure to reduce bacteria by removing and discarding (in a remote location) any infected plant parts. Decontaminate tools and hands with bleach, alcohol, or peroxide. Make sure you employ cultural practices by not overwatering, and reduce fertilizer in order to reduce juiciness. Always use slow-release fertilizers since quick-release fertilizers stimulate the rapid, tender growth preferred for bacterial attack.

Bacterial control with chemicals is not effective or practical for the landscape. You can try to sterilize or solarize soil, but it will not be effective for very long and is really not practical on a large scale.

Vascular Wilt of Annuals and Perennials

There are both bacterial and fungal vascular wilts of annuals and perennials. Symptoms similar to root rot are produced, but roots may still look healthy. Above-ground plant parts, however, are stunted and scorched, with leaves that wilt and die. Vascular wilts may appear on only one side of the plant or on half of the leaf. Because these diseases travel in the water tubes, a cross-section of the stem will reveal a series of dark dots and a lengthwise shave downward shows dark streaks. Shasta daisy may be often affected, and *Fusarium* wilt is highly specific to China aster, *Chrysanthemum*, *Dahlia*, and sweet William.

Fungal or Bacterial?

The critical difference between fungal and bacterial wilts is that fungi stay in the water tubes, while bacteria dissolve the tubes and move into adjacent tissues, causing pockets of bacteria, gum, and cellular debris. Yech! Cracks then form at the surface of these pockets, and the ooze leaks out and spreads. At this point, your plant is history!

Monitoring for bacterial wilt: How do you tell if your plants are suffering from bacterial wilt? Starting at the soil line, cut a chunk 2 to 3 inches long, place it in a clear glass of water, and then shine a flashlight through from the other side. If you see thin, white smokelike tendrils, the plant is afflicted by some form of bacteria. Or slice the stem horizontally, and then push the two cut ends back together. Carefully pull them apart again, looking for a sticky strand to remain between the cut ends. This indicates bacterial infection, as well. Plants often affected by bacterial wilts include those in the tomato family and those in the aster family. Bacterial wilts can be especially bad in ornamental peppers, sunflowers, marigolds, and *Zinnia*.

When determining whether you have a bacterial infection, remember that dicots (most trees, shrubs, and flowering plants—which have leaves with non-parallel veins) will have a circular or angular spot often with a yellow halo while monocots (grasses and bulbs, like lilies—which have leaves with parallel veins) will have streaks or stripes.

Bacterial Vascular Wilts

Wilts caused by bacteria often affect only herbaceous plants. Bacteria enter, move through, and multiply in the water tubes of host plants and interfere with the movement of water and nutrients, so you'll get drooping, wilting, and death of aboveground parts. Begonia wilt starts with small, glassy spots on the undersides of leaves that eventually develop a yellow halo. Disinfect if you take cuttings.

Fire blight. Ash, hawthorn, apple, pear, cherry, plum, *Cotoneaster*, and *Pyracantha*, to name a few, are affected by fire blight. It causes blackened, oozing, blighted areas; kills blossoms and branches; and creates cankers. The first symptom is usually blossom discoloration or a shepherd's crook. If trees or shrubs have many branches affected simultaneously, it looks like the plant has been scorched by fire. The woody parts of newly infected shoots are discolored reddish brown, which helps to distinguish it from other diseases.

The disease is vectored by insects, rain, or watering; control the disease, not the vector. If you get it, you need to prune 6 to 8 inches below the infected area or cankers, and then disinfect your pruners with bleach or rubbing alcohol. Prune out dieback during late winter. Canker removal disposes of a large amount of primary infectious material for the following year. Again, disinfect between cuts—or you'll spread the bacteria everywhere. Lists of resistant plants are available, so make sure you consult one before you plant!

During moist weather, bacteria ooze like used car salesmen from natural openings or wounds on infected surfaces, and, as I mentioned, the bacteria are very sticky. So when insects walk through it and move to another susceptible plant, they move the disease from place to place. This is yet another reason not to plant a bunch of anything that is all the same variety. Pollinators like bees and flies are the most common vectors.

Bacterial leaf scorch affects elms, oaks, sweet gums, and sugar and red maples. The scorch is caused by bacteria infecting water tubes, so the tree is not able to absorb water effectively. Discoloration begins at the leaf margin and moves towards the midrib, progressing from leaf to leaf near the tree's crown as dieback begins. The primary symptom is the browning of leaf margins from mid- to late summer.

Oaks and elms may especially develop a yellow margin between the outer scorched part of the leaf and the green inner leaf. On sycamores and oaks, you may see a red or brown interior edge of leaf tissue. Mulberry and oak

What Caused My Scorch?

One way of telling the difference between salt or environmental scorch and bacterial scorch is that all leaves on a plant affected by salt or environmental stress will be scorched, but a bacterial scorch will have some healthy, some scorched. Salt-scorched leaves will not have the characteristic yellow band. Scorch begins on basal leaves and progresses toward the tip. Oaks are likely to be affected on upper and outer branches, but scorched leaves are retained until autumn, unlike oak wilt. Scorch is also likely to occur on the coast, while oak wilt is found in the interior regions.

may drop leaves early, whereas sycamore leaves curl upwards but remain attached. The condition gets worse each year with growth reduction and dieback. You'll see no discoloration of wood, so that helps to separate scorch from oak wilt or Dutch elm disease.

Sharpshooter leafhoppers and spittle bugs are vectors, since they feed on water tubes. Scorch can spread from tree to tree by root graft, as well. The condition is reported nationwide in areas with moderate winter temperatures, predominantly in the mid-Atlantic region. It is especially bad in drought years, with oaks hardest hit.

Again, control of insect vectors is not practical. There is no cure, and even removing the affected tree may not solve the problem of spread to other trees. Pruning out infected limbs below the last scorched leaf, however, may cure an early infection.

Sycamores may produce leaves later than usual in spring when affected by scorch. Scorch predisposes elms to attack by bark beetles, and in fact, 40 percent of all Dutch elm diseased trees in one Washington, D.C., study were affected by scorch, as well.

Soft rot. Bacterial rot stinks—literally! Many times a serious problem already exists and the bacteria just come in and finish the plant off. Be careful not to wound plants with your weedwhacker because that is a great avenue for bacterial entry.

Crown gall. This bacterial disease is the only equivalent to a plant "cancer." The bacteria basically turns off the plant's ability to stop scabbing itself over, resulting in large woody galls produced on stems and roots. Crown gall occurs on many woody plants, especially stone fruits, apples, pears, quinces and their relatives, willows, brambles, grapes, raspberries, blackberries, *Euonymus*, and many others.

Most often you'll see crown gall at soil and graft unions. It doesn't kill the plants, but it is *uuuggly*. The moral of the story is not to buy bumpy plants. Prune during cold weather since bacteria are less likely to be active. Remove and destroy infected plants.

Other bacteria can cause leafy galls on annuals or perennial herbaceous orna-

Crown gall causes the plant equivalent of a tumor.

mentals and on olives and oleanders (these two will have hollow bacterial galls, while all others will be solid). Gall-forming bacteria are spread by tools like pruners and knives, soil, water, rain, and splashing. Crown gall disease is rare on annuals and perennials, but you may see it on yarrow, *Aster*, *Chrysanthemum*, *Dahlia*, *Delphinium*, *Phlox*, and rose.

Bacterial cankers are not always soft or sunken; they may be just splits in the stem, necrotic areas in the stem, or scabby areas on the surface of the tissue. They may have a slimy exudate, a dark gummy exudate, or nothing for much of the year. Sometimes canker-forming bacteria cause a syndrome called "gummosis" (I didn't make that up) on cherry trees where large mounds of resinous material will spontaneously appear on the bark.

Bacterial canker diseases are common, but they seldom cause much damage. There is an association with trees suffering from some other environmental stress. Areas attacked by bark beetles are a common site of infection.

Liquid seeping from a bacterial canker may have a sour odor and may also have a white froth with an alcoholic odor present at the surface of cracks in the bark. This situation is called "alcoholic flux" (I didn't make this up either) in elm, sweet gum, and oak in the Midwest.

Bacterial leaf spot. During wet weather, diseased tissue drops out of bacterial leaf spots, leaving round, shot-hole or ragged edges on the margin of the spot. The rim often turns brown within a few days of tissue drop out.

This disease is very common on ivy, *Zinnia*, *Begonia*, geranium, and hyacinth. You'll often see it with frequent rain, high humidity, or irrigation. The

Bacterial leaf spot is common in wet, warm weather.

hallmarks are red or brown angular spots surrounded by a yellow halo, surrounded again by a water-soaked halo. You'll see it on the older leaves first at temperatures of 60 to 80 degrees F. following prolonged leaf wetness.

Annuals and perennials usually do not develop severe bacterial problems, but bacterial spots and blights are much more aggressive in hot weather! If you do develop a problem, use sanitation as a control by removing infected leaves as soon as you see them. Scout plants, especially new ones, for signs of disease, and rip them out before they infect everyone else! *Delphinium*, monkshood, *Iris*, geranium, *Zinnia*, *Begonia*, and poppy are all prone to bacterial problems.

Lilac blight. This common bacterial disease affects Japanese, Persian, Chinese, and common (especially white) lilacs. Lilac blight also affects stone fruits (especially peaches), forsythia, mock orange, pear, and cherry laurel. The blight causes brown spots and blotches with yellow halos that eventually run together to involve the whole leaf. Young shoots may have black stripes, or the spots may be one-sided because only part of the shoot is infected. Sometimes young plants turn black and die quickly like fire blight infections. Flowers turn brown and limp. Buds turn black. Stems are infected through leaves and directly through bark. Black areas are seen on the stems.

Rain, frequent overhead irrigation, and succulent tissues from too much fertilizer all increase the incidence. Bacteria-causing blight overwinters in infected tissues and creates new infections with cool, wet conditions. Remove infected shoots several inches below visible cankers. Prune only when dry, and disinfect pruners between cuts. Prune to increase air flow within and around shrubs.

Ice crystals plus lilac blight lead to this lilac blight syndrome. If you have both infection **and** low temperatures, you get severe damage that would not occur if you had either factor alone. Bad or untimely pruning in autumn and winter may predispose plants to bud blight or cankers.

Geranium bacterial infections are very common and might begin with a small, circular leaf spot with a yellow halo. The spot is at first sunken but enlarges until the leaf wilts and collapses. You may also get a V-shaped yellow to brown lesion. Stem rot may appear where affected leaves remain attached. Geranium stems take on a grassy, gray-green color during midsummer, and leaves in the affected stem wilt and die. (You'll get the full scoop on geranium problems in Chapter 7.) Leaves in the upper part of the plant appear tufted, small, and dark green. Make a cross-section two to four weeks after infection, and look for discoloration plus yellow bacterial ooze. Roots turn black but don't rot. Whiteflies occasionally spread the disease.

The problem initially develops when weather is still, warm, and

Bacterial problems on geraniums are very obvious.

moist. **Absolutely do not** use overhead watering because this can spread the infection. If taking cuttings, sterilize tools in a 10 percent bleach solution.

Zinnias get a similar bacterial disease, but unfortunately, they can get fungal and bacterial stuff at the same time. You'll see water soaking around dead tissue in the morning; bacterial problems are easiest to see early in the morning when dew is still present. Look for the yellow halo!

Mycoplasma Diseases

Mycoplasma-Like Organisms (MLOs) are odd bacteria-like and virus-like organisms vectored by insects into the food tubes of plants. They are transmitted by aphids, leafhoppers, psyllids, treehoppers, and planthoppers, all of whom you will meet in Chapter 5. MLOs are mostly spread by leafhoppers. The diseases often overwinter in infected perennial plants.

The symptoms they cause are called "the yellows" because you'll see gradual, uniform yellowing or reddening of leaves that become progressively smaller than normal. The whole plant stunts, puts on less growth each year than it should, and in a characteristic particularly well associated with MLOs, produces an excessive proliferation of shoots called "witch's brooms." Oddly enough, flowers may turn green or be sterile and small roots may even die.

Weed control is a good option for mycoplasma diseases because it eliminates pools of the diseases hiding within the weeds and gets rid of alternate plant hosts for the vectors!

Aster yellows mycoplasma is carried by leafhoppers, and the disease occurs in pansy, marigold, and petunia, and in perennials *Gaillardia*, *Chrysanthemum*, *Bellis*, *Campanula*, *Coreopsis*, *Delphinium*, *Rudbeckia*, *Echinacea*, and *Salvia*. Often the **first** symptom is that leaf veins turn yellow. Other major symptoms are that the foliage yellows and witch's brooms are formed at the plant's base. Flowers look really weird with small petals partly or entirely green. *Allium* flowers lose their compact, globular shapes and look like they desperately need a haircut. You **must** remove infected plants entirely!

Ash yellows causes decline and dieback of many ash trees. White ash is especially susceptible, while green ash is more tolerant. The disease may not kill, but it weakens so that secondary problems take over. The first symptom is subnormal growth with very little twig elongation and trunk growth. You can expect death of the affected ash in one to three years.

Peach MLOs. Peach X disease affects sweet and tart cherries, nectarines, and chokecherries, as well as peaches. Leaves become mottled and get reddish-purple spots. Leaf spots eventually fall out. Leaves then turn red, and the margins curl up. Next, leaves drop off altogether beginning at the base of the branch. Eventually a tuft of leaves appears at the end of the bare branch. The fruit shrivels, and any left have a nasty taste. The disease is transmitted by leafhoppers and by root grafts with adjacent trees.

Elm yellows (elm phloem necrosis) infection begins with the death of fine roots and then progresses to larger roots so that yellowing and premature leaf drop occur. The eventual butterscotch discoloration of inner bark indicates the death of food tubes. American elms produce a diagnostic wintergreen odor when infected. To determine this characteristic, put a chunk of moist, fresh, inner bark in a jar with a lid for a few minutes; then unscrew the cap and take a whiff (the smell will not be present in dead trees).

This MLO affects American, slippery, winged, and some hybrids (Siberian is immune). Slippery elms may produce witch's brooms when infected. Symptoms may develop in just a few weeks. Most affected trees die within one to two years of showing foliar symptoms (but they may die in a single growing season if they show symptoms from June to July). Remove infected trees.

MLOs and lilacs. You may see leaf scorch and dieback in addition to witch's brooms. Plants die within a few years of brooming. Hungarian lilac and Japanese tree lilac have the worst symptoms, but you may also see evidence of disease in panicled red osier dogwoods, silky dogwoods, flowering dogwood, black- and heart-leaved willow, apple, ash, blueberry, Chinese elm, black and honey locust, papaya, peach, and sassafras.

Viruses

Viruses seldom kill plants, but they sure do look **weird.** Conifers are rarely affected. About 90 percent of virus transmission is by piercing sucking insects. Viruses can also enter plants through wounds.

The most common symptom is simply a reduced growth rate. Other common visual symptoms are bull's-eyes and mosaics (light green, yellow, white areas

Virus symptoms are easily seen on this leaf.

intermingled with the normal green of leaves or fruit, or white areas intermingled with the normal color of flowers or fruit), and ringspots. There is also a bizarre viral symptom that causes outgrowth on the leaf underside along the vein. Viruses can cause leaf galls. One very desirable viral symptom, especially in tulips, is flower "break" or color streaking.

Shoestring leaves, witch's brooms, yellow veins with green surrounds, or leaves with green veins while the rest of the leaf is yellow (looks like nutrient deficiency) are also all common symptoms of viral infection.

Viruses in redbuds. Progressive dieback of redbud is sometimes associated with short bands of yellow tissue along primary and secondary veins in leaves seen in spring soon after leaf expansion. Leaves may then become brown or have reddish-brown flecks, branches may lose vigor and dieback over the winter, or the tree will have abnormally small leaves and an open canopy.

Viruses in gladiolas. Yellowed, streaked, and mottled patterns and flower streaking are symptoms. Flowers may fail to open or fade rapidly. Severe stunting is a common problem. The viral yellows infection of gladiolas causes twisting and distortion of the flower spike, the plants are small and spindly, and flowers may remain green. Not sure whether you have virus or thrips damage? Look for thrips themselves within the flowers (see Chapter 5 for groovy thrips facts). Grow a tall ornamental between plantings of gladiolas to reduce insect transmission of viruses.

Viruses in *Anemone*, *Epimedium*, and *Hosta*. Tobacco rattle virus can cause strange yellow rings on *Anemone* and *Epimedium*, and *Impatiens* necrotic ring spot virus (INSV) does the same on *Hosta*. Of more concern, however, is a new viral disease of *Hostas* menacingly named "Virus X." This viral disease results in yellow splotches, blotches, browning, and collapse but, unfortunately, is the very factor providing color to the *Hosta* varieties 'Eternal Father', 'Leopard Frog', 'Lunacy', and 'Breakdance'. These varieties should be removed from your garden repertoire.

Nematodes

Nematode attacks usually leave plants yellow with stunted shoots and stems and cause the death of leaf areas between main veins. General nematode symptoms resemble nutrient or moisture stress. If you look at the roots, the root hairs are gone, unlike fungal infections where they're discolored but remain. You may often see nematode problems in boxwoods, especially in Washington, D.C., and farther south. Nematodes may also affect marigolds, salvias, verbenas, periwinkles, *Zinnia*, and a host of other herbaceous and woody ornamentals. Root knot nematodes are the most common trouble makers in landscapes in central and southern parts of the U.S.

Nematodes cause stress and create holes in the roots that allow secondary pathogens to enter, making them a major player in certain root rot situations. They are typically more numerous in warmer, sandier soils. Nematode-affected roots may lack feeder roots, which help to bind soil, collect water and nutrients, and keep the plant cool by moving water up through the top of the plant where it evaporates. Very few products are effective against nematodes, so management is best when resistant plantings are used.

Disease mimics can be tricky to properly diagnose. Here are a few of the most common ones:

Herbicide injury. One of the most common and easy-to-spot symptoms is the classic twisted look, tip yellowing, and dieback. Injury is dose dependent—with twisted, distorted leaves at low doses and shoot death at high doses.

Environmental wilt. Either drought or overwatering can cause wilt via root suffocation and decay so that the roots cannot properly supply the plant.

Edema. If the roots are still functioning properly and you have wet soil coupled with overcast weather, internal pressure can accumulate in leaves, causing a condition known as edema. Edema leads to the rupture of cells in the lower leaf surface, and scablike spots. It can happen **overnight!**

Issues of pH. Got a pH below 6.0? French marigolds and geraniums may end up with brown, black, or purple flecks on lower or middle leaves, or you may see yellow or brown margins on the plant. These symptoms can also be caused by numerous other things.

These leaf spots and marginal discoloration are caused by cultural issues.

Sooty mold is due to the excretions of piercing, sucking insects.

Sooty mold. Affected plants are covered by a black mold that resembles soot. It affects all parts of the plant, generally comes off with a finger or knife, may develop a crust that causes evergreen needles to mat together, and during dry weather may blow off in fragments. It can reduce photosynthesis and cause yellowing, but the yellowing is more likely due to the heavy insect load that results in the black mold. What you have, my friends, is sooty mold, a fungus that grows on a pseudo-poop of sticky plant sap that shoots out the back end of piercing sucking insects that have imbibed more than they can possible digest. Stay tuned for more on sooty mold in Chapter 5!

Other mimics. *Chrysanthemum* can appear to have fungal disease when really what they have is a cultural issue. They may end up with dead flower centers when temperatures are high and they have received too much nitrogen. They may also develop a cracked neck or develop deep cracks that girdle the flower stalk on plants whose buds have been removed to create larger flowers. This is related to water rather than disease. Temperatures drop overnight, but the soil is still warm, so too much water is taken up but never given off, leading to cracking. Watering in the morning hours rather than in the evening will be less likely to exacerbate the problem.

Nutritional deficiencies causing yellowing and stunting can also resemble disease. Excess nutrients can cause burning, particularly on gerbera daisy, and this can resemble a disease. Cold wet soil in spring causes temporary phosphorous deficiency, resulting in purpling of leaves that can be mistaken for disease. Galls can be caused by insects, mites, or disease. Bud mite infestation can look like virus activity. And finally, brick or masonry cleaning solutions may be toxic and produce an effect on leaves that resembles disease.

The Suckers Must Die

Insects in the Garden

Before you get out the pitchforks, holy water, and burning brands, the best thing you can do about insects in your garden is give yourself a lesson in entomology—the study of the little beasties. Yes, many people feel that the only good insect is a dead insect and would like to have each one pulverized by a giant mechanized shoe. Before you travel that same road, though, let me remind you of the parable of the common house cat. In ancient Egypt, they were revered, worshipped, and even mummified for travel into the afterlife. Why? Because they kept rodents from destroying grain stores and therefore helped people to be fed and happy. Fed and happy people generally don't revolt. Now let's fast forward to the middle ages where the enthusiasm for cats led people to burn them in baskets as witches' familiars.

The reward? **Plague.** Without cats to keep the rodents down, you can bet your sun-wrinkled sweet bippy (no, that's not a new variety of cherry tomato) that the level of plague increased dramatically.

This is exactly what happens when you use broad-spectrum insecticides in your garden. Think about it: When you go on an insect witch hunt, you kill off the good with the bad, leaving only resistant insects behind. Even if a few good insects survive, there will not be enough bad insects around for the good insects to eat—so they'll starve or go elsewhere. Then the resistant bad insect populations restock themselves and *voilà!* The problem is not only back, but stronger.

There are also broad-spectrum products that people generally consider safe, like soaps, oils, and garlic, but these, too, can wreak havoc on your good insect population. So the best way to go about insect control is through the cultural methods of the right plant in the right place with the right care.

Reducing Insect Pests

The key to successful reduction of insect pests is to understand the correct timing for your control methods relative to the insect's lifecycle. Think about how much food teenage boys consume—this will tell you that the juvenile stage is usually the most extensive feeder. Insect adults may not feed at all, in fact. People absolutely adore butterflies and moths, but they don't think about the destruction capability of a caterpillar and several thousand siblings. Therefore, targeting the insect as a youngster, regardless what types of control methods you use, is always the way to go.

The next problem you face is recognition. Unfortunately, no insect has ever stomped up to me and announced, "Tomorrow, I ravage the garden!" So you are the one charged with the twin tasks of recognizing the good insects from the bad at the proper life stage plus determining whether the problem is an insect at all.

What Makes an Insect an Insect?

Three body parts—head, chest, and abdomen—antennae, wings for the most part, and a hard outer skeleton are all sure characteristics of insects. Spiders, mites, ticks, and their relatives have only **two** body parts: a head and an abdomen. Consider this: Of all the world's insect population, only about 10 percent have any harmful effects; the rest are beneficial or don't bother us one way or the other.

Insect Lifecycle

Insects good or bad basically travel one of two developmental roads to maturity:

Down the first road, the insect—from egg hatch to adult—looks rather similar no matter what size it is. The color may be different and wings are usually no more than small pads in juveniles, but basically what you see is what you get. This type of insect development is primarily associated with symptoms of piercing and sucking. In other words, the insect's mouth parts are like a kid's juice box straw and can be poked into the plant to feed within the tubes that transport water or the tubes that transport sugar. A few insects that chew (like grasshoppers and earwigs) also have a development pattern like this.

The second road to maturity means no stage of the juvenile looks like the adult and no stage of the juvenile looks like the other stage of the juvenile in the same insect. Most insects that follow the second path to maturity are chewers, except for adult flies, who actually sponge. Yech!

The adult and egg stage of both kinds of development are **not** very vulnerable to control. Furthermore, the stage just before the adult stage in development path number two is also not especially vulnerable to control (think of a butterfly chrysalis). That, unfortunately, leaves you with a very small window for control of road-two insects. Road-one insects may have a larger window. For one important garden pest, the window for control is **extremely** small. Scale insects are vulnerable only during the stage when they are crawling around looking for a place to settle because the rest of the time they are protected like a turtle in its shell. Scales are in this single vulnerable stage at different times from each other, so proper identification is crucial to the success of your control.

Why Me?

Why do insects single out your plants to pick on? Here are four reasons:

1. Well, not to be a nag, but I did tell you not to choose that particular plant variety because it is susceptible to many different insect pests. That's because a lot of plants are bred for beauty rather than brains.

2. Other reasons that insects come to call may be cultural or environmental. Both kinds of problems can stress your plants so that they "vocalize" their dismay by releasing certain chemicals into the environment. Although undetectable to humans, this botanical "Help me" is a beacon to insects like borers, for example. (Borers are the ultimate party crashers. When they arrive and find the party atmosphere to their liking, they chemically call their friends.) A common reason for borer attack is drought in the previous season. Drought depresses the level of chemical resistance to attack, so the following season, the party is crashed.

3. Other often-overlooked reasons for insect attack are fertilization and pruning. Both practices can bring on a flush of soft, succulent tissue that screams "salad bar" to piercing, sucking insects. This tissue will be richer in nutrients and so will mean better survival of insects that feed on it.

4. Plant location can influence attack by pests. Both mites and lace bugs can be problematic on plants in full sun (south facing is worse) largely because the temperature and dryness prohibit the activity of predators that normally keep these vampires in check. Andromeda and dwarf Alberta spruce are particularly affected in these settings by lace bugs and mites, respectively. Transplanting the unhappy specimen can often work wonders.

No matter how well behaved your plants are and how good you are about following advice in this book, insects will still occasionally come to call. For example, the sad day I moved from Rhode Island, I took some seed heads from hollyhocks ravaged by hollyhock weevils and froze them to kill the weevils. I planted the seed on Long Island, and for two glorious years I had beautiful hollyhocks. Then one morning I woke up to ragged holes, aborted blossoms, and a thousand long-nosed little friends waving at me as they swayed like sailors on my hollyhock stems. Where did they come from? From someone else's hollyhocks.

My point is there is no shame in having insects attack if you have done everything right. Sometimes it's unavoidable. But there **is** shame in not attempting to distinguish the good guys from the bad guys and thus indiscriminately killing both. **Please read the section on beneficials at the end of this chapter before you become an anti-insect vigilante!**

Good Versus Bad Insects

It may be difficult without proper training to tell the difference between a beneficial insect and a harmful one, but you should at least be able to tell the difference between various groups of bad guys based on the signs and symptoms they produce. **A sign is the physical evidence that the insect leaves behind, and a symptom is the response of the plant to the insect.** (In practical terms, a sign is the dirty laundry someone leaves strewn on the floor and the symptom is the flush of rage in your cheeks). Signs of insects include chewing; notching; skeletonizing; borer holes; minute white or yellow dots from piercing, sucking insects probing the plant tissue; cast insect skins; and of course, **the sign of all signs, bug poop** (better known as frass), a many-splendored thing. Symptoms of insect damage may include wilting, curling, yellowing, or sap production.

Frass and Frass Wannabes

Frass can be a pretty good indicator of what you are up against. If the frass looks like:

- Sawdust or toothpicks, you've got a wood-boring beetle.
- Black pepper dots on the backs of speckled leaves (doesn't that sound romantic?), it's lace bug, but if the dots are on both sides of speckled leaves, it's thrips.
- Tiny black gnocchi, you probably have tree-dwelling caterpillars, especially if they are all over your picnic table and automobile hood. (It could be gypsy moth, if it's spring in the East.)
- Smears or liquidy dots concentrated in one corner of a landscape structure, it could be from a spider.
- A milky, sticky sap line, you have borers in conifers (but that is actually a symptom because it's something the plant produces).
- Sooty mold—well, many piercing, sucking insects drink up so much sap that it oozes out essentially unchanged. This sweet liquid dribbles down on the leaves below, sugarcoating them and providing a surface for opportunistic fungi to grow. This results in the leaves below a piercing, sucking insect invasion appearing as though they have soot or dirt on them, and their texture being sticky. The syndrome is known as sooty mold and can be a sign of insect presence on your plants.

Insect Anatomy

We need to know a few simple anatomical facts before we begin.

Beetles always have jaws. Adults have two hard outer wings that cover their backs in parallel positions, giving the beetles a tanklike appearance, with two membranous wings underneath. Beetles fly with the hard wings in a vertical position like two flaps lifted up and let the membranous ones do the work.

What's Bugging You?

Symptoms of insect invasion include adjectives that might also describe bad skin! They include spots, blotches, blemishes, blisters, and scabby areas. The thing to remember about all this plant acne is that disease or other problems can also cause all these symptoms. An insect-related problem is usually confined to a branch or two or will be uniformly distributed over the whole plant. Patterns straying from these two are likely to be something else.

A hole or a notch can easily be caused by an insect, but beware the hole or notch with a brown margin or holes that are arranged symmetrically inside the margins of the leaf. Both indicate strongly that the tissue died by disease or environmental issues such as frost and that the browned areas dropped out, leaving the hole or notch.

Yellowed leaves, perhaps the most common and hardest to properly diagnose, can be the result of piercing, sucking insects but can also be the result of root rot, nutrient deficiency, and plain old age.

Wilt and leaf drop can also be caused by excessive sap removal (sounds like a medical procedure!).

Deformed leaves can be caused by insect invasion, as well, either from feeding when the leaf is very young—resulting in stunting or abnormal shape or size—or by the effects of plant feeding on plant growth hormones.

A gall (a warty, horned, hairy, or smooth swelling) is formed when insect feeding affects plant growth hormones, and it is frequently inhabited by the insect as a free form of protection.

The **true bug** has a "straw" attached to its mouth region that tucks up under its body, and it never has jaws. The true bug adult also has wings that are half-hard and half-membrane; at rest, they all look as though they have an X on their back.

Adult flies have two wings rather than four.

Juveniles of **butterflies and moths** can be distinguished from juveniles of certain beetles by the presence of more than three pairs of legs; the excess legs (which are more like the bun feet on an ottoman) are located on the abdomen. Juveniles of butterflies and moths can be distinguished from juveniles of certain sawflies, who also have more than three pairs of legs, by the presence of tiny lines inside the "bun feet" located on the abdomen.

Who's on First?

Be aware that many pest insects enjoy more than just one plant! Woody ornamentals (trees and shrubs, to us) are a larger concern because they are more expensive to replace, have bigger eye impact in our landscapes, and are more likely to result in a hazard situation. I mean, nobody cares if a sunflower head falls off and bonks you in the bean, but a large tree limb is a different story.

So when you consider the laundry list of common pests that make their way into your landscape—either as refugees from other infestations, by invitation from common practices, or by virtue of the climates provided—recognize that they may be on **everything,** from the smallest annual to the tallest tree . . . or they may be specialized to a single plant or group of plants.

The most common pests for all landscape plantings are suckers, including mites, scales, and aphids. Vigilance can mean that pruning a single branch is the end of your misery. So let's have a little look-see at who's out in the garden and why we have to keep as many eyes as a potato on them. (And please see Chapter 7 for information on roses and their insect pests.)

Mites

You may see intermittent mite-feeding damage flares. Females can reproduce with or without males, so you can have a flare every three to five days.

Symptoms of mite damage include stippling (dotting), bronzing, flecking, premature leaf drop, and ultimately, webbing. Webbing may or may not be

Predatory Mites

Some mites are predators on other harmful mites, including the two-spotted spider mite. For this predator/prey interaction to take place, it is essential that some shade and humidity be provided for the predators. So this is a good reason not to site your dwarf Alberta spruce in a pot in full sun in the middle of a concrete slab—no matter how pretty it looks there!

Mite Control

A convenient way to monitor for mites is to tap branches of your plants over white paper to see how many fall off and start scurrying around. You also want to look at undersides of leaves for eggs and webs. Again, let me emphasize that damage does not mean mites are still present.

In general, when trying to control mites, do **not** use a class of insecticide called a pyrethroid. This insecticide increases mite populations like crazy by killing everything but eggs and young, resulting in a fitter population. The compounds also kill many natural predators. Horticultural oil at a 1- to 2-percent concentration works but may also be a short-term repellent to predators and parasites.

Oil may help to control mites, but **beware!** On conifers, oil removes the blue bloom from bluish varieties, and it takes several years for bluish needles to grow in again! You may also have difficulty with successful treatment related to timing, coverage, and frequency of sprays (repeat sprays at five- to seven-day intervals may be needed to control escapees and newly hatched mites). For a mite that is really not doing much but offending your sense of the aesthetic, a treatment plan is probably not worth it.

present, but if you do see it and **then** you treat for mites, it's too late and you are only comforting yourself—so go have a cinnamon bun and a cup of tea instead! The webbing is the point of no return because this means the damage is so extensive the mites are ballooning off in search of new adventure and new plants to pillage. Be aware, too, that just because you see damage does not mean the mites are still there—damage on the foliage persists long after the mites have picked up and left town.

In a wet, cool year, mites may show up late, and you may miss them until considerable damage has occurred.

Mites that are able to spin webs are generally divided into two groups—warm-season and cool-season—depending on when they occur. Warm-season mites include two-spotted spider mites, European red mites, honey locust spider mites, and bald cypress rust mites. Cool-season mites include southern red mites (upper leaf surface feeders on *Ilex* and *Rhododendron*), white pine sheath mite, and coniferous mites (which are bad news because once damage occurs, it takes the plants three to five years to lose those needles).

Probably the best-known mite is the spider mite—or red spider, as it is sometimes called. (Do not confuse these pests with the clover mites that run along the sidewalk and people's windowsills.) **These mites are seen in highest numbers from June to September and can complete one generation in less than one—count it, one—week!** Spider mites are first found adjacent to dusty roads or at margins of gardens on stressed plants. They are dispersed by wind, especially as the plants get worse. Fortunately, rain deters them, as does a frequent hard jet of water. You might also consider wetting or oiling down dust in roads to keep it off your plants.

If you use soap to control these mites, make sure you get the undersides of leaves because otherwise they just run underneath and hide like a gnome under a toadstool until the soapy shower passes. You also need to watch your fertilization patterns because high nitrogen content in leaves favors mites and all other piercing, sucking insects.

Mites on Trees and Shrubs

The best way to **invite** mites into your landscape is to plant something susceptible like *Euonymus* against a south-facing white wall with no vegetation around or under it. Bare ground under trees also makes mites multiply, so please mulch, but not excessively! Never add more than 3 inches of mulch under a planting—or the good you are doing for mite prevention will be outweighed by the smothering effects of too much mulch. The mulch also maintains humidity, which helps mite predators like pirate bugs, certain flies, lacewings, and good mites to thrive.

Two-spotted spider mites occur only on junipers in the tree and shrub category; almost all other plants have the spruce spider mite if they are suffering from spider mites. Heavy irrigation is the alternative to chemical control, but this can be difficult if you have a large specimen because it is rather hard to power-wash a 30-foot tree!

Spruce spider mites peak in spring and fall (as late as mid-November, depending on the weather!). You may be able to see orange eggs at the base of needles with your magnifying glass. Infested needles appear bleached, bled dry by these minute Draculas. Bright, dry areas get the worst infestations, but this mite has a tendency to hang around in shade until the end of March and then shift to sun, especially radiant sun. You should probably check your plants for mites twice a month by doing five taps of a branch on a sheet of white paper. Smear the specks you get on the paper; if you get greenish red streaks, you probably have mites.

Southern red mites attack broad-leaf evergreens, including hollies, Japanese holly, azalea, laurel, *Rhododendron*, and boxwood. You'll see them in cool weather. If you sample and get more than ten mites per tap on your white paper, a treatment with horticultural oil may be warranted.

Eriophyid mites are another piercing, sucking mite that can cause problems on your trees and shrubs, although these really cannot be seen with the naked eye or even a magnifying glass. They cause subtle injury at first, leading to odd growth or galling, and most tend to be specialized on one or a few plants.

They are referred to as gall, rust, blister, or bud mites, depending on damage symptoms and the feeding site, and may be found on the surface of foliage or live in galls, buds, berries, cones, or other protected sites.

Eriophyid mites on lilac bushes. Look for yellowed leaf margins, browning, curling, and leaf drop.

Eriophyid mites on trees. On maple leaves, they can produce truly amazing spindle-shaped projections; on beech leaves, they can produce beads; on Callery or Bradford pear, they can produce tons of tiny thickened blisters,

Eriophyid mite damage looks like something from outer space.

resulting in twisting and distortion of leaf tissue; and on birch leaves, they can produce swollen irregularly shaped magenta patches. You may see blistering on mountain ash and cotoneaster leaves due to the activities of these mites. Blisters are green at first, then turn reddish to brown to black over time.

Eriophyid mites on conifers. Bud mite on balsam fir and spruces causes buds to die before opening in spring and causes shoot proliferation on red pine. They can be affected by eriophyid mites, as well. One type feeds in, kills, or causes a swelling or crooking of tip growth. Another one causes yellowing or russeting of foliage. In the growing tips of junipers (especially *J. horizontalis* 'Plumosa', also known as Andorra juniper), eriophyid mite feeding might give way to dead tips and wavy injury to the base of needles.

Another eriophyid mite gets on *Chamaecyparis nootkatensis* (nootka cypress) and junipers, causing swelling and crowding at the base of needles, which can lead to stunting or killing of terminal buds, especially on low-growing cultivars.

Controlling Eriophyid Mites

Do these eriophyid mites hurt the plants? Not a bit. Some people find the distortions objectionable—so you could treat the leaf tissue with horticultural oil when leaves are about one-third expanded in the spring if you are really having a hissy fit about it, but the best thing to do is simply to leave it all alone. There is little information on control, and most of the time you don't even need to control them. Materials used to control spider mites are often **not** effective against eriophyid mites.

Another form may cause damage to oriental arborvitae similar to that seen on juniper; they cause crooking, bending, and distortion; or may result in distorted, shriveled cones.

Taxus bud mite can produce distorted shoots, a demented daisylike spray of elongated needles at the tips of branches, and dead brown buds with 1,000 mites per bud on yew shrubs. But it does not particularly bother the shrub.

Hemlock rust mite darkens then bronzes the foliage of Canadian hemlock, primarily in the spring. It is a further nemesis when, in certain states, the hemlock is already being attacked by the hemlock wooly adelgid.

Bald cypress rust mites prey on dawn redwood and bald cypress, make the foliage appear rusty, and cause distinct bronzing one to two months before regular leaf drop, especially in August and September. Small specimens get it worse, with bleaching at the base of the needles and death or stunting of inner needles.

Mites on Herbaceous Plantings

Web-spinning mites have their highest populations from June through September—unfortunately, this is when your herbaceous plantings are at their zenith. Two-spotted spider mites relish hot dry conditions in outdoor beds, alongside hardscape walkways, and within cement garden containers. In response to mite attack, flowers discolor and drop, and leaves become dry and leathery. Particularly hard hit are columbine, *Dahlia*, daylily, *Delphinium*, *Gaillardia*, *Rudbeckia*, hollyhock, *Iris*, *Phlox*, primrose, *Salvia*, *Verbena*, *Viola*, and mums. As recommended before, a regular hosing down, especially in dry, dusty areas, can really help. Marigolds are particularly fine fodder for mites in dry areas, so pay attention to your plantings!

Cyclamen mites are even more annoying since they are invisible even under a magnifying glass. They lay eggs in unopened buds and folded leaves. Their development is favored by high humidity and cool temperatures. Leaves curl and twist, and the tops of the plants become brittle and scabby. The *Fuchsia* Cyclamen mite causes stunting and puckering of new growth. *Impatiens* can become seriously distorted by Cyclamen mites. Flower buds may dry up and die. Light infestations may result in discolored or dark-flecked flowers, with the worst damage seen on delphiniums with leaves and flowers that are blackened or streaked. Monkshood, *Dahlia*, gerbera daisy, *Verbena*, mums, and *Viola* are often the most affected— remove and destroy infested plants! There is little you can do to cure 'em.

Mite damage is easily recognized by the stippled appearance on leaves.

Fuchsia **gall mite**, an eriophyid, ravages the plant by causing twisted, distorted leaves; seriously affecting blossoms; and causing pockets of swollen, red tissue.

True Bugs

True bugs are the next group of vampires. Bugs are divided into good and evil categories depending on whether they use that juice-box-straw mouth of theirs to poke into and suck dry a plant or another insect. Bugs in the good guy category are listed under beneficial insects at the end of this chapter.

The **four-lined plant bug and tarnished plant bug** are two of the most common bug pests for trees and shrubs, especially those that produce fruit. Their piercing and sucking activities can result in triangular patches of bumpy skin known as cat-facing, distortion, and stippling or dotting. You can look for them by laying out some

True bug damage caused by the four-lined plant bug looks like dots.

white sticky traps to which they are attracted (available from specialty companies). Remove plant debris promptly to reduce populations, and bear in mind that these true bugs can also be carriers of fire blight, a serious bacterial disease. They walk through the bacteria oozing from cankers and then track it everywhere they go.

Stink bugs are probably a bug with which most people are familiar, but they also come in good and bad. The good guys that prey on other bugs are often brown and have "epaulets" on their shoulders, while the bad guys are often green with no shoulder pads.

Box elder bugs, quite simply, are a pain in the neck. They gather in vast quantities on the side of a trunk or a building but really do no harm. They eat seeds that have fallen on the ground.

Lace bugs are a common landscape pest, particularly on andromedas and azaleas! Look for silvering, flecking, and stippling as a key to potential problems, particularly on plants in full sun. You will also see black pepper dots of bug poop on the undersides of leaves.

Lace bug damage, seen here, lessens when plants are given a little shade.

Transplanting the affected shrub to a location with a bit more shade is often enough to alleviate the problem by introducing an environment that is tolerated by predators. Varying the kinds of plantings around affected specimens, especially when some flowering plants are added, can really boost beneficials. Lace bugs are also referred to as tingids in some parts of the country.

True bugs on herbaceous plantings. Feeding results in spotting that is similar to small fungal leaf spots of different diseases, depending on the plant fed upon. For example, monkshood may develop dark, depressed spots, while mums, *Gaillardia*, and *Echinops* may develop tan spots. *Perovskia* develops purplish or silvery spots.

Four-lined and tarnished plant bugs produce the worst damage on herbaceous plantings and may spend their winters under large leaves of weeds. In early spring, true bugs may also feed on the buds of fruit. Damage from bug

Predicting Insect Outbreaks Like a Landscape Psychic

Insect development corresponds not just with the temperature on any given day, but with the temperature of all the days combined during the whole growing season. Like a bank account that bears interest, heat also makes a profit, accumulating gradually in the "bank" of the growing season.

You have to start with a base account of fifty bucks (50 degrees F., usually beginning March 1); from there, deposits are made each day. Your balance is what determines which insects are at what stage. Some insects will be active or susceptible (these two may or may not be the same) at a very low balance, but others need a higher heat balance.

While you can gain over the course of the season, you never subtract. If you are below a certain amount for the day, you simply gain nothing. The formula for calculation is simple, and the name we give this heat accumulation is Growing Degree Days (GDD). While we know the heat accumulations for some insects, others are not as well known. You can calculate your own GDD by this easy method:

1. Add the Maximum Temperature to the Minimum Temperature (find these from a weather website or the newspaper).
2. Divide that number by 2.
3. Subtract 50.
4. The answer is the amount of heat that accumulated over the course of the day!

Start keeping track of this March 1, and you'll always know where you are with respect to insects whose lifecycles have been well correlated with the GDD method. This is a particularly effective way to scout for pests because it helps you predict when you are most likely to have to keep an eye out for them.

probing occasionally occurs on *Heuchera*, *Dahlia*, mums, *Rudbeckia*, *Heliopsis*, lavender, lupine, peony, *Coreopsis* and geranium, as well. Angular brown spots may also result and may even coalesce to look like a disease.

On mums, the *Chrysanthemum* lace bug causes similar damage as it feeds on the undersides of leaves and bleaches them out. You will also find dark fecal specks on the undersides of leaves.

Aphids and Their Kin

You never, ever want this huge piercing, sucking family to have a reunion in your landscape!

Ever wonder where aphids come from? They seem just to materialize from thin air, but they actually overwinter as eggs, which hatch as females that do not need males to reproduce (watch it guys—your days are numbered!). After several generations, winged females are produced, which then go off to different plants. Now get this: Later in the season, they migrate back to the original plant and produce males, mate, and lay eggs, which then overwinter.

Aphid feeding results in leaves that are curled and twisted under. Look for honeydew and sooty mold, and particularly for cast skins as signs of aphid activity. You can tap branches to look for them, use strong jets of water to knock them out of your plants, use horticultural soap, or simply prune 'em out. Aphids seldom kill plants; they just weaken them.

You can also look for large numbers of ants climbing into trees. They tend the aphids and protect them from harm because they are looking for that sweet sap shooting out of the back end. (Bleah!) Control ants to reduce aphids by placing a masking or other tape wrong-side-out around the tree so that ants will be deterred from climbing. Keeping weeds away from plantings is also a great idea because the aphids use the weeds as an alternate snack station.

Aphid infestations usually result in twisting of leaves and lots of sticky sap.

Wooly and gall-making aphids can be seen on twigs, branches, and roots. They also produce honeydew. On elm trees, you might see rolled, twisted leaves at the tips of shoots or you might see them on beech trees, as well. Simply use a strong jet of water to knock them off.

Cicadas produce those noisy nuances with which most people are familiar, but folks don't often know what kind of damage they do. Cicadas deposit eggs in the twigs of trees and shrubs, causing twig terminals to die. Eggs hatch in a month, and then young drop to the ground and feed on roots, especially those of perennial plants.

The cicada remains a juvenile for thirteen to seventeen years. When ready to become an adult, it digs its way out, climbs onto a flat surface, and molts (sheds its skin). Adults survive a month or more. The principle problem is caused by egg laying, which can cause damage to young trees and nursery stock by causing twiglets to drop off.

Treehoppers look like small aliens, thanks to the weird "thingy" on their backs; they look like a thorn or a tiny dinosaur. Most feed on trees and shrubs; some may feed on grass and herbaceous plants. The buffalo treehopper is a pest of apples, with damage similar to that of the cicada.

Leafhoppers are small, wedge-shaped insects that tend to feed on shrubs and herbaceous plants, resulting in five types of plant injury:

1. Sap reduction, resulting in leaves with white or yellow spots followed by the whole leaf turning yellow or brown.

2. Plugging of the plant's water and food pipes, resulting in browning of the leaf's outer margin followed by browning of the entire leaf. This is known as "hopper burn" (sounds more like what you get after the three-alarm chili contest, if you ask me!).

3. Damage similar to that done by the treehopper and cicada.

4. Transmission of diseases like elm yellows (which we covered in Chapter 4). **This is very significant to your landscape.**

5. Simple stunting and leaf curling due to leaf growth inhibition on the undersurface, where leafhoppers feed.

Many leafhoppers produce honeydew. Juveniles may be covered with wax filaments, so it is easy to mistake them for other pests.

Froghoppers are also known as spittle bugs and primarily feed on shrubs and herbaceous plants. Young surround themselves with a frothy mass that comes from their butt and from mucus-producing glands on the abdomen. They use their feet to produce air bubbles and cover themselves with this foaming mess while standing on their heads (don't you wish you could do that at the next staff meeting?).

Most are harmless, but a few important pests of pine may cause shortened twigs or deformed foliage. The pine spittle bug attacks Scotch, jack, loblolly, Virginia, slash, white, and oriental pines. It deposits eggs in twigs; when juveniles hatch, they withdraw sap from phloem and produce spittle. Adults suck sap and produce honeydew, which then leads to sooty mold on the leaves below. The main symptom is yellowing foliage followed by dead twigs. Heavy infestation may lead to twig, branch, and tree mortality. A strong jet of water may help the development of natural fungal controls of the blasted things!

Hoppers in herbaceous plantings. Trouble comes in the form of the garden fleahopper. The juvenile looks like a green aphid, and the adult looks like a flea beetle, but it jumps when disturbed. The injury that it causes corresponds with $1/16$-inch-wide coarse spots on leaves, which may be bleached, dark, or red. Damage in shady areas is worse; the plant may be badly stunted, experience early flower drop, or even die. Plants that suffer the worst effects include *Scabiosa, Verbena, Chrysanthemum, Helenium, Helianthus, Heliopsis,* and *Rudbeckia.*

The aster leafhopper vectors (transmits) aster yellows (caused by mycoplasma) to *Anchusa, Aster, Coreopsis, Dahlia, Gaillardia, Centaurea, Lobelia, Phlox,* poppy, *Rudbeckia, Scabiosa,* and *Dianthus.* Potato leafhopper causes the infamous "hopper burn," with whitening of leaf veins; a triangular area of the leaf tip browns and becomes flaccid. *Dahlia* affected by the potato leafhopper may be stunted and fail to flower. Tips of other plants may curl down and be killed, and *Alcea* and lupine may be seriously damaged.

Boxwood psyllid damage is easy to recognize.

Psyllids, also called jumping plant lice, look just like miniature cicadas. They can also secrete a waxy covering so that they look a bit like wooly aphids superficially. Hackberry psyllids may be noticeable because of the galls they make, but pay them no mind. Boxwood psyllids are much more a concern because they produce distorted foliage tips. They can be recognized by their bright orange eggs around the bud and the extremely characteristic strange cupping of the leaves. Try soap in early May, but the boxwood psyllid is very hard to control!

Whiteflies outside unfortunately produce honeydew and sooty mold—just like on our houseplants. Azalea whitefly attacks azalea, *Rhododendron,* and andromeda, covering the backs of leaves with round papery structures. You'll see honeydew, sooty mold, yellowing leaves, dieback, and curling over as a result of a whitefly attack. Crawlers settle in twig crotches, bark crevices, and the axils of leaves. Horticultural oil may be of some help, but watch your timing. Apply oil as a dormant treatment, and then treat again in June to late July. Make sure you actually have whitefly and not azalea bark scale!

Whiteflies may hop off your infested houseplants to your outdoor annual and perennial garden if you bring your infested houseplants outside for a summer vacation. Defoliation can result from whitefly involvement, as well as yellowing, stunting, and good old sooty mold. Whiteflies primarily target *Hibiscus*, lupines, primroses, *Salvia*, *Verbena*, mums, and *Rudbeckia*.

Aphids in herbaceous plantings. Aphids are key in transmission of the disease *Botrytis* by tracking it around on their feet and by the vessel of honeydew. Peonies may be particularly hard hit by this one-two punch. Flowers especially susceptible to attack and damage by aphids include *Anemone*, rock cress, wall flower, columbine, *Delphinium*, *Doronicum*, foxglove, *Iris*, *Penstemon*, *Rudbeckia*, *Hibiscus*, poppy, primrose, *Sedum*, *Helianthus*, *Echinops*, *Verbena*, *Chrysanthemum*, *Dahlia*, *Dianthus*, forget me not, and *Viola*.

Phylloxerans, while a **huge** problem on grapes, are more of a curiosity to the home landscape. These insects do **not** feed on conifers! Their little bodies are all covered in waxy powder but no waxy threads. They do cause galls, such as hickory stem gall *Phylloxera*, but for the most part, they do not need to be treated.

Adelgids are strictly conifer pests. They form galls only on the primary host plant, but they usually have two hosts. Unlike the phylloxerans, their bodies are covered with waxy threads. There are two very important adelgids in our home landscape. One is the spruce gall adelgid on Douglas fir. It causes little yellow spots and bent needles; general yellowing; and small, pineapple-shaped waxy balls. It needs a Colorado blue spruce nearby to complete its lifecycle. There are two management times. You can use soap from mid-September through October or in April before new growth.

Spruce gall adelgids make a characteristic pineapple-shaped gall.

Hemlock wooly adelgid creates cottony bits like dryer lint on infested plants.

The second is the hemlock wooly adelgid, a terrible pest of Canadian hemlocks in certain parts of the country. This piercing, sucking insect secretes a fluffy, white, waxy covering and will turn your healthy green hemlocks to dying yellow sticks in a matter of a few years.

Nitrogen from fertilizers makes the problem much worse—so **do not fertilize.** Use humic acid or bone meal if you must give them something. You also do not want any bird feeders in or near your hemlocks because the adelgids often hitch a ride on the birds. Water trees during hot, dry periods.

You can get 95 to 100 percent control with horticultural oil or soap, but you really have to stay on top of the problem. Apply your horticultural oil at 7 Growing Degree Days. (See page 103 for more information.) If the wooliness is not gone within two weeks, treat again. Another option is to simply get rid of the hemlocks.

Pine bark adelgids are another ugly but less damaging pest, which affects white, Scotch, and Austrian pines. It even makes the trees look white-washed! The infestation can result in stunted or bushy trees, but primarily it simply weakens them. Infestations will be heaviest in well-shaded areas. You can use oil in the later part of May, but you may need to repeat the treatment every two to three weeks.

Pine bark adelgid is more common in shady sites.

Taxus mealybugs look very similar to the ones you get on your houseplants. They attack yew, as well as dogwood, *Rhododendron*, *Prunus*, maple, andromeda, and occasionally crabapple. They look like sugar-frosted pill bugs! You'll see sparse foliation and needles, and twigs caked with honeydew. They feed on the inner bark of the trunk and branches and may cluster in crotches of plant branches. Use dormant oil at 7 to 9 Growing Degree Days in a dormant spray and again at Growing Degree Days 246 through 618. (See page 103 for more information.)

Scales

Scales do their damage by using their mouthparts like a juice box straw and sucking up plant sap. The two largest scale families we need to worry about are the armored scales and the soft scales. Armored scales suck up individual cell sap, but soft scales suck up enormous volumes of food tube sap, so they are the ones who produce honeydew.

What kind of damage will you see besides sooty mold? If scales are on foliage, you will see yellowing of the foliage around the site infestation, especially if armored scales are feeding. If there are a ton of armored scales, you may see browning and defoliation. If scale is on the bark of the plant, slow dieback, leaf shedding, and unthriftiness are evidence. Injury is exacerbated by environmental stress and excessive fertilization, which increases the number and survival of eggs and offspring of the scale.

The euonymus scale is a fine example of an armored scale.

You're Surrounded by Scales

Scales are everywhere: No gardens are exempt. Let's start off with a scale fact or two. Many people know that the original material for lacquer was produced from scale insects. Cochineal scales feed on prickly pear cactus, which secretes a chemical, which deters insect feeding. This chemical is extracted from the scale insects to make a crimson or carmine dye used as a food colorant and for cosmetics.

Scales are masters of disguise. They are flatter than a preteen, and their color often blends right in with whatever they are sucking the life out of. Adult scales don't move around. They find a spot suitable to settle down and stay there for life. The juvenile, however, has several stages. The first stage is called a crawler. This may be the only mobile point in the scale's entire life, and this stage often occurs at a predictable point based on accumulation of heat in the environment (that is, at a certain number of GDD). A great monitoring tool is a piece of electrical tape wrapped around a few branches sticky side out. The crawlers meander over this trap and become stuck and much more easily visible to you. Extra nitrogen can really increase your scale problems, so don't be too lavish with the fertilizer!

The best way to get rid of scales is early detection. This means examining new plant material before it is installed. Ants and wasps are attracted to honeydew, so their presence on plants can mean soft scale or mealybugs. Armored scales may resemble normal plant parts like pores in the bark or look like the spore splats of artillery fungus. Try to pop off the cover. If you can, and you have an orange, pink, or yellow body underneath, you have a live scale. Black, brown, or shriveled scale bodies are goners.

White prunicola scale and its nearly indistinguishable relative white peach scale are very serious pests in suburban landscapes.

White prunicola scale and white peach scale are similar scales and very destructive to fruit trees, flowering cherry, plum, peach, privet, *Aucuba*, lilac, walnut, *Catalpa*, chinaberry, *Hibiscus*, honeysuckle, golden raintree, redbud, *Spiraea*, dogwood, mulberry, and beautyberry. The species most hard-hit are Japanese flowering cherry, privets, and lilac. The scales commonly feed on the bark of the trunk and large branches. Scale builds up rapidly and may cause the death of large branches in short order. There are two to three generations per year.

San Jose scale infestations can be problematic on *Pyracantha* and *Cotoneaster*. Often found on boxwood, dogwood, hawthorn, linden, privet, walnut, roses, and mountain ash, these scales may have five generations a year. High populations cause branch and twig dieback. Heavy infestations may kill the plant.

Pine needle scale set up camp on host pines and some spruces. Mugo and Scotch pine get it the worst; Austrian and red pines are often attacked. Plants in dusty areas near roads are most at risk. Heavy infestations of these skinny white scales cause needles to turn yellow to brown, and then branchlets or whole branches may be killed. A very heavy infestation can kill a tree. Inspect plantings twice a year. Red eggs are present under the scale cover. Eggs hatch in May or June, and reddish crawlers disperse. A second generation of crawlers may appear in late July.

Oystershell scale looks like, well, an oyster shell. Over a hundred types of plants can be infested. Twig dieback is the most common symptom. There are two forms, which vary in their appearance and seasonal development. The "lilac" type is larger and later in its development. You commonly see it on lilac, ash, willow, poplar, and maple. The "apple" type enjoys apple, dogwood, and poplar. With either type, entire branches may become completely covered before it moves on to other parts of the plant. They produce one to two generations a year.

Other common hosts include boxwood, birch, *Cotoneaster*, elm, horse chestnut, linden, mountain ash, *Pachysandra*, pear, plum, sycamore, tulip tree, *Viburnum*, Virginia creeper, and walnut. The twice-stabbed lady beetle is an important predator, but may not appear in huge numbers until a large population has built up.

Juniper scale is circular and white and looks like a poached egg. Infested junipers do not develop new growth, and the old growth is off color. Branches turn yellow and die. Crawlers appear in late May or early June. A close rela-

Identifying Scale

If you are trying to identify which scale you have, one easy way to determine the difference between hard or armored and soft scale is the presence of a wax cover on the hard scale that can be popped off with a needle or a thumbnail to reveal the female scale's legless body beneath (eeeww!). Soft scale and mealybugs always retain their legs. If there is no separate wax cover or powdery white wax hanging from the margin, you are probably dealing with a soft scale.

Soft scale females produce fifty to a thousand eggs per batch (or sometimes live young!). Crawlers are mobile for only twelve to twenty-four hours, which offers you but a tiny window for effective treatment. And, once again, these are the honeydew producers, so look for sooty mold below infestations.

Armored scale is the largest scale family. They also tend to be host-plant specific, unlike the soft scales and mealybugs. Their shape ranges from elongate to circular. Males tend to be narrower than females, and coloring may vary slightly between males and females. Armored scales do not produce honeydew since they suck individual cell contents rather than tapping into a sugar pipeline in the plant. Crawlers can be carried on air currents to new plants. Plants with overlapping foliage make a great bridge for scale crawlers.

tive attacks arborvitae, spruce, and juniper. These scales are white to brown, and females have a dark spot in their center.

Hemlock scale at maturity are always found on the undersides of hemlock or spruce needles and resemble tiny snails. Symptoms include small yellow spots on the upper sides of the leaves. Needles fall off with a load of four to six scales.

Euonymous **scale** infestations are extremely common and will get on other plants, including *Camellia*, boxwood, yellowwood, *Daphne*, ivy, *Hibiscus*, holly, jasmine, privet, honeysuckle, *Pachysandra*, and *Prunus*. A light attack will cause yellow or white spots on the leaves. A heavy infestation causes premature defoliation. Plants close to a building tend to get more damage, possibly due to a lack of air circulation. Stems closer to the ground are more severely affected, for the same reason. (I can give a personal testimonial to this principle as it relates to *Pachysandra*. I had propped a glass door against the side of a garage where *Pachysandra* was growing. The scale went wild!) Eggs hatch in early June. A second generation develops toward the beginning of August.

Elongate hemlock scale is primarily a pest of eastern hemlock (as if this tree didn't have enough problems). It will also occur on yew, spruce, and fir located near heavily infested hemlocks. Infested growth yellows, drops prematurely, and slows. Scale mouthparts are three to four times the length of the body! Many of the crawlers are present in late May, but crawlers may be present at many other times of the year.

Tulip tree scale attacks . . . tulip trees, but also *Magnolia × soulangiana*, *Magnolia stellata*, linden, and occasionally shrubby St. John's wort. It kills numerous branches, leading to the rapid decline and death of the host plant. This very large scale looks like an orange or yellow helmet and may be mistaken for the *Magnolia* scale. Adults are gray-green to pinkish orange. Young are born alive in August and September, and there is only one generation per year. Dieback and branch death occur with the most active feeding season, spring through late summer. One unusual natural predator of this kind of scale is a caterpillar!

Magnolia **scale** is the largest scale insect in the U.S. (up to about the same length as two-thirds the diameter of a penny!). It looks like a blob of yellow insulation. Huge amounts of honeydew are produced. A single generation is produced each year, and females produce living young. Crawlers overwinter and are gray with a red edge and two spots of white wax. They usually mass beneath one- and two-year-old twigs. The massing of scale will give normally green twigs a purplish tinge.

Fletcher scale, also called the arborvitae soft scale, is a caramel-colored pest of yew, juniper, arborvitae, and hemlock. It very occasionally gets on pachysandra. Though seldom causing visible injury to arborvitae, on yews fletcher is a serious pest, causing foliage drop and a heavy coat of sooty mold. Twigs and stems are usually the most seriously infested. There is one generation per year. Eggs hatch mid-June, and yellow crawlers concentrate on a particular branch or part of the infested plant. Plant damage is most obvious in spring, which is when you see the most sooty mold. The one good thing is that the eggs all hatch around the same time, so a single application of a control is likely to eliminate most crawlers.

European fruit lecanium scale causes the worst feeding damage spring through early summer. Crawlers emerge in June and July, with one generation each year. They look a bit like a stationary pill bug without legs. They have no cover per se, just the shriveled body of the female covering the eggs. This scale is primarily found on small branches, and, unlike other scales, its population can collapse from natural predators.

European fruit lecanium scales are a good example of a honeydew-producing soft scale.

Cottony *Taxus*/cottony *Camellia* scale can be on *Camellia*, holly, *Hydrangea*, Japanese maple, *Euonymus*, *Magnolia*, and beautyberry. One generation per year occurs. Adults are a mottled, tannish yellow and are shaped like an elongate convex oval. The ridged egg sac is produced on the underside of a leaf or needle. Eggs hatch in June. Settled crawlers are visible by mid-July. Damage is mostly seen in early spring and late summer, appearing as off-color, light-green foliage. You will realize they are there only after the egg sacs appear.

Cottony maple leaf scale and cottony maple scale should be considered together since they often cohabitate. Cottony maple scale favors soft maples, like silver maple, but it will also get on alder, box elder, hackberry, dogwood, hawthorn, *Euonymus*, beech, apple, mulberry, Virginia creeper, sycamore, poplar, *Prunus*, pear, oak, black locust, rose, sumac, willow, lilac, linden, and

Cottony maple leaf scale is present on the leaves of many plants.

elm. Crawlers appear in late June and July. They feed on either side of the leaf in warm weather and on twigs during cold weather. There is one generation per year. Sooty mold is a common symptom, and premature defoliation may occur with heavy infestations.

Cottony maple leaf scale also gets on dogwood, hollies, andromeda, honeysuckle, and sour gum, causing premature leaf drop and twig or branch death. Before egg sacs form, adult females are maroon with a yellow-brown keel in the middle of the back. After eggs hatch at the end of June, pale-green crawlers settle along leaf midribs and larger veins, blending in with the leaves. They will migrate to the bark in autumn. You'll find them on the undersides of leaves. The cottony maple leaf scale produces its white egg sacs on leaves, not on twigs or small branches. This is an important characteristic for telling the cottony maple scale and the cottony maple leaf scale apart.

Beech scale has a woollike appearance and is associated with *Nectria* canker, which we talked about in Chapter 4. Heavily infested trees appear to be covered in a mass of white wool. One generation is produced a year, and crawlers are spread by wind. In combination with *Nectria*, it can kill the tree.

Calico scale, in late summer, bothers ornamental stone fruit, Persian walnut, elm, *Zelkova*, maple, *Pyracantha*, pear, gum, Boston ivy, Virginia creeper, redbud, *Magnolia*, hornbeam, dogwood, buckeye, *Wisteria*, honey locust, scholar tree, and crabapple. Calico gets its name from its white and brown mottled colors, which are brightest just as it reaches maturity and then darken with

Scale Tips

* With any scale insect, if you remove its cover, it dies, so use a fingernail or a scrub brush to wreak havoc.
* A spray is not as effective as a bath, so if the plant is containerized and manageable, wrap the base of the plant with foil and dip the plant to control crawlers.
* Scales that overwinter as eggs will not be as susceptible to treatments you apply before the plant has broken dormancy in the spring (often a recommended time to treat for scale).
* Scale is extremely common on Henry Lauder's walking stick (lecanium and oyster shell scale are the worst). A severe infestation can kill one of these expensive plants within two to three years.

age. Only one generation occurs each year. These scales produce huge amounts of honeydew in the spring.

Azalea bark scale belongs to the same group as the European elm scale. It attacks *Rhododendron*, andromeda, hawthorn, poplar, and willow (look in crotches of twigs, bark crevices, and leaf axils.) This scale feeds on the bark of twigs and stems. Eggs hatch mid-June through late July and produce red crawlers.

Scale in herbaceous plantings. Purple scale sometimes gets on *Monarda*, oyster shell scale can bother *Iberis* and peony, cottony cushion scale can nourish itself on your *Helianthus* and *Verbena*, and black scale sometimes gets on *Phlox*. Cutting back herbaceous perennials to get rid of scale may result in a beneficial second flush of growth and extended flowering!

Beetles

Remember that beetles have two hard outer wings covering two inner membranous wings and they have *chewing* mouth parts. This means plants with ragged holes, notches, or roots with fewer hairs than your cousin Artie's bald pate.

Scarab beetles are generally stout and somewhat oval, with antennae that look like golf clubs. They chew holes or skeletonize leaves. Oriental beetle young, which are generally a turf pest, can also be a problem in beds, where they chew roots off herbaceous materials and can even girdle small shrubs like *Ilex*. Asiatic garden beetles can be problematic as adults and young. The young feed much as the oriental beetle young do, but the adults may chew large holes in flowers or make them ragged, especially roses. Japanese beetle adults, which we will also discuss at greater length in the rose section in Chapter 7, skeletonize many plants in the rose and apple family and are particularly fond of grapes.

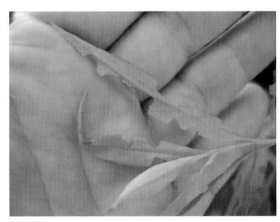
Weevil damage is characterized by notching.

Weevils, with their long, narrow, curved noses, look very much like Gonzo of Muppet fame. Often their antennae are attached halfway down these noses like a pair of *pince nez* on Aunt Harriet. Weevil juveniles resemble a turf grub that's had a bad accident with a band saw: no legs! Whenever you see a small legless grub with a brown head capsule, it is typically a weevil juvenile (except for certain wood-boring beetle juveniles). These beetles make small notches in leaves as adults.

Bark beetles leave tiny pinholes in the bark of stressed trees. They tend to be minute, dark, and cylindrical, with square-ended bellies. Their young have no legs. The general symptoms of bark beetle invasion are fading foliage, reddish brown bug poop, and on evergreens, hardened streams of resin on the trunk. Lots of woodpecker work on bark is a warning of bark beetle infestation. Few pesticides are very effective against bark beetles or other types of borers.

Flat-headed borers, as adults, tend to be very metallic, especially on their bellies. Flat-headed borers also have broad, flat chests. You'll find their handiwork in unhealthy or dying fruit and on shade and forest trees. The tunnels of the juveniles are oval in cross-section (which you may notice if you split your own firewood). The bronze birch borer is a member of this group. The juveniles sport a head shaped like a calculator battery with a wormlike tail attached. The adult's antennae are short and often threadlike.

Branch and twig borers attack living and dead trees, branches, and seasoned lumber (and sometimes your house, too!). They look like Brahma bulls from the side, their heads bent low, giving them a hump-backed appearance. These borers possess clubbed antennae and tiny bodies. The apple twig borer belongs to this group.

Round-headed borers are the juveniles of **long-horned beetles,** a very important pest group. With just a few exceptions, the antennae of these beetles are at least half as long as the body! The heads of the juvenile forms—those round-headed borers—are . . . you guessed it, round. The larval tunnels in wood are also circular in cross-section. Linden borers, twig pruners, and the Asian Long-Horned Beetle are all part of this group.

Leaf-eating beetles superficially resemble tiny long-horned beetles or may resemble lady bugs. Their threadlike antennae are less than half their body

Elm Bark Beetles and Dutch Elm Disease

Two kinds of elm bark beetle spread the fungus causing Dutch elm disease, so it is particularly important to remove dead and dying elms and to trench around adjacently planted elms to get rid of roots that may have grafted together with neighboring trees. Elm logs should be stripped of bark so that stockpiles don't attract beetles and become reservoirs of fungus.

Borer Savvy

Most borer or bark beetle problems come a year after a drought. Look for sawdust or sap, especially in trees you believe were stressed. Drought causes bark beetle attack in pine, spruce, elm, basswood, ash, redbud, serviceberry, dogwood, cherry, purple sandcherry, crabapples, hickory, willow, arborvitae, and *Chaemacyparis*.

The most important borer deterrent is a healthy tree. Healthy trees initiate heavy sap flow at attacked sites; stressed trees don't. Infested trees often have secondary problems. If a tree has lost more than a third of its canopy, get rid of it.

Woodpecker work can mimic borer damage.

The woodpecker can be a borer look-alike. In declining maples, it is common to see evidence of both, resulting in darkened, stained, oozing bark with sooty mold below. If the holes are in an ordered pattern, you are looking at work by a sapsucker or woodpecker. Random holes indicate an insect borer.

length—and boy, can they eat! Adults feed on flowers and foliage, and juveniles feed on roots. Many of our common vegetable pests like Colorado potato beetle, bean leaf beetles, flea beetles, and asparagus beetles belong to this group and will happily feed on herbaceous annuals and perennials, as well.

Ladybird or lady beetles are often beneficial, with just a few members causing problems in our home landscapes. They tend to be broad, nearly round, and flat on bottom and are distinguished from the leaf-eating beetles by their round rather than oblong shape and their clublike antennae. The Mexican bean beetle and the squash beetle are harmful members of this group and will happily feed on herbaceous annual and perennial plant materials.

Black vine weevils create notches in the leaves of *Rhododendron* and yews in particular, while the juveniles feed on roots. Look for damage early in the season; heavy feeding by the young may result in poor plants with off-color leaves. To screen for adults, wrap the base of the plant with burlap, which encourages the adults to hide in it during the day. Then simply unwrap the weevils with the burlap and drop them happily into a bucket of soapy water to get rid of them. Adult feeding is unsightly, with lots of notching, but not dangerous like the juveniles feeding on roots. In a small planting, it is possible to exclude them altogether. Bury 6-inch-wide aluminum flashing 2 inches in the ground and coat the top 2 inches with lithium grease (available at your local hardware store . . . I checked!).

Bronze birch borer, a flat-headed borer, is a menace to paper white birch trees already maxed out with stress from birch leafminer defoliation and drought. The birch borers produce D-shaped exit holes, which you can look for on the trunks of your trees. Feeding by this pest also causes ridges to form on the bark. Attack weakens the structural integrity of the tree. Usually trees are not attacked until a few years following installation, but the borer will eventually kill the tree.

To reduce stress and therefore susceptibility, never plant birches in shade. The canopy should be in the sun and the roots in shade. Make sure you irrigate if the plant is likely to become water stressed! Some research shows birch can be immune to birch borer with as little as 1 inch of water a week in summer.

River birch and heritage birch aren't bothered by the borer, or you can try planting Japanese white birch or monarch varieties.

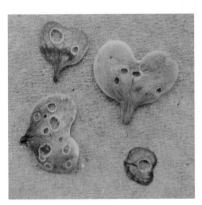

Flea beetle damage can decimate new plantings.

Flea beetles create pinholes in foliage with their voracious feeding and can also cause wilting and stunting. Frequent scratching of the soil around the base of the plant and removal of dead or discarded plant material helps. The beetles also don't like shade, and according to some studies, a sprinkling of wood ashes may deter them.

Viburnum leaf beetles happily and quite severely defoliate European highbush cranberry *Viburnum*, Guelder rose, arrowwood *Viburnum*, American highbush cranberry *Viburnum*, and maple leaf *Viburnum*. Adults and juveniles alike devour leaves, with high numbers of juveniles eating everything but the major veins. The beetle overwinters as an egg. The females chew square holes in twig bark and then cover the eggs they lay with a little hat of black beetle dung, chewed bark, and wood. Eggs hatch in May, and juveniles feed together in a clump, systematically stripping *Viburnums* for eight to ten weeks. Adults appear in mid-July and are seen until first frost. About half a pencil eraser long, they are dusky with a broadly round shape and moderately long antennae.

Beetles in Your Herbaceous Plantings

Scarab beetles are usually not thought of as a problem in herbaceous perennials. But because Japanese beetles are so ravenous for things in the rose family, *Astilbe* can sometimes be attacked rather badly. Other flowers attacked by Japanese beetles include *Aster, Dahlia,* daylily, foxglove, *Gaillardia, Hibiscus,* hollyhock, and peony. Another turf pest, the Asiatic garden beetle, can be problematic as both adults, which feed on flowers, and juveniles, which feed on roots. *Aster* is the preferred host, but they also feed on columbine, *Dahlia,* mums, *Delphinium,* foxglove, *Gaillardia, Rudbeckia, Penstemon, Phlox, Physostegia,* and *Salvia.*

Imported long-horned weevils will sometimes feed on columbine, Chinese lanterns, and daylily by nibbling on the edges of leaves. These are black beetles with gray-green scales. The strawberry weevil nibbles strawberries and *Potentilla,* while the strawberry root weevil munches on *Heuchera.*

Japanese weevil may notch the leaves of lily of the valley, obedient plant, Chinese lantern, *Veronica,* and mums. Black vine weevil, the scourge of the *Rhododendron,* will, as a juvenile, munch the roots of primrose.

Hollyhock weevils—ahhh, back to my friend, the hollyhock weevil! Black, covered with gray hair, a long snout that makes small round holes in leaves— priceless! Soapy water goes a long way toward alleviating the problem.

Cucumber beetles, both striped and spotted varieties, feed on flowers, particularly those of *Dahlia,* mums, daylily, hollyhock, Chinese lantern, and *Coreopsis.* Make sure you clean up weeds in fall to keep populations down.

Hollyhock weevils are a great example of an irritating pest that is not dangerous to the plant's health and so is not really worth treating.

Cucumber beetles readily make the switch to the ornamental bed.

Other Beetles in Your Herbaceous Plantings

These pests might also create issues for your herbaceous plantings. Blister beetles can destroy *Anemone, Phlox, Verbena,* and mums with their infernal chewing. The beautiful golden tortoise beetle does some unlovely feeding damage on *Phlox* and Chinese lantern. Potato flea beetles nibble pinholes in forget me not, *Phlox,* primrose, *Helianthus,* and *Viola,* while strawberry and steel blue flea beetles work their ugly jaws in primrose plantings.

The golden tortoise beetle is a frequent diner in the garden.

Rose chafer beetles sometimes chew hollyhock, foxglove, *Iris,* peony, poppy, and mums, while the June beetle gnaws *Iris* and *Phlox,* and can actually disturb mum roots in the juvenile stage. Grape *Colaspis,* a large, spotted scarab beetle, will nibble *Dahlia.* This jumbo-sized bird snack will usually be found in the vicinity of domestic or wild grape vines.

Caterpillar Pests

Caterpillars are butterflies and moths when they grow up. They are also chewing plant feeders. Although people perceive butterflies and moths as things of beauty, the juveniles can trash a garden in a hurry if populations are high.

Bagworms hatch as caterpillars the first week in June; if you are vigilant, you may not need any treatments. Prune out the largest bags early—these have the eggs. Bagworms tend to like evergreens in warm, sheltered spots. Bacterial pathogen *Bacillus thuringiensis* Kurstaki (*Bt* K) is very good against tiny caterpillars less than 1 inch long, but **never** use pheromone traps—they don't help.

Eastern tent caterpillars break out every eight to ten years with unsightly nests in crotches of branches of cherry, apple, crabapple, peach, and plum. They feed gregariously (all together in a clump just like your cousins' kids at the family reunion) six to eight weeks after cherry leaves come out.

Use this gregarious behavior to your advantage: A strong jet of water really messes up the nest and knocks caterpillars to the ground where they can be gobbled up by hungry birds. Water also vastly increases diseases, which turn very hungry caterpillars into very icky goo. If you are having a bad day, simply don a pair of rubber gloves and squish them with your hands. It's better therapy for a bad mood than cooking liver and onions for the kids! In fall, prune out and bury egg masses, which appear as shiny dark swellings surrounding a 1- to 3-inch area of a small branch.

Gypsy moth, with egg masses that look like little camel-hair-covered sacs, are very easy to transport on camping equipment. Juveniles eat pinholes in leaves when young but devour the entire leaf as they get older. The best control is obtained by treating caterpillars less than 1 inch long, but mechanical disruption of egg masses is also an excellent control. An old-fashioned hand-held whisk broom used for dusting crumbs from the table makes an excellent tool for this purpose. Gypsy moths are spread by wind or storms—like spiders, they can balloon in on silk threads and easily infest previously treated areas. This means you must continuously monitor your susceptible trees. They feed on oak, sugar maple, beech, and aspen from mid-April to mid-May. You may see a sudden resurgence of gypsy moths after drought years due to drought knock-back of a natural fungal disease that helps to keep the populations in check.

Rhododendron **borer** can be very problematic in older *Rhododendron*. The borer is the caterpillar of a clear-winged moth and emerges between 192 and 298 GDD (Growing Degree Days) see page 103,, usually from mid-May to

mid-June. One method of combat is to prune out infested wood before emergence. Infested plants look drought-stressed, with dull-green or yellowed leaves and stunted branches. Infested branches often break off easily. Look for small holes near branch crotches and rough bark. Look for sawdust on branches or on the ground at the base of the plant. You might also see it on azalea or mountain

Rhododendron borer damage is more common on older plants but may also infest stressed plants of any age.

laurel, as well. Infested plants may also display a dark purple leaf spot that is physiological rather than fungal, resulting from the stress of the borer attack.

Spring canker worm is the group we officially know as inch worms; their principle claim to fame is defoliation leading to stress, which opens the door for other problems. For example, feeding on elms predisposes the trees to Dutch elm disease through the stress of leaf loss. A fun way to reduce inch worms is to use strips of sticky paper on a burlap base wound around the trunk from March-May. *Bacillus thuringiensis* (Bt) will also work if the caterpillars are less than 1 inch.

Dogwood borers are also a species of clear-wing moth, and I should note that clear-wing moths resemble bees or flies rather than the traditional moth. You can peel back the bark around the holes in the wood and find the black pepper dots characteristic of the dogwood borer. They lay eggs in wounds and scars on the trunk, so watch that weedwhacker! Mulching (no more than 3 inches deep) around the base of the tree helps, as does decorating the trunk with white latex paint before eggs are laid in June. The dogwood borer particularly likes to colonize swellings on the trunk, so look there first for signs of infestation.

Boxwood leafminer is a frequent visitor to boxwood plantings.

Boxwood leafminer is not the same as boxwood psyllid. Instead, you'll see deformed, discolored leaves which shed, leading to winter injury and sunscald. Try the 'Handsworthiensis' and 'Varder Valley' varieties to avoid the issue altogether.

Juniper tip midge overwinters in terminal galls on tips. To confirm their presence, keep your eye out for $^1/_4$- to $^1/_2$-inch-long terminal buds and break them open to look for mining by reddish maggots. To catch the next generation, treat in mid-May, again in mid-June, or in early August and mid-September.

Caterpillar borers in herbaceous plantings. All borer problems in herbaceous perennials are related to moth juveniles. The stalk borer (now there's a new one for the cop shows!) is a member of the large, nocturnal, dun-colored noctuid moth family. The caterpillars are responsible for boring into *Dahlia, Iris, Aster, Monarda*, columbine, *Centaurea*, mums, *Delphinium*, foxglove, *Gaillardia, Rudbeckia*, hollyhock, *Phlox*, and *Salvia*! Not a picky eater, apparently. Getting rid of weeds can help to reduce problems with this pest. The Burdock borer is similar but can severely injure *Iris* leaves.

The *Iris* borer is a very different problem. It hatches in late April when *Iris* is 5 to 6 inches tall and then in June and July tunnels into the rhizome, introducing soft rot bacteria! That's not fair! The plant wilts and discolors and generally looks terrible. You can divide *Iris* periodically (every three years or so) and discard parts of the rhizome that have the characteristic pinholes signifying borers. Destroy old leaves and other debris in fall to reduce populations.

Good old European corn borer doesn't just stick with what's on the cob: it injures bud ends, stems, flowers, and leaves of *Dahlias, Aster*, hollyhock, and mums. Columbine borer bores into crowns and casts out sawdust. A great way to rid yourself of this problem is to scrape the soil around the base of plants in spring to destroy overwintering eggs.

Caterpillars in herbaceous plantings. The legendary appetite of the caterpillar (second only to my own) is not something to be trifled with in the flower garden! Beet armyworm, corn earworm, red banded leaf roller, yellow wooly bear, variegated cutworm, and regular cutworms can all do a number on your herbaceous plantings. Tobacco hornworms so strongly desire your lovely petunias (same family) that they will decimate them overnight since most caterpillars are primarily nocturnal feeders. Plants may wilt due to this activity, especially *Anemone, Delphinium*, mums, and *Dianthus*.

Beet armyworm is a quick defoliator, leaving plant bits webbed together with silk as its calling card. Caterpillars often bore right into flower buds of *Gypsophila* and *Dianthus*.

Nocturnally motivated **painted lady butterfly caterpillars** chow down on *Hibiscus*, hollyhock, lupines, *Helianthus*, and *Echinops*. They bind terminal leaves with silk and feed on foliage.

Yellow wooly bear comes to call in summer and autumn, damaging *Dahlia*, daylily, hollyhock, lavender, *Salvia, Helianthus, Verbena*, mums, and *Viola*.

Celery or greenhouse leaf tier caterpillars cheerfully and preferentially chew up *Anemone, Dahlia*, mums, *Leucanthemum*, forget me nots, *Lobelia, Echinops, Viola*, mums, *Dianthus*, and *Tradescantia*. They do not enjoy dining *al fresco*, so they bind leaves together and feed inside *à la carte*.

Other caterpillars and hosts include the checkerspot butterfly caterpillar, crunching on mums, *Penstemon*, and *Veronica*; the orange tortrix, which makes its meal on lavender, goldenrod, and *Tradescantia*; the verbena bud moth caterpillar, with a craving for *Iris, Physostegia*, and *Verbena*; and the diamondback moth, with its nosh of *Iberis* and wall flower. Don't forget about the swallowtails and their lust for all things in the carrot and dill family!

To continue in this vein, the beautiful columbine gets troubled by the very hungry caterpillar of the columbine skipper, as well as the white-lined sphinx moth. Corn earworm, tiring of corn, will happily dine on *Hibiscus, Phlox*, poppy, and *Helianthus*. The red banded leaf roller has a taste for hollyhock and *Lobelia*, and the oblique banded leaf roller finds *Helianthus, Echinops, Verbena*, and *Dianthus* oh so tasty!

Wasps

Although most wasps are beneficial predators or pollinators, a few can cause problems on your plants. Here are some of the bad guys:

Birch leafminer is also a sawfly. It produces blotch mines on birch leaves and causes the tree to defoliate early in the season. The tree will refoliate, but the repeated cycle of two flushes of leaves each year weakens it and makes it susceptible to bronze birch borer. Again, the ever-popular but short-lived

Flies in the Garden

Most flies are actually beneficial as predators and pollinators, but a few can cause problems, like leaf mines and galls.

Yes, Virginia, there is a fly in your herbaceous planting. Lesser bulb fly maggots hang out in *Iris* corms but are usually confined to already rotting areas. Sunflower maggots cause stems to fall over on each other. (Tiiiiimber!)

Leafminers are normally not a crisis in herbaceous plantings. Columbines may suffer from serpentine mines, caused by a type of small fly. Your best option: the old squish and pinch maneuver. The miners are seen primarily after bloom, a few years after they have been planted.

Leafminer on columbine leaves spectacular trails.

Chrysanthemum leafminer is another dang blasted fly, but instead of leaving long winding trails, it leaves blister mines so that leaves dry up and hang down the stems. These little buggers also hang out in *Dahlia, Dianthus, Eupatorium, Lobelia,* primrose, *Salvia,* and *Verbena.* The Larkspur leafminer chows down on *Delphinium,* monkshood, *Verbena, Heuchera, Dianthus, Gypsophila,* and primrose, once again causing large areas of the leaf to discolor and then collapse. Remove infested leaves pronto!

paper birch is the most susceptible. Yellow and black birches are resistant. An important step in reducing leafminers is to remove the birch suckers that proliferate at the base of the tree and harbor the leafminers. It is also important to avoid excess fertility because all that nitrogen benefits the insect's reproductive capabilities. To determine when the adults are out and about, hang yellow sticky cards at branch tips.

European pine sawfly is as voracious as any caterpillar. Recall that the difference between caterpillars and sawflies are little lines inside the feet of the fleshy abdominal legs of caterpillars versus none on the footies of the sawflies. European pine sawfly eats old needles and the bark of new shoots. It seldom kills because it doesn't eat new growth. Like eastern tent caterpillar, it feeds gregariously and will rear back on its hind legs with a "what's up?" expression when disturbed. Trees up to 15 feet are most severely affected, especially Scotch, mugo, and jack pines. When flowering quince is in bloom, you'll see sawflies (late May).

European pine sawfly can easily win an eating contest.

Again, a strong stream of water is the answer because when they fall off the tree, they generally can't get back up. You could always shop-vacuum them off, and there is also the thumb and forefinger tango if the water method doesn't float your boat. If you see sawflies later than June, it is the red headed pine sawfly that is noshing on your conifers.

Cynipid gall wasps are tiny yet mighty wasps that produce strange swellings known as oak "apples," horned oak galls, and hedgehog galls. Oak apples are a common sight in the fall. With the last of the foliage blown off the oaks by fall storms, it is easy to see little papery brown balls produced by the wasp *Amphibolips* (what a wonderful insult!). The life history of these wasps is not well understood. Two broods are produced, one all female, one both sexes. The large galls are attached to the midrib or petiole of a leaf and filled with a spongy, easily sliced mass. The juveniles inside the "apple" are in a hardened capsule in the center. No serious damage is done by these wasps.

Horned oak galls are warty with sharp points or horns sticking out of them. They are very woody. Hedgehog galls are softer and fuzzy, occurring only on leaves. Black oaks may be affected by producing abnormally large leaves, and the attack may weaken trees so that a fungal infection kills them, particularly when combined with drought stress. Clean up leaves to reduce populations.

Sawflies and wasps in herbaceous plantings. Hornets can tear *Dahlia* stems for nesting material, while sawfly can cause blistering or flagging of viola and *Doronicum* leaves and occasionally defoliate *Rudbeckia*.

Thrips

Tiny tubular thrips are likely to make a big impact on your landscape plantings should you get them, but perhaps not as bad on trees and shrubs as on herbaceous plantings. Thrips creep around flower buds even before the buds open, sucking and rasping away tissue. Leaves become mottled with silvery or papery stipples, and you'll see tiny black fecal specks on both sides of

Insect Pests of Annuals

When we consider herbaceous annuals, most people simply rip up and toss out plantings infested with insects since the plant is only going to be there for one season anyway. It is always important to know what is affecting them, however, because if you rip out the annuals, chances are the pests may simply move on to your perennials or into your vegetable garden!

* *Alyssum* is affected by cabbage maggots and flea beetles, while *Calendula* may suffer from blister beetles, cabbage loopers, corn earworms, and *Cyclamen* mite.
* China asters may fall victim to Japanese beetles. Ever-popular cosmos gets nibbled by earwigs, European corn borer, and Japanese beetles.
* Geraniums, while unpalatable to some insects, is a favorite of cabbage loopers, *Cyclamen* mites, four-lined plant bugs, Japanese beetles (white geraniums are poisonous to them), root mealybugs, tarsonemid mites, and western flower thrips, which carry viral diseases.
* *Impatiens* suffer the wrath of *Cyclamen* mites and western flower thrips.
* Nasturtiums fall prey to bean aphids, cabbage butterflies, flea beetles, and serpentine leafminers.
* Petunias are likely to be devoured by Colorado potato beetles and tomato hornworms, so think twice about rimming the garden patch with them.
* *Annual Salvia* gets leafhoppers.
* Snapdragon twists up with *Cyclamen* mites.
* The old-fashioned favorite, stock, is fodder for cabbage maggots and flea beetles.
* Sunflowers can suffer from leaf-curling aphids and sweet peas from garden chumps like pea aphid, pea moth, and seed corn maggot.
* *Nicotiana* will be ravenously consumed by Colorado potato beetles.
* *Verbena* is bothered by western flower thrips.
* Wall flower will suffer from cabbage maggots and flea beetles.
* Poor, hard-working *Zinnia* are set upon by blister beetles, European corn borers, four-lined plant bugs, and Japanese beetles.

Thrips damage mimics a lot of other conditions, including viruses and leafhopper feeding.

leaves that are fed on. Shoots are distorted, flower buds drop, or blooms are deformed. Thrips suck cell contents rather than tapping into the plant's sugar conduit. They vector viruses (mainly *Impatiens* necrotic ring spot virus [INSV] with black, brown, and red concentric rings and other symptoms).

Thrips often resist pesticides but may be deterred by plant-based repellents like those from the neem tree. These insects also tend to attack drought-stressed plants. Thrips are attracted to blue sticky cards hung just above the canopy; place the cards in areas of air movement. If you blow gently into flowers or on buds to draw out thrips that are hiding or tap a plant over a white piece of paper, you will be able to determine the extent of their presence.

Thrips are often in dandelion flowers, so if you want to see what they look like, start there. Adults are most active at the beginning and end of the day, so that's when you should apply your controls. Given thrips' cryptic habitat and resistance to control, pesticides might not be the best option.

Pear thrips are the biggest issue for trees and shrubs, resulting in flecked, dwarfed leaves (one quarter their normal size), with crinkled, mottled, discolored areas between veins. The end result is thin, yellow crowns, defoliation, and stress. Some of the palliative measures you can take are water and light fertilizer applications in the fall after leaf drop.

Thrips rasp leaf and flower surfaces, then suck juices that flow out, giving the plants a silvery look. They feed gregariously, particularly on *Dahlia*, *Dianthus*, *Campanula*, foxglove, *Gaillardia*, hollyhock, peony, *Verbena*, mums, daylily, and *Delphinium*. They will turn peony petals brown, and flowers may remain balled, never to open no matter how hard you beg. Tops of *Iris* are russetted or blackened by thrips damage, and flowers fail to open. White or brown streaking on flower petals especially indicates thrips.

Beneficial Insects

No chapter on garden insects would be complete without a little education on beneficial insects. Lots of confusion exists over whether an insect is beneficial or harmful. Since many insects that are pests get all the publicity, just as corruption and crimes get publicity in the media, I thought it might be useful to give a quick round of applause and recognition to the good guys.

Lady beetles come in all sorts of patterns and sizes. Although most people know what the adult lady beetle—or lady bug, as popular literature refers to it—looks like, few recognize the immature versions, which look a bit like spiny little alligators. They are pointed on both ends, blue or black with orange spots, and range from $1/4$ to $1/2$ inch long. Both adults and juveniles eat aphids, scale insects, mealybugs, mites, and insect eggs. It takes about one month to go from egg to adult. They overwinter as adults, sometimes together in hedges, under rocks and bark, or even in buildings. Eggs may be cream, yellow, or orange and may resemble the eggs of some harmful vegetable-eating insects, but they are usually much smaller. The eggs are normally laid near an area infested with prey. The stage just before the adult stage usually resembles a VW Beetle. They are most effective with high numbers of pests, or else they disperse in search of more things to eat. Pollen is a staple in the diets of some lady beetles, so having flowers (even dandelions) may entice them to stick around.

Rove beetles often resemble earwigs without the claws. The primary prey of these long, narrow, short-winged, and slinky-bodied insects are soft-bodied insects, especially root maggots. The juvenile stage resembles the beneficial ground beetle juveniles. The adults are easily recognized by the very short wings over very long bodies (think of a bolero or short cloak on a dress uniform). Rove beetles are found under rocks, in debris, in compost, near water, or even in the foliage itself. Hedges make excellent hiding places. The beetle ranges in size from a little less than $3/4$ inch to less than $1/10$th of an inch.

Ground beetles, like tiger beetles, have dark or metallic, flat, shiny bodies with ridged wing covers and can range in size from $1/4$ to 2 inches long. Juveniles are similar to turf-infesting grubs but are very active compared to these pests. Some juveniles also look a bit like tiny scorpions because of their pincer jaws. All stages are more active at night and are common in heavily mulched landscapes. Juveniles hide in soil, grass, debris, and dead bark. They prey on a wide variety of insects and caterpillars, and some species will even climb trees to go after pests hiding there.

Aphid mummy wasps are less than $1/8$ inch long—you're more likely to notice the fruits of their labors than the wasps themselves. Look at aphid colonies to see whether they appear to be brown or white bloated aphid bodies or mummies; these are the end product of the wasp juveniles eating the aphid from inside out. Yum! These parasites are specific to aphids and should be conserved if possible by allowing the process to go on without interference.

Aphid midges look like tiny mosquitoes (less than $1/8$ inch) as adults and are indeed true flies. Adults fly at night. Aphid midges are very beneficial. They have bright orange or red, wormlike juveniles. Aphids are paralyzed then sucked dry (anyone see *The Mummy?*). They are most effective when temperatures range from 68 to 80 degrees F., with high humidity and strong winds. One youngster may eat ten to eighty aphids. You'll most commonly see juveniles from mid- to late summer. Mass releases of commercially available aphid midges have successfully controlled aphids in small backyard areas. Adults need a source of honeydew.

Large wasps are usually long and slender with extremely long, coiling ovipositors. They may also have a single black pane in their wings. They are parasitoids, which means that the juvenile lives within a single host that it eventually kills. They may be host-specific or broadly parasitic, utilizing moth, fly, or beetle hosts.

Syrphid flies, also called hover flies, may resemble bees or wasps by being yellow and black striped with short antennae and large eyes. They are generally only 3/8 to 3/4 inches long and can be distinguished from true bees or wasps because they have only two wings. Adults are not predatory; they feed on nectar and pollen. The sluglike juveniles more than make up for this by eating up to 400 juvenile aphids per day! Eggs are laid near aphid infestations, where the juveniles feast for two to three weeks before pupating in soil. Attract adults by planting from the carrot family, including Queen Anne's lace, dill, and angelica or horseradish.

Tachinid flies look like houseflies in that they are hairy and grayish brown, with possible lighter markings on the abdomen. Wings are usually semispread. When the adults are looking for hosts, they usually walk rapidly over surfaces or in hops or short flights. This naturally agitates nearby caterpillars and beetle juveniles (including the Colorado potato beetle). Adults feed on nectar or honeydew secreted by aphids or scale. They range from 3/8 to 1 inch long and attack corn borers and earworms, cabbage loopers, imported cabbage worms, armyworms, Japanese beetles, leaf eating beetle juveniles, and squash bugs. They deposit eggs just behind the head of the host, and when the egg hatches, the larva bores inside to enjoy the host's innards.

Braconid wasps are small parasites that are usually dark and may attack the host internally or feed from the outside on the innards of the prey. The adult may have a single black pane on its wing. The most widely recognized braconid is the one attached to the outside of the tomato hornworm. What we are actually seeing is the cocoon phase. The female wasp injects her eggs into the caterpillar's body, where they hatch and feed until they are ready to pupate, at which point they chew their way to the surface of the caterpillar's skin and spin their cocoons. Hollywood horror movie directors take note! Different species may attack eggs, juveniles, pupae, or adults. The best thing to do is to leave parasitized insects where they are so that the parasite can complete its lifecycle.

Predatory stink bugs feed on caterpillars, beetle juveniles, and slow-moving insects. They may feed on plants too. Not all stink bugs are bad guys, although it may be hard to tell them from their plant pest cousins. The spined soldier bugs and the two-spotted stink bug are particularly important predators. Stink bugs have a shieldlike back and five segmented antennae. Juveniles look much like the adults except for the gradual development of wings. Bad guys are often green, while good guys are brown or gray. The spined soldier bug is pale brown to tan as an adult, with spurs on the shoulders and a dark line on the tip of each wing, which distinguishes it from pest species. The young are rounded and marked with yellow, orange, and red. The two-spotted stink bug has a shieldlike body that is red and black or yellow and black. Juveniles are red and black. They are especially useful against Colorado potato beetles.

Damsel bugs are elongate brown bugs $1/3$ to $1/2$ inch long. Wings have a series of cells on their edges. They eat small insects like beetle juveniles, aphids, leafhoppers, and caterpillars. Their method of capture and feeding is similar to other bugs, and the juveniles look much like the adults except for the gradual development of wings as the insect approaches maturity. These bugs are frequently encountered in many habitats, but you may find them more often in low-growing grasses and ground covers.

Assassin bugs have wide stomachs and long, narrow heads. They look almost as though they have a neck. Assassin bugs may have spines on their chests (wheel bugs). The eggs look like old-fashioned brown glass milk jugs with white caps. The juveniles look similar to adults, and both stages feed on a wide variety of insects by spearing the host with a hypodermic-like mouthpart, ejecting enzymes that digest the body contents, then sucking the predigested guts from the insect that has become the meal. Ain't nature grand?

Robber flies are true flies with 4,000 species. They have hairy bodies with long, tapering abdomens and a depression in their heads behind their eyes. They are large, $1/2$ to 1 inch long. Wormlike and predaceous juveniles inhabit soil with large amounts of decaying organic matter where they can prey on other insect juveniles in the soil. Adults eat leafhoppers, small beetles, wasps, bees, and grasshoppers, so they obviously consume beneficials. They will also bite you if mishandled. You can encourage robber flies in your landscape by having flowering plants, since the flies need sugar and protein to lay eggs.

Ambush bugs use a similar method of dining on their prey. Their coloring allows them to hide their small stout bodies with wide rear ends (my kind of camouflage!). They are all predatory, feeding on bees, wasps, butterflies, and flies, so unfortunately their menu also includes beneficial pollinators. They camouflage themselves inside flowers (leading to their name). The juveniles look very similar to the adults.

Big-eyed bugs look so much like chinch bugs because they are closely related and because they hang out with chinch bugs in order to make a meal of them. These little black or gray guys also eat mites, leafhoppers, aphids, insect eggs, and other small insects. They eat plant sap and seeds when pests aren't around for snack attacks. Juveniles look very like adults.

Lacewings eat pollen and honeydew, along with insects. Immatures are actually called aphid lions and are far more frightening than even the cheesiest sci-fi movie on a lonely Saturday night. Immatures are mottled, pointed on either end, and possess awesomely large, sicklelike mouth parts. Rock on, dude! Unfortunately, *Night of the Aphid Lion* doesn't make a title anyone would want to watch, so we'll simply have to settle for enjoying the battle in miniature on our plants. The egg-to-adult cycle takes only one month, so there may be ten generations per year! The eggs look like tiny cotton-tipped swab heads on gossamer stalks, which is protection against sibling cannibalism. Adults are attracted to flowering plants, so the more of these you have in your garden, the better your beneficial population will be.

The brown lacewing is smaller and does **not** lay its eggs on stalks; it tends to be found in wooded areas. Brown lacewings tolerate cooler temperatures and are responsible for keeping pests low early in the season, including the aphids. The juveniles are similar to those of green lacewings. Adult lace-wings need a source of honeydew before egg laying and may be attracted to flowering plants.

Insidious flower bugs and minute pirate bugs, at less than $1/8$ inch long, truly are "minute." They are black with white wing patches and extremely mobile. Young are teardrop shaped and yellowish orange to brown. They feed on thrips, aphids, spider mites (as many as thirty per day!), and insect eggs, taking a bit of sap from time to time without harming the plant. They also enjoy biting humans, especially in late summer or fall, but don't take it personally. They are simply so numerous then that they are more likely to encounter you—and are just trying to defend themselves from that "really big predator."

Fireflies, as most people know, are harmless and make for pleasant company on a summer evening, but these beetles are also predaceous in their larval form. Adults usually don't feed, except for the occasional nip of pollen or nectar. Juveniles are flattened and may resemble the tower of Pisa without the lean. Juveniles live in soil and may also glow, accounting for the nickname (also given to other insect juveniles) glowworms. They eat insects and snails.

So there you have it, the *in*complete guide to insects in your landscape. We can only ever hope to cover a mere fraction of insect and plant interactions in a user-friendly fashion, but read on to find out about other vertebrate and invertebrate pests. *Bon Appétit!*

Deerly Beloved (Not!)

A Few Other Pests

As much as *you* would like to blame all our problems on insects and diseases, and as much as *I* would like to blame a lot on cultural practices, we also have to consider a few other garden miscreants. The biggest vertebrate gluttons are deer and rabbits; in the invertebrate group, slugs and snails pack a mighty wallop. For underground pillage, we have the vole and its voracious appetite and its cousin the mole, who is often blamed for offenses committed by the vole. Although many others (such as squirrels) need to be chased around with a rake while you scream like a banshee, the creatures listed in this chapter are the biggest delinquents.

De"feel" Your Deer

Deer do not like the feel of good old chain link underfoot. The next time someone is pulling out his chain link fence, harvest the pieces and cut them in strips to place along the margins of your garden. Covered with a skim of leaves, you'll never know the chain link is there, but the deer will and may not be as willing to walk in those areas!

Deer

For some of us, Bambi and his kin are a major garden pest, and although we try to put in deer-resistant plantings, the sad truth is that if they're hungry, they will come. Interestingly, deer do tend to prefer fertilized plantings, so a heavy hand with the fertilizer may once again bring a bad outcome. The reason deer prefer the fertilized plant is probably the excuse that insects use: succulent tissue. (Would you prefer a dry old twig or a nice, juicy apple?)

Deer will eat leaves as high as they can reach.

Deer Repellents

Deer across the country are actually different from place to place, so behaviors and repellencies may be different, as well. A fence to keep out neighborhood browsers will usually have to be about 8 feet tall, which may conflict with city, village, or county codes or neighborhood covenants. Check before you erect!

Deer do not like plants from the mint family, medicinal plants, anything with a lemony taste, or sticky or hairy leaves. The problem with this happy solution is that many plants that answer this description are moderate to low growers. Therefore, Mr. and Mrs. Deer can simply reach over them and grab whatever tasty little treat is growing just beyond.

If you want to use these kinds of plants as a living fence, back them up with plants rarely damaged by deer, such as barberry, boxwood, American holly, drooping leucothoe, Colorado blue spruce, or Japanese andromeda. Take into account which plants will do better in cooler versus warmer climates. This double deterrent to the delicious fodder that lies within may be enough to make your resident herd form a munch bunch for lunch elsewhere. Other repellents are marketed, such as one made from rotten eggs, but they have to be renewed after rain or irrigation. On the whole, a physical barrier affords more consistent protection.

Rabbits

What about those wascally wabbits? Peter, Harvey, Thumper, and Bugs are all hungry, and their real-life counterparts are even worse! These sneaky little bleeps can really do a number on your plantings and leave you totally mystified as to what struck in the night!

Why is it so hard to tell that a rabbit is the culprit? It's because they eat the **entire** plant, leaving absolutely no trace behind that there ever was a plant in the first place. If they leave any clue, it looks like someone took a penknife and cut the plant cleanly and low to the ground.

Rabbit Repellents

Dogs and cats that patrol the area are quite good at scaring away your hoppy friends. You can also try the pet fur method, which offers mixed results. Troop down to the local pet grooming salon and ask for their clippings. Strategically place some of these around favored fodder, and weigh them down with rocks. If the animal fur doesn't scare away the bunnies, it will at least give your pets (and the neighbors) something to wonder and worry about. Another potential repellent is the organic fertilizer, dried blood meal. This also may have some rabbit deterrence, but like the rotten egg product for the deer, it has to be renewed after rain or irrigation.

Rabbits are repelled by plants in the tomato/potato/eggplant/pepper family, so perhaps a few of these surrounding your most vulnerable plants might be helpful. Datura or *Brugmansia* (angel's trumpet) is also in this family and highly ornamental, so a planting of these may also help with your rabbit problems if veggies amongst the ornamentals spook the aesthete in you. Gourd plantings may also repel.

Remember how Peter got into Farmer MacGregor's garden? He squeezed under the fence. So the protocol for a rabbit fence is $1/2$-inch wire mesh buried to a depth of 6 inches and extending 2 feet above ground. Otherwise, you are likely to wake up to a nice neat harvest of all your favorite stuff.

Slugs and Snails

There's another powerful set of villains out there that feed by night. To a slug or snail, those new, soft, tender plants look like a salad bar. Adding to the problem, perhaps no experience is as unpleasant as stepping on a slug in one's bare foot!

Slugs are actually econo-snails—with no shell (they're probably trying to avoid property taxes!). Slugs feed mostly at night and in cloudy, damp weather. During the day snails with shells like to hang out on smooth, shaded surfaces,

Mulching May Encourage Slugs

Mulching, although a practice we like to promote, may make your slug problems worse since the cool, damp confines of a mulched bed are just the kind of roadside pit stop that appeals to slugs. If you have a problem year after year with slugs and snails, try using mulches that compact, like rice hulls or pine needles, or try mulching with an irritating substance like egg shells, gravel, sand, oak leaves, cedar or oak bark, or sawdust. Bear in mind that these mulching materials may change the pH of your site. If you are growing strawberries, sawdust may be a good choice since the berries like the acid and benefit from having a barrier between them and the soil.

Composting slug-infested plant material can also be a source of reinfection if the compost is not properly cured.

while slugs clamber into moist crevices. Many are hermaphroditic so that every single one lays eggs, and in as little as a few months, those eggs are more reproductive adults. Eeek! Additionally, eggs, which look like tapioca, are not especially vulnerable to small predators. If weather becomes too hot or cold, snails can become dormant for up to four years. They are most active in the spring and fall.

Slugs and snails both leave slime trails, with slugs eating large holes in plants or defoliating them entirely. Snails are daintier, eating irregular holes in the middle or at the edges of leaves. They need the slime they manufacture in order to move. The ripple of their muscular foot allows them to slip slowly along the slime they have made.

Slug and Snail Repellents

Slugs actually prefer decaying vegetable matter and (gulp) doggie doo, which they effectively demolish. So to reduce slug populations, remove dead leaves and debris, particularly around seedlings.

A Switzerland study looked at the palatability of different plants to slugs and found that slugs love plants in the cabbage family, but don't care so much for plants in the bean and grass family, the buttercup family, or the snapdragon family. Specific garden plants that are minimally bothered by slugs are azaleas and *Rhododendron*, apricots, almonds, basil, beans, cigarette plants (*Cuphea*), corn, chard, Jerusalem cherry, daffodil, *Fuchsia*, *Freesia*, grape, gopher plant and other *Euphorbia* species, holly, *Hibiscus*, Swedish ivy, Peruvian lily, parsley,

Typically slugs rasp holes in leaves as they feed on them.

pumpkin, plum, sage, sunflower, and many poppies. Interplanting palatable plants with prostrate rosemary and wormwood also helps.

If you wish to hand-pick slugs, leave an old board lying around—they often congregate under it.

Slugs can also be excluded from plantings by using corrugated lawn edging with a 1-inch lip that has been bent away from the plants. A very thin piece of copper cut into strips will act as a slug deterrent, as well, or can be wrapped as a collar around trees at about $1^1/2$ feet off the ground (remember to expand this as the tree grows). The copper gives off an electrical charge to the slug.

Slugs hate rough surfaces, so using a piece of hardware cloth with a bit of the wire sticking up can deter slugs from feeding, as can collars made from old window screen.

If baits that act by dehydrating the slugs and snails are ingested during humid or rainy weather, the slugs can counteract the effects and rehydrate themselves. One iron-based product causes the snails and slugs to stop eating and starve to death—and it's not harmful to dogs and cats, which is a huge issue with most slug baits. Diatomaceous earth may be another good source of irritation for them by compromising the slugs' health. (I like to compromise them with the heel of a wooden garden clog, heh-heh-heh.)

Moles

The next time you are tempted to do a *Caddyshack* thing or two, **bear in mind that moles are beneficial!** They feed exclusively on meat like grubs or earthworms, aerate the soil, and enrich the root zone with minerals. They do not—repeat, **do not**—eat plant roots: It's the gophers and voles of the world who are the vegetarians dining on your prized garden plantings.

Moles also get a bad name for damaging turf. They tunnel under the earth looking for insects or earthworms; unfortunately, turf disturbed in this way may shrivel up and die during hot weather. "Blind as a mole" would be a better phrase than "blind as a bat" since moles can detect only light and dark. They have no external ear flaps, which makes it that much easier for them to ignore nagging relatives. You can tell if moles are extremely active in an area by tamping down tunnels with a shovel and then watching over the next day or two to see whether tunnels reappear. Eastern moles prefer well-drained, loose soil in lawns and gardens and may also nest in the edge of woodlands. The star-nosed mole prefers wet areas in woods, fields, or swamps but will nest in higher ground. The presence of star-nosed moles may indicate that you are overdoing the irrigation a bit. Both kinds use earthworms as a major food source. Their tunnels are on two levels, with upper tunnels used for

Moles Are Beneficial

Controlling mole populations by flooding tunnels with water, car exhaust, or chewing gum is not an effective management option. Fumigation with poisonous gas can be detected by the mole, which may fill in the tunnel to prevent poisoning. Moles do not eat peanut butter or bran baits.

If the mole tunnels bother you, roll the area lightly and water it. The mounds shouldn't interfere with mowing unless your mower blade is set too low, which isn't good for the grass anyway. Multiple tunnels can be evened off with a shovel. Mole populations are not constant. Extra rain will cause a temporary increase in numbers and possibly activity since it will also cause grubs to stay near the surface—mole smorgasbord. Once the moles have moved on, you can expect your grass to thrive better than before, thanks to the effect of tunneling.

transportation and lower ones for living space. Mostly nocturnal, moles tend to be solitary (as you would be too, if you had nothing but almost blind dates!). They mate in spring and produce two to six young.

Voles

Now many of you are grumbling that I don't know what I'm talking about and that you **know** the moles are eating your roots and bulbs because you've seen the tunnels and the half-eaten bulbs at the ends of them. Well, say I gloating, **wrong!** You've got voles riding the subway of the moles' tunnels to avoid predators!

Voles, also known as meadow mice, have plump bodies, short hairy tails, and small eyes and ears in proportion to the head (with the exception of the tail, this is starting to sound a good deal like me!). Fully grown, they are about 7 inches long and have rather coarse hair. They eat a variety of grasses, broad-leaf weeds (every pest has a plus), seeds, tubers, bulbs, and rhizomes. They also eat tree bark, including bark on roots.

Voles do not hibernate but remain active all year, mostly during the day. They can produce a new generation in about sixty days. Like moles, their populations fluctuate from year to year and may pose a significant threat to fruit trees when populations are high. Fortunately, many are consumed by natural predators, and the mortality rate of the young is more than 80 percent before reaching one month. The lifespan of the vole is also short, ranging from two to sixteen months.

When trying to tell the difference between rodents, bear in mind that moles have greatly enlarged front feet, including prominent claws for digging; shrews (another rodent present commonly left by Kitty on the doormat) have long, pointed snouts and needlelike front teeth; and voles have a blunt snout with chisellike front teeth (sort of like my high school prom date).

Mole and Vole Repellents

So how do you rid yourself of moles and (perhaps less easily) voles? Okay, boys and girls, this one sounds like it's straight from the annals of Mother Hatchet's Home for Unfortunates. Apparently, moles are repelled by the smell of castor oil (aren't we all?), an accidental discovery made when researchers working with castor bean plants noticed that moles tunneling near plants stopped short when approaching the plants themselves. Look for mole repellent that contains castor oil as an active ingredient; the oil is held in an unrefined state, suspended in a fatty acid carrier (slimy yet satisfying) for extra staying power.

Current recommendations for homeowners are to water the lawn before applying the repellent. Use at least 1/2 inch of water; after applying the repellent, water at least another inch. The window of efficacy is thirty to seventy-five days. Areas under constant irrigation are not good candidates for this solution, nor are very sandy soils where the scent washes through fast.

Another option is to ring mole-infested areas with the actual castor bean plants, highly decorative, large tropical annuals. The seeds, although very pretty, are highly toxic (ricin is derived from them, to many a spy thriller novelist's glee), so this may not be the best choice for those with children or animals who might eat the seeds. Voles are less likely to be repelled by castor plants or castor oil, but they are unhappy with plantings of *Euphorbia*, squill, and fritillaries for the same reasons of peculiar and unattractive scent.

Clematis, Geraniums, Impatiens, Roses, and Oaks

Problems of Popular Plants

There are a few plants that almost everyone tries to grow. Unfortunately, like the relatives that always show up at the most inopportune times, these can be some of the most problematic! *Clematis,* roses, geraniums, *Impatiens,* and oaks are all very popular, but each has some specific problems.

Clematis

Remember Mary, Mary quite contrary and her garden? They didn't mention anything about *Clematis* because *Clematis* is an old fusspot when it comes to growing conditions. Your neighbor might have the greatest success, while every one you have ever tried dies quicker than yesterday's PTA raffle goldfish.

The best overall time to plant *Clematis* is early spring using bare-root stock, although container-grown plants can be stuck in at any point. Choose the east or north side of your property, in a location where filtered sun will be available for the upper part of the plant yet roots will be kept cool. Unlike other plants, the crown should be covered with 2 inches of soil so that new buds can emerge from a protected section if something bad happens to the top (the neighborhood Spring Slugathon comes to mind.)

Clematis are very slow to establish, so you will see little or no top growth or flowers during the first year after planting. *Clematis* also like soils that are not acidic.

Soak your plants for an hour or so in a bucket of water before you plant, and if stems are longer than 1 foot, cut them back to encourage side branching and to make plants less prone to snapping off at the base. *Clematis* with purple or red blossoms will bleach in the sun, so use these varieties in shadier spots. Set a growth support for plants to twine around in place before you plant your *Clematis* to avoid disturbing the roots and crown later unless you are planning to use the *Clematis* as a ground cover.

Along with incorporating organic amendments into the planting hole, mulch around your installed plant—but not right up to the stem, which encourages the fungal diseases to which *Clematis* are prone.

Clematis should never be allowed to dry out in the root zone, or the plant quality will severely suffer. Slugs and snails can also be annoying, especially in springs following mild winters.

Clematis Pests

Earwigs chew holes in flowers and leaves, or in buds, ruining flowers before they open. They can be especially bad if plants are located next to brick buildings or other construction with cracks and crevices ideal for the earwigs to hide in. Try stuffing a discarded plant container with newspaper and placing it on a stick near where damage occurs. Earwigs will hide inside this and can be removed daily and destroyed. Or roll up newspaper and secure either end loosely with rubber bands for the collect and discard routine.

Mice, those rotten rodents, can nip *Clematis* off at the base, especially where they grow up through other ground covers. Damage is most noticeable in spring. New growth will initiate from the base, though, so ignore the problem.

Spider mites bother *Clematis* especially if it is dry, causing distortion of leaves and flowers, as well as flecking. Hosing off the plant on a regular basis can keep spider mites down.

Clematis Diseases
***Clematis* wilt** is the most serious problem, especially for large-flowered varieties. The fungus attacks the plant at the soil line or just above, entering through a crack or a point of previous damage. The stem's plumbing is blocked up and the stem collapses, turning black, then brown. *Clematis* plants collapse overnight, usually in early summer just before flowering and just after you were bragging to the neighbor! Affected stems need to be removed immediately and destroyed (no composting!); then drench the base with a recommended fungicide in a 2-foot diameter around the plant. *Clematis* with a good set of growth buds below the soil will usually recover if the drenching program is continued.

Get the stems as woody as possible as quickly as possible; when stems reach 9 to 12 inches, remove tip growth to encourage side branching. Keep stems from damage as much as possible, treating the entire plant as though it were newly planted in terms of feeding, watering, pruning, and training on the support. *Clematis vitacella* cultivars like 'Blue Belle' are not susceptible to wilt, so they are the best choice for carefree gardening.

Powdery mildew is the bane of the large-flowered varieties. Use baking soda-based pesticides at recommended rates to control this disease, and increase air circulation around your plants.

Roses

Many of the self-same problems that plague our weediest plantings often occupy our prized plantings with even more vigor, precisely because we are paying so much attention, like a lavish hand with the fertilizer and water.

Insects on Roses
Borers include rose stem sawfly, curled rose slug, rose stem girdler, and small carpenter bees. These pests bore through canes and lay

Rose midge damage looks like a burn.

Rose Pest Tips

* Clean all debris from around roses while they are dormant (during a winter cleanup) to reduce next year's crop of insects.
* Bear in mind that moles can disturb rose roots by tunneling and that voles may actually cut off underground roots. Examine your plants for these pests before leaping to the conclusion that an insect is your problem. Scilla bulbs can sometimes repel rodents.
* Weak necks or stems in roses are not caused by insects but rather by a phosphorous deficiency or too little sun.
* Leafcutter bees cut perfect circles of leaf tissue but do no other harm; simply prune out wilted shoots they cause.
* Don't segregate your roses; mix them with plenty of diverse plantings to encourage beneficial insects. Use hedgerows, barriers, or a row of sunflowers to repel insect pests and provide cover or alternative food for beneficials.
* If you have already been attacked, a little stinky fish emulsion fertilizer may help roses grow out of problems encountered earlier in the season.

eggs; then the juveniles eat through the canes. Simply cut out canes below the infested portion when you see evidence of the pests in late spring. The miscreants lay eggs in small punctures made in the cut tip of a rose cane; then the juveniles tunnel down the pith and finally hibernate until next season. The stem eventually dies. If you cut the cane, you'll see the hole; it will be either a few inches deep or descend all the way to the crown!

Raspberry cane borers can also be an issue in roses, especially if you have a nearby raspberry patch. Once again, cut infested canes below the bored-out area. In some cases, it may be helpful to seal the cut canes with waterproof glue.

Rose midge, as an adult, is a tiny ($^1/_{20}$-inch) yellowish fly, which lays eggs on succulent new growth and under sepals of flower buds. Rose midges hatch in just two days and feed on new growth, which turns brown and dies, preventing bud development. Curses! They reach maturity in a week, fall to ground to become adults, and then more adults emerge again in three to seven days to start the cycle over!

Infestations lead to very few blooms since immature buds are destroyed. A major sign of midge infestation is a tiny, crisp, burned-looking tip to new growth. The juveniles use sicklelike mouthparts to slash tissue. Examine your roses daily in spring and fall, and remove "burned" foliage immediately. Mulch around plants, and look for black, deformed flower buds as a sign of invasion.

Thrips can be a huge issue for roses, especially if they are surrounded by other thrips-susceptible plantings such as gladiolas. Leaves may be mottled with silvery or papery stipples, and you'll see tiny black fecal specks on the fronts and backs of the leaves.

Shoots will be distorted, flower buds will drop, and blooms may be deformed. Blooms are discolored, with white or brown streaks. Blow gently into flowers or on buds to draw out hiding thrips, or tap a bloom over a white piece of paper. The juveniles look a bit like lice. White rose varieties are especially likely to be affected. Cut off and dispose of spent blooms promptly, give the bud a quick squeeze, or breathe on it to look for thrips. Insecticidal soap may help!

Mites are a big issue on roses, especially miniature ones, but if you follow all the mite protocols in Chapter 5, you should be able to successfully reduce mite populations. Just remember to prune judiciously so you don't get a surge of juicy growth during mite prime time, avoid fertilizing plants that are already infested with mites, and mulch to maintain humidity, which supports beneficial populations. If you switch to roses that are a trifle more tolerant of less bright sun (most are not), you may also reduce mite populations. Try 'Abigail Adams', 'Danae', 'Gloire de Rosemanes', or 'Iceberg' roses. 'Iceberg' makes an excellent foundation planting choice.

Japanese beetles *looooove* roses but fortunately are not distributed over the entire country. They also like Pennsylvania smart weed, crapemyrtle, grapes, and lindens, so if you have all these choices in one small garden, the problem intensifies. Get rid of Japanese beetles by underplanting your roses with white geraniums because they are both toxic and irresistible to Japanese beetles. If you want to plant a linden tree nearby, choose 'Rancho' or 'Chanticleer' varieties rather than the common 'Greenspire'. Adults also like wild grape, blackberry, crabgrass, ragweed, cattails, apples, cherries, peaches, plums, maples, birch, crabapple, sassafras, and mountain ash.

Caterpillars cause damage on roses that is often evident simply as eaten flower buds or leaves rolled or tied around the caterpillar and eaten from the inside. You'll see the damage most often in late spring. Simply cut out infested buds and leaves or use a preparation of *Bacillus thuringiensis* (*Bt*) bacteria to kill young caterpillars, which are very small (less than 1 inch). Budworms are green or whitish orange and about ³/₈ inch long. The rose leaf-tier is pale green and about ³/₄ inch long. All caterpillars and budworm pests cause similar damage.

Leafhoppers cause the tops of leaves to pale and become speckled yellow, which looks similar to spider mite damage. Check out Chapter 5 to get the skinny on leafhopper biology.

Rose slugs are a kind of sawfly juvenile. By July these pests have become adults and will torment you no more. During their voracious juvenile stage, though, you'll see holes eaten into leaves from the underside, leading to a skeletonized, glazed effect, followed by consumption of large parts of the

Leafhopper damage on rose foliage resembles virus injury.

leaf and finally destruction of the veins by larger juveniles. If you catch them in the act, you'll see bristly, plain, green-white, $1/2$-inch caterpillarlike juveniles. Wash off plants with a strong jet of water, and clean up garden debris.

Scales on roses cause darkening and premature drop of foliage and may cause extensive sooty mold. Again, refer to Chapter 5. Scale infestation of roses responds well to simply being pruned out and removed. Or scrub them off with an old, soft toothbrush or nail brush.

Aphids on roses are like mustard with hot dogs—you might feel something was missing if they were not on your roses! The biology of this pest is reviewed in Chapter 5, but try hosing off your plants with

Rose slug damage looks a bit like true slug injury on rose foliage.

a strong jet of water every couple of days and take it easy with the fertilizer. Wait to prune roses until later in the season; early pruning causes a flush of succulent growth most attractive to aphids. Aphids tend to live in colonies, so simply pruning out your colony may suffice. Before that, though, check to see whether you have beneficials, like the aphid mummy wasp or juveniles of lady beetles. If these beneficial insects are present, leave the whole system alone and let nature take its course!

More Beetles That Love Your Roses

Several other beetles can attack your beloved roses. The rose curculio is $1/4$ inch long, red with a long black snout; the rose chafer is $1/2$ inch long and a muddy yellow-brown; while fuller beetles are grayish brown and less than $1/2$ inch long. A two-banded Japanese weevil can also get cozy with roses; spread a white sheet under the plant, shake the stem, pick up dislodged beetles, and destroy them. The two-banded Japanese weevil feeds on new and inner foliage, beginning in April. The pest lays its eggs inside a folded leaf, which you can search for on your routine inspections.

The two-banded Japanese weevil often notches roses.

Rose chafer skeletonizes leaves just like the Japanese beetle. It is found only in light, sandy soil and likes peonies and roses, particularly. Unfortunately, birds are often killed by eating them due to a toxin in the beetles' bodies. The rose curculio also feeds on wild brambles, but the greatest damage occurs on rose buds. Flowers end up riddled with holes if they are even able to open at all. The adult is only about $1/5$ inch long. The fuller rose beetle overwinters under debris. It feeds primarily at night.

Mossy rose gall is a rather bizarre insect problem caused by tiny Cynipid wasps, which create a very hairy gall by messing up plant hormones. It looks like a crown gall, but if you cut into it, you can find wasp juveniles. Prune infested stems and burn them!

Earwigs are not exactly beloved, but they aren't that harmful, either. They can eat many wee holes through rose petals. Excessive mulch can attract them, but they really need other insects for food and moisture. If your roses are near your foundation, make sure downspouts are draining well away from them and that irrigation is not hitting the building. Clogged gutters and ivy or *Clematis* growing on the sides of buildings or within the rose bushes can provide attractive harborage for earwigs. See the information on *Clematis* in this chapter for disposal methods.

Diseases of Roses

Black spot on roses is the biggest rose fungus problem in the eastern half of the country. Hybrid tea roses are particularly hard hit, and you'll need to inspect foliage of susceptible varieties starting in late spring for fringed dark spots and leaf yellowing. Don't forget to check for infected canes, as well. Improve air circulation and reduce leaf wetness time.

Black spot on roses is the bane of the gardener's existence!

Remove and destroy fallen leaves, and prune out infected canes. Treatments will not work well unless diseased parts are removed first. "Resistant" roses may give mixed results due to races of the pathogen that are regional. Repeated defoliation weakens the plants so that you get poor bloom or the rose succumbs to other stresses or winter damage. Hybrid teas, hybrid perpetuals, and polyanthas are very susceptible. For some reason, yellow and orange cultivars are the most susceptible. *Rosa rugosa* is very resistant, but *rugosa* hybrids have diluted resistance.

Plant your roses in sunny locations to encourage drying of foliage. By all means, use resistant *rugosa* varieties like 'Ballerina', 'Blanc Double de Coubert', 'Dortmund', 'Hastrup' (aka 'Frau Dagmar Hartopp'), 'Hansa', 'John Cabot', 'New Dawn', 'Pierette Pavement', and 'Therese Bugnet'.

Prunus necrotic ring spot virus / rose chlorotic mottle virus / rose line pattern virus / rose vein banding virus / rose yellow vein mosaic virus—yep, they are all synonyms for the same virus. In roses the disease causes chlorotic lines and rings, or even oak leaf patterns on foliage. You may see enhanced winterkill. Vein banding may be seen with prolonged high temperatures. Symptoms are usually most evident in spring and may be in association with infection by other viruses. There is no treatment or cure.

Strawberry latent ringspot virus is usually spread by infected rootstocks or possibly by nematodes. If your roses have stunted shoots and leaves with a leathery texture and are distorted, strapped, or have small, angular flecks, they may have this virus. It is best to pull out these plants.

Rose streak, a disease transmitted by graft, causes brownish green rings and vein banding in expanded leaves that tend to drop prematurely. Remove and destroy infected plants.

Yellow leaves. Watering problems are the usual cause of yellow leaves in great numbers. If leaves turn yellow around the edges but the centers remain firm, the plant is not getting enough water. If leaves turn yellow and wilt, then over-watering is likely.

Edema. No, we're not talking about the ankles of your great-grandma. Edema is corky brown patches on leaf undersides that occur when the plant is getting too much water. This is especially common in ivy-leaved geraniums. Reduce watering.

No flowers. If your plants refuse to flower, they may not be where they get enough light or heat, or they may be overfertilized so that all their energy goes into the production of green tissue.

Leaves of geranium redden due to a drop in temperature.

Red leaf edges. This phenomenon is caused by sudden temperature drops, especially in zonal geraniums. The normal color will return soon after the temperature climbs again for a few days.

Rose leaf curl is a widely distributed virus that affects antique roses. Symptoms in spring include reduced leaf size, shoot tip necrosis, twisting and distortion of leaves, yellow flecked veins, and easily detached leaflets. Symptoms come back in the fall with the addition of cracking and longitudinal corky areas in the canes. Remove and destroy plants. The progress of this disease is very slow.

Geraniums

Although geraniums are relatively trouble free, there are some other things that "bug" them besides the bacterial and fungal diseases discussed in Chapter 4.

Geranium Problems

Aphids and whiteflies. Aphids are likely to be found along the stem, and whiteflies on the undersides of leaves. You may see sooty mold on the leaves from excreted sap. Use insecticidal soap, making sure to cover the undersides of leaves.

Blackleg. Stem bases rot due to overwatering, nonsterile potting mediums, or dirty pots. Reduce watering, discard infected plants, and keep sanitation practices top notch.

Botrytis. Outbreak is mostly due to cool, damp conditions. Fluffy gray growth on leaves and stems, and brown flowers followed by gray mold on affected petals are common symptoms. Reduce watering, increase ventilation, and don't overcrowd plantings. Pick off dead material and discard, and wash your hands and equipment to avoid spreading the infection.

Rust. Zonal geraniums (the ones with multicolored leaves) are the most susceptible to this fungus, which starts out as pale spots on the upper leaf surface with rust spots beneath. Cut off affected leaves and discard, and if you are receiving a large order of geraniums for planting, don't accept those that have rust. Geranium rust is worse in shade, potentially causing severe defoliation.

Viruses. Piercing, sucking insects like leafhoppers and aphids spread viruses that manifest themselves as mottled, yellow-spotted, distorted, or crinkled leaves. If leaves are curled, check to make sure no aphids are rolled up inside. Destroy infected plants so that the insects do not pick up more viruses and spread it to other plants.

Everyone Loves *Impatiens*

Thrips are the primary threat, particularly for double *Impatiens*. These tiny insect gangsters are packing *Impatiens* necrotic ring spot virus with its characteristic black streaking and leaf spotting. Stressed plants are much more likely to show symptoms. The thrips also carry tomato spotted wilt virus. Don't be tempted to carry over garden *Impatiens* because they can reintroduce the virus to your plantings the following year.

Impatiens also fall prey to fungal and bacterial diseases that result in stem rot, particularly in heavy, wet soil. The plants are girdled and fall over. Combat this by mulching under the plants (to reduce splashing) but not all the way up to the stem. If your *Impatiens* wilt each time you put them in a particular spot, switch to containers because there is a soil-borne disease afoot!

Oak Problems

The oak tree, for many of us, represents a stalwart forest giant that cannot be felled by anything less than a chainsaw. But like the famous Goliath, many oaks are being felled by something a good deal smaller and subtler than a chainsaw.

Armillaria is identified by the presence of thick strands of fungus that resemble shoestrings and grow similarly to roots. These strands can penetrate roots only after stress-induced chemical changes occur within the tree, which alter the plant's susceptibility. Defoliation of oaks by gypsy moths or leaf rollers encourages this shift, which leads to stimulation of *Armillaria*. Once this sequence of events is off and running, the fungus can spread from 1 to 2 yards a year. The fungus can also persist in the soil for decades in chunks of decaying wood.

Growth reduction usually becomes visible after more than half the root system is already dead. Large trees may alternately win and lose to *Armillaria* by containing the fungus in compartments in the roots and root collars. Stress will allow the fungus to begin to win the battle again. *Armillaria* grows as much as 2 yards above the ground and results in stress cracks around the root collar caused by the pressure of wind, snow, or ice on a tree already weakened by internal decay. Trees that successfully fight *Armillaria* produce callus tissue at the canker margin.

Spores of some strains can colonize recently wounded sap wood (watch those weed whackers!). Occasional infections of wounded roots also occur. Avoid planting conifers where *Armillaria* has felled stressed oaks. New trees are at high risk for ten to fifteen years. Prevention is difficult due to *Armillaria*'s persistence in woody debris and its broad host range. In the landscape, minimize stress, remove stumps and any other debris, and monitor trees.

Oak wilt affects most species but is seen in the interior parts of the country rather than on the coast, where you are more likely to see bacterial scorch. Red oak group members experience wilting, tanning, and bronzing over the whole canopy. Symptoms of this disease begin at the leaf margin and then spread toward the mid vein. Leaf loss follows soon after. Brown or black streaks appear in the wood of branches. The poor trees are dead several weeks after the first symptoms are seen. Eventually, the bark cracks from the pressure, revealing gray or black mats of fungus. White oaks decline over several years and do not produce the mats.

The fungus survives up to four years in dead trees and is spread by sap beetles feeding on newly killed trees. Bark beetles also transfer the fungus, which clogs up the water tubes and spreads by root grafts just like Dutch elm disease. Trench around the sick ones to prevent transfer by root graft. There

Sudden Oak Death

Another serious and frightening oak disease has extended its range to include many more plants. It is our old friend *Phythophthora* again, the soil-borne fungus wreaking havoc on everything from petunias to potatoes. It began on the West Coast in June 2000. The disease is called sudden oak death and causes two kinds of disease: bark cankers that kill, and leaf blights that serve as a disease reservoir. Canker hosts include tanoak, coast live oak, California black oak, Shreve's oak, coast red wood, and Douglas fir. Leaf blight hosts include blueberries, *Manzanita*, *Rhododendron*, bay laurel, Oregon myrtle, big leaf maple, toyon, California buckeye, coffeeberry, honeysuckle, *Viburnum*, western starflower, *Camellia*, madrone, and andromeda.

Unfortunately, the list does not stop there. Obtain a more complete list at *www.ncpmc.org/sod*. Transmission occurs through infected plant material, rain, and soil; moist, cool, windy conditions seem to increase infection, as with most other *Phytophthora* infections. In fact, the severity of the Irish potato *Phytophthora* blight was in part blamed on cool, wet conditions resulting from a remote volcanic explosion!

Host death may occur several months to several years after infection, and the infected plants are often prey to other stress-related organisms such as bark beetles and sapwood fungi. Leaf blights appear as dark gray-brown areas with distinct edges or spots with dead areas extending from the leaf stem into the leaf tissue, but the problem can appear anywhere on the leaf. Some hosts will show premature defoliation and twig dieback. If you suspect you have the disease on a plant, contact your local university or Cooperative Extension office. Currently only the West Coast is afflicted.

is no cure. Try to avoid trimming or wounding oaks during spring or early summer when sap is flowing. Destroy infected oaks as soon as they die to prevent spread.

Green Obsession

Caring for Your Lawn

Chances are if you are too old for summer camp but too young for Florida, you're dealing with a lawn of some sort. Depending on your climate, you'll deal with primarily warm-season or cool-season grasses, which are managed differently! Cool-season grass does most of its growing of leaves and roots during spring and fall when temperatures are cool. During summer, much of the root growth and function slacks and sloughs off, leaving grass vulnerable to desiccation and disease. These grasses are best suited to temperate regions.

The warm-season grasses do most of their growth during warmer temperatures and go dormant or die during cold temperatures. Most warm-season grasses are suitable for growth only in the southern regions of the country where cold temperatures are minimal. A few warm-season grasses can be grown in the north, and even more can be grown in what is known as the transition zone, the middle of the country, where a mixture of warm-season and cool-season grasses are usually grown.

Let's begin by looking at cool-season grasses.

Cool-Season Lawn Care

The lawn is like a high-maintenance haircut. Yeah, it looks good, but you have to fuss with it . . . constantly! So back off buckos, and start thinking like a grass plant.

Here's one way to think about it: You know what you have in your basement (and I'll bet you don't want anyone down there with a camera, either). But if you don't inspect the basement, there's a chance the whole house could fall down because the basement is the foundation of the life and health of your house, right?

The roots, and the soil surrounding them, are the foundation of your lawn. Without roots, the whole lawn falls down. And you know what the greatest source of root death is?

The lawn mower!

Mowing

Primary food storage for grass isn't in the crown or roots; it's in the blade, so when you cut grass too short, you remove all its stored food. You have also just removed most of the surface area that the grass plant can use for making more food by photosynthesis. Added to that, you have stimulated growth from the cut tip of the existing blade and stimulated new blades to grow from the base of the plant (the crown). So where does all the little bit of existing food left in the nub go? You guessed it: to the new growth, so the roots suffer malnutrition.

Without food, a portion, sometimes a large portion, of the root system dies, taking with it water to hydrate and cool the turf and nutrients to support photosynthesis in the remaining part of the blade and the new tissue that's been stimulated. This loss results in grass thinning out, which results in sun penetrating the thinned areas, as well as greater heating simply due to a shorter canopy.

The soil surface dries out in response to the heat from the sun, and because short grass equals short roots, the grass thins out further. The heat and light stimulate weed seeds that hang out primarily in the upper 2 inches

Sharpen Your Blade!

A dull blade crushes and shreds the tissues at the tips, inviting disease and massive water loss. Sharpen your blade at least once a season—and maybe more, depending on how much you need to mow and how often!

Nature abhors a dull blade. What if you were stuck in one of those awful horror or sci-fi movies where the mad scientist has you all tied up and is going to harvest your body parts? Would you rather he used a nice sharp scalpel or a rusty Swiss army knife?

Dull blade injury can mimic disease.

of soil and *voilà!* the vicious cycle has begun. Now we need to apply all the usual lawn elements that keep us running all season long—herbicides for weeds, extra water to offset the short roots—which of course results in more fungal diseases, so we need a fungicide; and let's not forget the insects that are attracted to the short-cut grass that we fertilized in a vain effort to try to get the lawn to "perk up."

The kindest thing we can do for our grass is to start with changing our mowing height. For every $1/8$ inch your mowing height is raised, you get a 30 percent increase in leaf surface area. (Wish I had a 30 percent increase for every dollar I saved!) Keep your grass 3 inches high during the growing season except for one short mow at the beginning of the season and one short mow at the end of the season after the grass has gone dormant again, both of which reduce disease.

So when do you mow? Just about the point that your grass reaches $3^3/4$ inches, mow it back to 3 inches and leave the clippings.

Clippings less than 1 inch long sift back into the canopy and provide free food (yes, no cost to you, you bargain shopper). Ever see Mother Nature vacuuming? I think not! What you are really doing when you "clean" your yard is removing valuable organic matter, which in turn increases compaction potential of your soil, making it that much more difficult for your roots to grow and your grass to thrive.

Thatch and Dethatching

Thatch is one of those things that people lie awake at night worrying about, along with tax breaks and gingivitis. What is thatch? It's dead and dying roots that build up because they are being manufactured at a rate faster than they can be broken down because your microbes are slackin'.

Now you really don't need to worry about thatch until it hits the $1/2$-inch and longer mark. At that point, the thatch can become a nest for disease and insects or become water repellent and interfere with water or other lawn applications that must travel through it in order to get to the soil. Does this happen often? Not really.

Then why are people obsessed with dethatching their lawns? Because it looks like you are doing something good. But if I stand in front of you, rip out great handfuls of hair, lay them on the table before you and say proudly, "Look! Just look at what I have done!" you'll scratch your head and answer, "Given yourself a bald spot and a sore scalp?"

Precisely. Dethatching rips up the root system of the turf—usually at a time when the roots can ill afford to be disturbed. You stress the turf just as it's going into its slump, you bring weed seeds to the surface, and you generally mess up the health of the turf.

If you have a genuine thatch problem ($1/2$ inch or more), the best bet is to use a rototiller-like machine to poke holes in the ground (core aeration). This machine punches a bunch of relatively large holes in the thatch layer, providing an avenue for water to get in and air to be exchanged, and it also brings soil and its microbes into direct contact with the thatch layer. Check your pH because sluggish microbes may mean a pH range that is less than ideal. Less than $1/2$ inch of thatch is not such a bad thing. After all, you wouldn't buy an expensive carpet without a carpet pad, would you? A little bit of thatch cushions the crown of the plant and lessens damage due to heavy foot traffic.

Watering

Turfgrass, like every other plant I could hope to meet, wants about 1 to $1^1/2$ inches of water each week total. Nature may do all the work, or you may supplement with irrigation. This is best applied on a deep and infrequent basis. If your soil is too heavy, it may not take that kind of water all at once and you may have to shut down your system temporarily. So if and when you see runoff, wait thirty minutes and start up again.

Everyone's irrigation system delivers water at a different rate, and each zone of the system may deliver at different rates depending on how the system was designed. You can figure it out by setting out tuna or cat food cans and seeing how long it takes for your system to fill them. The cans are

1 inch deep. I prefer to let the grass do what it naturally would do during times of drought—go dormant. The grass will not die; it will simply turn brown until sufficient rain causes it to break dormancy, usually about two weeks after the rain returns.

When and How to Water

The "when" of watering has a huge bearing on how much disease you have. Running your system in the evening results in grass being wet all night long. Think about what would happen if you slept in wet clothes and wet socks and shoes. If you water anytime between midnight and about eight in the morning, you will correspond with the natural dew period when grass will be naturally wet anyway.

Deep, infrequent irrigation is key to turf health. Light, frequent irrigation is nothing but a secret-disease-and-weed benefactor in mature turf, but it is the kind of irrigation that many homeowners see fit to give their grass. Light, frequent irrigation on established turf causes surface crusting, with moss and algae buildup; plus it creates a shallow profile for soil moisture, resulting in

Irrigation Systems

When you set the sprinkler system at a single rate early in spring where cool-season turfgrasses grow and don't change that rate all season long until November or October, you do your plants two disservices. First, you are not taking advantage of normally rainy springs and delivering water to the grass when it definitely doesn't need it. Second, in the fall, when we generally have rain again, moisture in excess of normal rainfall can lead to increased disease susceptibility. At the very least, your irrigation should be equipped with a rain sensor so you don't have the classic "sprinkler twitching in the rain" scenario. Ideally, the amount being delivered to your grass should change with the seasonal fluctuations in natural precipitation.

Additionally, overirrigated, closely mowed lawns are the favored site of egg deposition by Japanese beetles. Reduce the water, and the beetles may not even lay eggs, or the eggs, which are laid in a partially dehydrated state, may not survive at all.

dry areas deeper in the soil profile and a dead zone for roots in those areas. It stimulates weed seeds, which hang out in the upper 2 inches of soil, it attracts grubs to the zone where they will crop off roots and cause turf death, and it's associated with poor wear tolerance.

Sun and Shade

Many of you are trying to grow grass in shade. This is simply a no-win situation because grass, even in full sun, is not very effective at absorbing light.

Grass needs a minimum of four hours of light each day to survive, but six hours of light to thrive. Morning light is best—it has the highest intensity.

To improve grass growth beneath trees, prune tree branches lower than 10 feet to get air circulating. Rather than rake leaves off of grass in shade, blow them off because grass is easily uprooted in shade. Use a full inch higher mowing height (4 inches) on grass growing in shade to provide more area for photosynthesis. Or just eliminate the headache of grass in shade by installing shade-tolerant ground covers or mulching beneath trees instead.

Remember, too, that objects other than trees cast shade, especially in winter. Fencing can be a major problem. Open fencing is always better for grass growth because it lets light in.

Fertilize at half the normal rate in shade unless you have heavy traffic in these areas, and reduce traffic in shady areas as much as possible because of shallow root systems and low recuperative ability. Apply potassium to help the turf regulate water; this also helps shade-grown turf resist certain diseases. Any wet areas should be raked out in the spring to promote drying and to reduce snow molds and leaf spots, which will almost always occur first on shade-grown, weakened turf.

Compaction

The lawn area is one of the most likely spots to find compaction. Use your cheap compaction test (the screwdriver test—see Chapter 1) to see what level of problem you have; in the spring look for compacted areas to green up more quickly than the surrounding areas.

The best remedies for compaction are to poke holes that remain open (that means core aeration or core cultivation—and be sure to hold onto the cores) and add some fiber in the form of organic matter. For the most part, aeration on a home lawn is best performed in the fall when soil is a bit drier. Leaving holes open during winter will allow freezing and thawing, which provide additional decompaction.

You can core-aerate in the spring, as well, but wet soils may compact even further, so watch your step. In all cases, if you can, do not break up the cores

Your Best Friend?

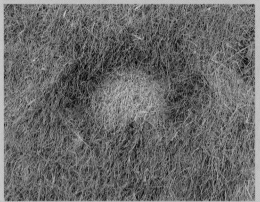

Female dog spot damages turf unless you wash it away immediately.

The biggest issue with dog urine is salt. A female dog releases most or all of her pee in one squatting, so you end up with a brown spot (salt kill) with a green ring around it. This syndrome can easily be mistaken for disease if you are not observant.

Male dogs tend to pee a little at a time, and while they can kill small trees or shrubs with repeated small doses of urine (thank heavens we're not trying to grow turf near our bathroom fixtures, eh, ladies?), their impact on turf is usually less. The worst situations occur on Kentucky bluegrass, which is very intolerant of salt, or during periods with little water to wash the salts through and dilute the urine to a simple fertilization.

Water is the answer. If you can water anytime up to eight hours after your pet has relieved herself, you will dilute the pee to a fertilizer effect. Delay watering for twelve hours or more, and you will see progressively worse burns. A motion-activated sprinkler may be enough to deter both sneaky dogs and neighbors!

and return them immediately . . . this is sort of like getting your ear pierced and then not putting the earring in. The hole closes up very quickly. Instead, stockpile the cores so that if you need soil for any operation, you'll avoid the incompatibility issue by having some already on hand.

Topdressing following aeration with $1/8$ to $1/4$ inch of compost (no more) will also, over time, help amend the soil. You should have ten to twelve holes per square foot; if the area is **very** compacted, then core-aerate, irrigate, let the water settle in for twenty-four hours, and core-aerate again. In a normal situation, core-aerate one day after a normal rainfall or irrigation for best results.

Fertilizing

So far I have skirted the issue of fertilization for turf because it is such a misunderstood issue. I went over the whole N-P-K thing in Chapter 2. I won't shove it down your throat a second time here, but I will remind you that a recommendation for a pound of actual nitrogen doesn't involve a pound of product. Each product has different amounts of nitrogen, so head back to Chapter 2 if you feel confused!

One of the biggest problems with turf fertilization is understanding that fertility is intimately linked to turf growth patterns, not visual stimuli (unlike human relationships . . .).

Proper Timing and Amount of Lawn Fertilizers for Cool-Season Grass

The correct amount is 1 pound of actual nitrogen per 1000 square feet of lawn three times a year: Memorial Day, Labor Day, and Thanksgiving. The correct rate of actual potassium is half that of the actual nitrogen per 1000 square feet; phosphorous for mature turf is unnecessary, so go for as low a phosphorous number as possible. Instructions for calibrating a spreader are in Chapter 2—so on to the reasons for the timing!

Three holidays coincide with the proper schedule for fertilization of turfgrass:

Memorial Day. Grass growth is slowing down in response to heat, and the grass is ready for a snack after all that spring activity. This makes for an ideal time to fertilize. The grass is hungry, has established its root system, and will take up the fertilizer and use it to get through summer. Apply no more fertilizer during summer unless it is 100 percent slow-release natural organic fertilizer. Otherwise, you'll get a rapid flush of growth that is quite susceptible to fungi thriving in the hot, sticky reaches of summer. Plus the root system that has declined in response to hot weather will never be able to support or cool down all that top growth.

Labor Day and Thanksgiving. The Labor Day fertilization goes hand in hand with the Thanksgiving fertilization, sort of like Jack and Jill going uphill. Late-fall fertilization is much less effective if the grass is already yellow and hungry from missing out on the September fertilization. Those chlorophyll reserves need to be pumped up (picture Arnold Schwarzenegger's head on top of your grass plant) by the early-fall fertilization in order to achieve maximum food storage that occurs as a result of late-fall fertilization.

We use Thanksgiving as a loose window. Late-fall fertilization should be applied after the last mowing but before brown dormancy, so as a general

Early-Spring and Weed-and-Feed Products Are Not Cool

Cool-season turf growth of blades and roots occurs primarily in spring and fall, while growth slacks off in summer. So fertilizing in early spring pushes shoot growth at the expense of root growth during a time when the top is growing like a house on fire anyway but you need to establish a nice strong root system to get you through summer. Fertilizing early in spring also causes the grass cuticle to thin and makes it that much easier for fungus to penetrate top growth made all the more juicy by overfertilization early in the season. This doesn't even begin to account for the fertilizer that will be washed away by spring rains before the grass plant can take it up. So why, why, why would you fertilize early in spring? The answer is simple: the media.

People get the gardening itch early in the season, so the media market lawn fertilizer to scratch that itch, often in the form of weed-and-feed products. Everyone competes for whose lawn can "green up" first in spring, not realizing that spring greening is a function of soil temperatures, not fertilizer. Moreover, weed-and-feed products deliver fertilizer at the wrong time of year, causing your grass to make lush top growth with a weak root system that will keel at the first sign of hot, dry weather and be unable to support all that top growth. But if you wait to use a weed-and-feed product later, around the end of May, when cool-season grasses **should** be fertilized, then the weed-fighting pre-emergent herbicide is useless because the weeds are already up and running. The take-home story? **Avoid combination weed-and-feed products.** Instead, apply them separately and at the correct time for the health of your turf.

rule, try timing your fertilization this way: Look for seven to ten days with daytime temperatures consistently below 50 degrees F. and night temps around 30. Then do your late-fall fertilization.

Occasionally, grass can become yellowed between early-fall and late-fall fertilizations, particularly if we have a prolonged Indian summer. If this occurs, you can get away with applying $1/2$ pound actual nitrogen per 1000 square feet as an in-between snack that won't over fatten shoots or end up in groundwater.

Warm-Season Lawn Care

Many facets of cool- and warm-season care are the same. For example, thatch, compaction, watering, dog issues, sharp blades, the principles of mowing, and shade information are all interchangeable. Other factors are specific to warm-season grass care.

The most important time to fertilize warm-season grasses is late spring, and a second application in summer is recommended. Alternatively, apply slow-release nitrogen products (2 to 3 pounds of nitrogen per 1000 square feet) in late spring for summer-long release.

Even in the South, warm-season grasses become dormant during winter months. For winter color, cool-season species are often overseeded over the dormant warm-season grasses at the onset of cooler temperatures so turf areas stay green all winter. Then as temperatures soar, they die off and warm-season grasses take over again.

Lawn Renovation

Whether you have warm-season or cool-season grass, an awesome amount of work goes along with making a poor site into a good site, particularly in terms of the vast size of even a small lawn. Those of us who have had good success amending a flower bed or enjoying the productivity of a raised vegetable garden will look at such a lawn and say sure, I can do this in a weekend. No sweat.

Wrong! Lots and lots of sweat, back-breaking labor, and earth-moving tools are more like it. A complete renovation, done right, is a week's worth of work, and then about six weeks of intensive care afterwards.

Can it be done? You bet. And the rewards of stress-free lawn maintenance for many years after are ultimately worth it. But like triple bypass heart surgery, make sure it's done right the first time. Cutting corners will invite weeds and other lawn health disasters.

Why Is Fall Fertilization Important?

With fall fertilization, you have more uniform turf cover the following spring, which helps reduce weeds. You'll also notice less leaf spot damage the following spring. Another major benefit is enhanced rooting and color, both in fall and the following spring, accomplished by sufficient food reserves which maximize photosynthesis. This makes the turf more durable under drought or traffic stress.

Steps Before Renovation

Step 1. Time your renovation correctly: Early September is ideal—but don't plan to go away for about two months afterwards. You should also get a pH of the existing topsoil so that you know how much lime to amend with if you need any. A final pH of 6.3 to 6.8 is crucial for the soil structure and for nutrient uptake by grass.

Step 2. Do you want an in-ground irrigation system? Now is the ideal time to have one installed. I do not recommend that you do this yourself. Despite the kits that you can buy from local suppliers, irrigation technology is very fine tuned and requires extensive training to produce efficient, well-constructed systems. Make sure your contractor is certified by the National Irrigation Association—to ensure proper training and good results!

Step 3. The fastest way to get rid of the old lawn is to rent a sod cutter and strip it off. Do you lose some topsoil this way? Certainly, but if you are sitting on a poor site anyway, replacing the little you lose this way with an organic amendment is a better bet. Set the sod cutter on the lowest setting so you get as much of the old root system as possible. Spread your organic amendment on the surface, using a 2- to 3-inch depth of material, or 6 cubic feet per 1000 square feet of lawn area. Spread starter fertilizer on the soil, using 40 pounds of 5-10-5 or 5-10-10 N-P-K or its equivalent per 1000 square feet. Spread lime based on the recommendation of your soil pH test.

Step 4. Fire up the rototiller. Plow in your organic and other amendments to a depth of 6 to 8 inches. Do not over-rototill, or else you break down the soil structure, leading to compaction and drainage problems. You want soil clumps from the size of a pea to the size of a golf ball. If you have a slope, don't plant it in grass; instead, install a low-maintenance ground cover. Holes and dips in the landscape should not be filled in with pure organic matter or topsoil brought in. Mix equal parts organic matter and topsoil shaken from turf that was removed from your site, and use this mix to fill in those

Renovation and Herbicides

When you renovate, you won't be able to use most herbicides for six months before or after because they interfere with germination and growth. That's why it is critical to renovate in fall—you won't have the weed pressure that you experience in spring. The bottom line is to avoid herbicide applications to newly seeded areas until the seedlings are practically grown up and off to college.

depressions. The site should slope only slightly away from the house to promote drainage. Try to avoid piling extra soil on top of tree or shrub roots, or scraping excess earth away from these plants since both actions can damage or stress the plants.

Step 5. Now you are ready to go take a break and let your spouse do the really annoying part: rake the seed bed. Rake out root clumps, as well as stones over 2 inches in diameter; then rake again to smooth the bed. Apply a light fertilization of about a third of the amount that you put down before the incorporation of your neighbor's dog waste and other amendments. Freeze your seed for forty-eight hours before you spread them. The freezing cracks the seed coat and encourages more rapid germination. Make sure to compensate for seed that will never sprout. Divide the seed mixture in half, and sow each half in opposite directions so there is good overlap.

Step 6. Allow the bed to settle for twenty-four hours. Rake a final time for levelness, and then seed with a mix of grasses that are appropriate for your site and at rates appropriate for the type of grass you have selected.

Step 7. Now mulch your newly seeded lawn using a $1^1/2$ bales of straw per 1000 square feet. You should be able to see about half straw and half soil. You will not need to remove this unless you have applied it too thickly. Don't use hay—it contains lots of weed seeds.

Step 8. Just after seeding is the one time we recommend light, frequent waterings (and make sure the waterings are gentle since seed is easily washed away). Initially, water to a depth of 5 to 6 inches, and then water lightly several times a day. You will not be able to back off this regimen until the grass is at least $1^1/2$ inches long! When grass reaches a height of 4 inches, mow it back to 3 and begin to treat grass like a normal lawn. Six weeks after you have seeded, fertilize again with $1/2$ pound of actual nitrogen, using starter fertilizer. This snack makes sure that your rapidly growing turf doesn't run out of food and succumb to disease. You can then make your normal fertilization at Thanksgiving with regular fertilizer and from then on treat your grass as mature turf.

Sodding

To sod, you must prepare for exactly the same way as for seeding. Skipping preparation of the soil up to Step 5 can result in sod failure, which is annoying and costly.

The worst mistake you can make is to lay sod over existing turf (don't laugh, I've seen this done) or to only lightly scratch the existing turf before laying sod. Once you have prepared the sod bed and laid out the sod (pieces should be laid in a staggered pattern like bricks, not parallel to each other),

Damping Off Can Ruin Your Newly Seeded Turf

Post-emergence damping off occurs when the stem and roots form, but the grass is girdled at the soil line. The seedlings yellow, the plants lose turgidity, you get secondary invasion of pathogens, and the new stand goes down faster than the Titanic. Damping off is favored by a poor seed bed, or one that is too wet, where seeds are planted too deep (never plant deeper than 1/8 inch), where too much fertilizer has been applied so that the cuticle is very thin, and most importantly, where too much seed has been planted! When you think you'll do yourself a favor and spread seed on thicker than cream cheese on a bagel, you set the seed up for high competition for light, which leads to spindly plants with thin cuticles; you also increase the humidity, which leads to rot, as well as extreme competition for water and nutrients. All this leads to weak grass, which means that the opportunistic diseases are going to move in.

Before planting, freeze seeds for twenty-four to forty-eight hours to crack the seed coat and speed germination. This really gives an advantage over scourges, such as *Pythium*-induced pre-emergence damping off in cool soils. Another important trick to avoid post-emergence damping off is to fertilize with 1/2 pound of actual nitrogen per 1000 square feet in the form of starter fertilizer about four to six weeks after establishment.

lightly roll the sod with an empty roller to rid yourself of air pockets, which will later become dead spots.

New sod needs at least 1 inch of water thirty minutes after installation so the soil beneath should seem sopping wet. Watering the area **before** laying sod isn't a bad idea unless heavy equipment will be driving over it. Use your screwdriver to pierce the sod and the soil beneath during the rooting period so that there is no need to keep lifting the edge of the sod like a flap jack to peek at the water situation and thus interfere with rooting. Simply run your fingers along the barrel of the screwdriver: There should be moisture for at least 4 inches. Light, frequent watering is the rule for freshly cut sod, as well, since it has no root system upon installation. After a few weeks, you can change over to deep, infrequent watering because the roots will have grown back.

Fertilizations should be performed just as for a newly seeded area.

One extra operation must be performed on newly sodded areas. As weird as it sounds, **you must core-aerate new sod about four weeks after it has been laid.** This provides avenues for roots to channel into the soil beneath. Failure to do this results in incompatibility between the soil brought in on the sod and the soil beneath—even when you have properly prepared the bed below. The roots remain only in the soil that was brought in on the sod, and eventually the sod succumbs to root pathogens. When you take a sample of the ailing sod, it falls off the soil below like a bad toupee, and a vertical section looks just like a two-layer fudge candy.

Weeds

Weeds are not all bad. They are just fulfilling their biological destiny as Soil Erosion Prevention Devices (S.E.P.D.—sounds like a James Bond villainous organization, doesn't it?). For example, deep-rooted weeds like thistles, pig-weeds, and nightshades mine the soil and bring deep minerals to the surface. Others can be habitat for beneficial insects or act as trap crops, improve nitrogen fixation, and prevent desiccation.

The secret to weed control is to evaluate which species are at a site and whether they are aggressive or spreading. Drip irrigation discourages weed seeds by delivering water deeper than the upper 2 inches (where most weed seeds hang out), but few people have drip irrigation on their lawns. Weeds are happiest with light sprinkling. Evaluate and correct watering practices, and you may have much less weed pressure.

Another great way to reduce weed pressure in lawns is to raise the height of your cut to shade 'em out. Weeds have a serious Achilles heel in that they

Dormant Seeding

Dormant seeding during winter means flagging off bare or very thin spots in your turf and putting some seed down in order for it to be up before the weeds root.

The critical factor for dormant seeding is to make sure there is good "seed-to-soil" contact: This means putting seed down with a melting snow or just after a major rainfall (to make sure your seed won't be washed away) while the ground is still wet. As the soil dries, it pulls the seed into contact with itself, increasing the chances of germination.

have tiny seeds with little stored food. They use all their available food to sprout, so by reducing available sun (or changing the type of light that filters through), as well as heat, you prevent the weeds from being able to grow fast enough to support themselves with more food generated by photosynthesis.

Weeds have several different kinds of lifecycles, and knowing which pattern your problem weeds fall into is critical to successful control.

Reducing Weeds Through Management Practices

It is never necessary to set a 100 percent weed-free threshold since even highly managed turf has 1 to 2 percent weeds. A practical goal is 4 to 10 percent weeds—more, with a no-pesticides program.

If your weeds are increasing from year to year, it's time to look at management practices. A common cause of increased weed pressure is simply not having enough water. Clumping of weed growth is due to heavy wear on turf or structural problems like heavy compaction, broken irrigation or sprinkler heads, or scalping due to an uneven grade.

Fighting Weeds with Herbicides

As much as I would like to think that everyone will wait until cultural improvements produce a thicker stand of grass or other plants that will help to crowd out weeds, I know that some of you impatient souls will demand that your weeds die immediately, for better or worse. If you must use a herbicide, the most important thing to remember is that herbicides do not prevent weeds from germinating—they kill the weeds as they grow through the herbicide-treated zone. Because of this and other inherent difficulties in controlling weeds on a site that has not had the proper cultural amendments put in place, even herbicide treatments often fail. Also remember that, in general, herbicides are degraded in sixty to seventy-five days: Your product may simply run out of steam.

Types of Herbicides

Selective herbicides are those that target one or a few weeds without injuring desirable turf or ornamentals. Nonselective herbicides kill all vegetation. Contact herbicides kill only those plant parts to which they are applied (most effective for annual weeds). Systemic herbicides are absorbed by roots and shoots, and move throughout the entire plant (most effective for perennial weeds).

Indicator Weeds

Indicator weeds are those that indicate a particular characteristic about a site. Try to rely on the presence of more than one indicator species, and use the healthiest plants as indicators.

Dry conditions are indicated by bird's foot trefoil, crabgrass, silvery cinquefoil, rabbit foot clover, pigweed, speedwell, leafy spurge, prostrate spurge, yarrow, yellow wood sorrel, goose grass, and curly dock.

Wet or poor drainage is the case with nutsedge, barnyard grass, creeping bent grass, buttercups, corn chamomile, coltsfoot, docks, lady's thumb, and plantains. Excessive surface moisture can result in algae, moss, creeping bent grass, annual bluegrass, and cinquefoils.

Low pH is shown by sheep sorrel, rabbit's foot clover, coltsfoot, docks, and English daisy, as well as hawkweeds, knawel, lady's thumb, common mullein, wild parsnip, wild radish, foxtail, and mallow.

Low nitrogen results in clover species like black medic.

Compaction is indicated by prostrate knotweed, goose grass, pineapple weed, corn speedwell, annual bluegrass, broad-leaf plantain, and prostrate spurge, which can be distinguished from knotweed by its milky sap.

Mowing too low results in annual bluegrass, chickweeds, speedwell, moss, and creeping bent grass.

Shade can encourage violets, moss, chickweeds, and creeping speedwell.

Pre-emergence or Post-emergence Herbicides?

Pre-emergence herbicides are applied to the soil before weeds appear and form a chemical barrier at or near the soil surface so that when a germinating weed contacts this barrier, it dies. These products will not kill established turf, but you may have a problem if you are seeding. Post-emergence herbicides are applied after the weed has already germinated and are usually used to kill perennial broad-leaf weeds and occasionally annual grassy weeds. The rule of thumb: Use pre-emergence herbicides to kill annual weeds, and post-emergence ones to kill perennial weeds.

If you use pre-emergence herbicides, wait two to four months before over-seeding; then wait—for at least three mowings or preferably a full year—before using them again, while the turf establishes.

Very Bad Weeds

Crabgrass control is determined by turf density—bare, thin, or too closely mown areas, as well as areas damaged by insects and disease, excess traffic, poor drainage, etc., are the spots likely to have the most crabgrass, which then becomes a self-fulfilling prophesy of endless crabgrass renewal.

The system works like this: Weeds, including crabgrass, invade thin turf which dies off in fall, leaving bare soil in winter. This bare soil is still there in spring, causing these areas to warm up more quickly and thus allowing the weed seeds to germinate and fill in, including even more crabgrass. When spring rains come, these bare areas are eroded just slightly, giving a cultivating effect so that more crabgrass seeds are exposed to warmth and then germinate, resulting in, you guessed it, more crabgrass. The warm-season crabgrass out-competes cool-season turfgrass seedlings, which are moving into a stressful time as we go into summer. The crabgrass also uses all the extra resources we put down to try to help our cool-season turf along and, in response, produces massive amounts of seed, which fill in gaps we produce during the summer from edging, scalping, and other stressful practices.

Warning: If your undisturbed turf will be disturbed by planting activity, realize that you have to guarantee sustained protection by reapplying crabgrass herbicides when the barrier is broken or by using a product with a residual if you expect heavy wear.

Commercially acceptable control of crabgrass is considered to be 85 to 90 percent. Once crabgrass is past six plants coming from a single crown, save your money and cultivate the crabgrass—it is going to be impossible to control, so just wait for the first frost and then cackle with glee when it croaks.

Nontoxic crabgrass control is possible through cultural means. When turf quality is acceptable to begin with, a routine fertilization program reduces crabgrass populations by an average of 84 percent because of turf density. When turf quality is unacceptable to begin with, a routine fertilization program reduces crabgrass populations by an average of 31 percent by virtue of turf density. Not too shabby either way, if you ask me, all for the price of a little fertilizer!

Irrigation is very important to crabgrass control: **Deep infrequent irrigation discourages crabgrass because it has shallow roots.** If you keep turf on the dry side and encourage deep roots by deep infrequent irrigation coupled with high mowing to shade it out, you are less likely to favor crabgrass invasion.

Plenty of nontoxic ways can reduce crabgrass invasion on a permanent basis. For instance, you can use rapidly germinating ryegrass to compete with crabgrass seedlings in bare areas and to improve density. This approach can provide 30 to 80 percent crabgrass control. Neither crabgrass nor ryegras can tolerate shade, though, so as long as they are in the sun, the rye has a pretty good chance of duking it out with the crabgrass and winning.

Increase mowing height to reduce light, especially in spring and early summer during peak germination. You can decrease the height you cut in heavily infested areas, and collect clippings that contain seed heads during late summer and early fall as an effective way of reducing viable seed. Fertility is extremely important. Avoid high levels of nutrients during the summer, but ironically this is when you get the major kick-in from organic fertilizers. If you have a heavy infestation of crabgrass and thin turf, consider increasing fertility levels in fall as the crabgrass dies in order to support the vigor of the remaining turf. Aeration can also bring crabgrass seed to the surface, so consider removing cores when core aerating during

Predict Crabgrass Emergence and Amaze Your Friends!

Initial emergence begins when soil temperatures in undisturbed turf are between 54 and 58 degrees F. for three consecutive days at the 1-inch depth. The most effective way to predict emergence is to use a meat thermometer! (Yes, your neighbors may be watching you again.) Jam it into the soil to a depth of 1 inch, and you will always have an accurate and site-specific way of tracking optimum conditions for crabgrass emergence. The length of time that seedlings emerge in undisturbed turf is greater probably because the soil temperature warms at a much more moderate pace when shielded by dense turf. This means you have a greater window for successful pre-emergence control of smooth crab in undisturbed turf, compared to a short window of opportunity in turf with large gaps.

peak germination time, rather than breaking them up. And you can always try the tactic of an increase in shade by letting branches grow over susceptible areas. Crabgrass cannot survive shade. If you do this, make sure your existing turf has some shade tolerance.

Above all, reduce edging practices on turf, especially parallel to sidewalks and other hard surfaces. When you edge, you expose turfgrass roots to heat and drying conditions, which makes them shrivel up and die. And you expose crabgrass seed to heat and light—just what it needs to germinate! Remember that the crabgrass is always going to be able to out-compete the turf in the hot, dry conditions surrounding the edged areas. So don't do it!

Nutsedge, in addition to being very difficult to get rid of, is also awfully hard to mask due both to its chartreuse color and to its more rapid growth rate than surrounding grass. (If we could bottle this stuff as a hair-growth formula, we'd make a fortune!)

Nutsedge is not a grass. Sedges have three-sided leaves and stems, and are often found in wet habitats. Once again, watch that irrigation!

Because nutsedge grows more rapidly than desirable grasses, it is readily apparent two to three days after mowing. Hand removal is laborious, expensive, and usually unsuccessful due to buried tubers unless soil is removed to a depth of 3 feet and replaced with tuberless soil. Tubers are hard, round, and brown; they vary from 1/2 to 3/4 inch long. Any topsoil you bring into a site should be screened for nutsedge. Without interference, yellow nutsedge can produce 4 million to 12 million tubers per acre. This works out to about 1000 tubers from a single plant.

Yellow nutsedge also thrives at high temperatures where cool-season grasses encounter difficulty. In warm climates, you might rid yourself of nutsedge by covering moist ground with one to two pieces of clear plastic for four to six weeks during hot weather—hot enough to raise the temperature of the top 2 inches of soil to 100 to 103 degrees F. and 90 to 97 degrees F. at a depth of 18 inches. Temperatures in the North never reach a sustained level for long enough to fry the little buggers.

Drainage is one of the best bets for containment. Keep an eye on irrigation systems because a sudden surge of nutsedge in an area that has not been disturbed recently or that never had nutsedge before might signal a break in the irrigation head or line.

Tubers rarely last more than two years in the soil, but only 1 percent of tubers from a previous infestation are sufficient to bring back an overwhelming population once unloosed onto an unsuspecting yard.

Algae and moss—that green gooey stuff on the surface of the soil underneath some meager grass blades—are not good signs, either. Just like a bottle left out in the rain and sun, the soil is collecting enough water on its surface for a long enough time to grow algae. The algae are not going to hurt the grass but do indicate poor conditions for the grass to grow in.

Poorly drained, compacted soils are especially susceptible to algae growth. Water sits on the soil surface, and sunlight provides additional warmth. Therefore, growth occurs even more rapidly. Standing water and algal growth further impede air penetration into the soil, resulting in even less oxygen for roots and a buildup of toxins that are produced by anaerobic bacteria in the soil. Copper-based products control algae, but when copper builds up in soil, it is also toxic to plants, particularly when the pH is not where it should be.

Some mosses will grow in dry areas, as well as wet. If the soil becomes too dry, the moss can become dormant. Mosses indicate low soil fertility or scalping or drainage problems. On the plus side, mosses are very beautiful and can colonize areas where turf just simply won't grow well. If the moss has to go, iron sulfate will control it. Because moss has no cuticle, it will scorch easily. Be sure to select a rate that will kill the moss but not the surrounding turf. Moss may also form in response to acidic soils.

Ultimately, getting rid of moss and algae depends not on stop-gap chemical measures but on soil renovation. Compaction and drainage problems can be improved by amending the soil with fibrous organic materials or core aeration (or both).

Turf Diseases

Fungi, like every other pest, are opportunists—the ambulance chasers of the plant world. Although other microorganisms can occasionally make grass sick (bacteria, viruses), most of the diseases we worry about in turf are fungal.

In general, look for thinned areas of turf or bare ground. You should also tug on turf to see how well it is rooted and look at weeds as an indicator of site problems that could lead to stress-related disease.

Be sure to survey the site below the ground! Remove a chunk of sod in several areas and in trouble spots, wash off the roots, and observe whether they are black, brown, slimy, dry, or brittle. The roots should be white and healthy, with a bit of tensile strength like a piece of hair.

Fighting Diseases

The commonsense ways to reduce turf disease attack are the same things I've been screaming about like an alley cat on a fence all chapter long (my psychic turf sense says someone is going to throw a shoe at me soon). Core-aerate to

Is the Problem a Disease or the Soil?

Turf has a problem with soil when you have a shallow but extensive root system, few or no roots below 4 inches, little or no top growth, off-color yellowed tissue, easy wilt, low density and high weeds, a poor response to fertilizer and soil applications of pesticides, prolonged wet periods limiting recreational uses, and easy run-off. It sounds like a disease event has caused these symptoms, but actually it's a cultural problem with the soil.

reduce compaction and thatch and to improve drainage. Increase air circulation. Use no light or frequent irrigation. Irrigate early in the a.m. rather than in the p.m. Use proper fertilization (back to *Goldilocks and the Three Bears*—juuuuuust right!). Pay attention to pH: High pH promotes some turf diseases, and low pH promotes others. And of course, increase organic matter and use organic amendments!

Many of the visually spectacular fungal diseases you'll see are mere history once the weather changes. A fungicide application for these is costly—and unnecessary—not to mention potentially ineffective. Make sure you have correctly identified the disease. Certain turf diseases respond only to certain fungicides, and even then, lots of things can mimic a turf disease, such as dog spot, dull mower injury, and insect problems. Misidentification means you might also use the wrong formulation: Liquids or water-dispersible granules are best for leaf diseases; granules are best for root and crown diseases. And the list goes on.

One tip I suggest is that **if you really do feel compelled to apply a fungicide, do it between mowings or just after a mowing instead of before** so that you do not cut off product after application—you'll have more product-to-surface area.

Common Turf Diseases

Now take a look at this list of common turf diseases. You'll be surprised how few you really need to pay attention to, provided you were paying attention to the cultural factors I was yowling about earlier in the chapter.

Red thread is visible to the naked eye and gets on bents, bluegrass, fescues, and rye during cool, wet weather. You'll see red or pink strands near tips of leaves binding them together or fuzzy pink on dead leaves. Infected leaves turn straw colored. Fertilize properly, reduce compaction, irrigate, and use organic amendments like composted poultry litter. The grass is unlikely to die, and you can probably forgo a fungicide treatment. Most grass outgrows the symptoms of red thread with a weather change. Grass may take on an overall bleached appearance.

Brown patch (*Rhizoctonia*) appears as irregular brown lesions, tip blighting, or smoke rings on closely mowed turf. Bents, blue-grasses, rye, fescue, and *Zoysia* all get the disease in cool, wet conditions. A

Red thread is a startling color.

different type occurs in warm, wet weather (75 to 95 degrees F. during the day, 70 at night). Blight or dieback from leaf tips may occur, or you may see brown patches with a dark border, especially in the morning. Kentucky bluegrass may appear to have reddish blades or whitish spots with red margins (a bit like dollar spot but the spots don't go all the way through the blade). In warm weather, the size of the patch affected may increase in size rapidly over a day or two. Blighting of leaf tips may last one to three weeks.

Brown patch can cause permanent damage.

Improve drainage, reduce compaction, do not over-fertilize—and avoid excess soluble nitrogen. Irrigate deeply and infrequently, and not every day; mow early in the morning to speed leaf drying; get rid of excess thatch; and use organic amendments like composted poultry litter, compost, or animal and plant meal.

The grass may possibly die since brown patch affects roots and crowns. Should you use a fungicide? Possibly, since root health and turf density can be seriously affected.

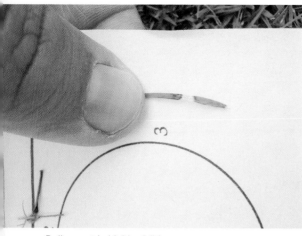
Dollar spot is highly visible.

Dollar spot is highly visible, affecting bents, bluegrasses, rye, fine fescue, and *Zoysia* (can be very severe). Warm temperatures, high humidity, cool nights, and persistent drought all bring the disease on. You'll see hourglass-shaped spots with brown edges, irregular straw-colored patches, tip blighting, and "cobwebs" on the lawn in the morning (these are actually fungal threads).

What should you do? Reduce compaction, raise the mowing height, do not water in late afternoon and evening, avoid light frequent sprinkling, reduce shade, increase air circulation, and use natural organic fertilizers and amendments of animal and plant meal.

The grass will die, but fortunately only small areas are usually affected. Also, new roots may decline from dollar spot. Should you use a fungicide? Probably, since dollar spot is easily spread on mowers, shoes, and other objects.

Rust is also highly visible, getting on bluegrasses, rye, and *Zoysia* (can be serious). Cool, wet weather, moisture for ten to twelve hours, and fog bring it on. Yellow, orange, or red spots on leaves are surrounded by green, yellow, or brown borders, depending on age and susceptibility of grass; severely affected grass has a red or yellow cast, and there may be huge clouds of spores, which turn shoes and clothing orange.

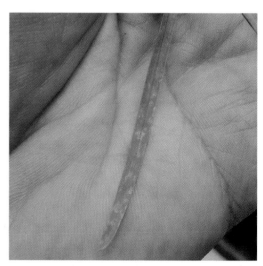
Rust produces lots of spores.

What should you do? Mow frequently, avoid prolonged drying, irrigate, reduce compaction, and increase light and air circulation. The grass is unlikely to die, and no fungicide treatment is really necessary.

Leaf spot, another highly visible disease, gets on bents, bluegrasses, rye, fine fescues, and *Zoysia*. Cool, wet weather favors simple spots, while hot, wet weather can foster massive damage. You'll see browning, thinning, circular-to-elongate purple spots, with brown, red, white tan, or straw centers. You may see leaf blotches or tiny red or purple spots on blades and sheaths. Seedlings are the most susceptible and often

Leaf spot can be found all year long.

die. *Zoysia* dies back from the tip during hot, wet weather. Look for the first signs of leaf spot on bluegrass. Leaf spot may look like dull mower injury on bents.

In hot weather, you may see tip blighting or a reddish brown to black crown root rot, and there may be only a few shallow feeder roots. Older leaves are more susceptible than young. In warm weather, leaf spot is restricted to roots and crowns. Kentucky bluegrass is more susceptible with overcast weather or succulent growth.

Avoid planting grass in shade since leaf spot appears first on shaded grass. The disease is also worse on closely mowed turf, so mow high, reduce thatch, and don't overfertilize. Apply higher rates of nitrogen in fall than spring. Avoid soluble fertilizers like urea or ammonium nitrate. Do improve drainage, irrigate deeply and infrequently, but try not to mow or irrigate when the disease is active. For fine fescue, be sure not to overirrigate or keep the grass wet. Avoid all light, frequent irrigation. Don't sprinkle in the early evening; the more often the grass is wet or remains wet, the greater chance of leaf spot establishment. And for goodness' sake, increase air circulation!

Leaf spot attacks roots and crowns, so in hot, windy weather, plants die and you get what is known as melting out. Discrete spots seen in spring and fall will not kill the plants. Usually you do not need to use a fungicide since most varieties of grass are now somewhat resistant. If you do use a fungicide, only **contact** fungicides are useful against leaf spots.

Smut is visible (ask any tabloid reporter) and gets on bluegrasses and bents. Cool, wet weather is best for infection, but you will not see a progressive decline until hot dry weather sets in.

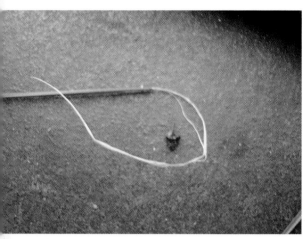

Smut can cause a progressive decline later in the season.

Smut symptoms include shredded, curling leaf blades down the length of the leaf and gray parallel lines along the length of the blade that split open. You may see a swirling pattern in the turf similar to summer patch, usually the third or fourth year after seeding.

What should you do? Check your pH, since low pH promotes the disease. Check potassium levels, manage the water, and increase soil moisture levels since progressive decline sets in during hot, dry weather. Avoid heavy nitrogen applications in late spring and summer, and decrease thatch. The grass may die if the water is not managed.

A fungicide may be necessary, depending on the extent of the problem.

Anthracnose is readily visible . . . if you have a hand lens. Bluegrasses and bents are likely to suffer from it. Warm temperatures, excessive moisture, stress, and abrasion bring it on. You'll see elongated reddish brown spots that eventually become small, black hairy dots on dead and dying leaf tissue. The disease is common with excessive moisture combining with factors that slow grass growth. It is more common on annual bluegrass, but also seen on bents. You may see it in conjunction with leaf spots.

What should you do? Increase your mowing height, and reduce abusive practices. Reduce traffic.

Will the grass die? On a home lawn, probably not. Try to fix stress factors to improve chances for survival. You probably won't need to use a fungicide in a home lawn setting.

Anthracnose *is a common turf disease.*

Necrotic ringspot disease is similar in symptoms to summer patch. You may see only a swirling area of browned-out grass or thinning since the disease affects the roots. Bluegrasses, bents, and fine fescues are affected in mild weather in fall and spring. You may see frog eyes, which are tan circles with apparently healthy grass growing in the center, or sunken bronzed patches in lawns less than four years old. The roots will be discolored dark brown or black.

Necrotic ringspot attacks young lawns.

Overseed with resistant varieties, avoid serious fluctuations in soil moisture, use slow-release fertilizers, avoid excessive watering, avoid compaction, and top-dress with compost. The pathogen attacks the roots, so the grass will die, but a fungicide should probably not be used until the following season around the middle of April—once the symptoms are obvious, the grass is already dead.

Pythium root rot is very sneaky because the disease is not readily visible as anything more than yellowing. Bluegrasses, bents, and rye all get the disease, which is most prevalent during cool, wet weather (this is not the same as *Pythium* blight, which occurs during hot, wet weather). Your grass will have thin, off-color turf, yellowed areas, and roots that are short and off color in areas that have poor drainage and shade or in low spots near surface water. If soil has been amended with topsoil or sod has been laid, you may have what look like two or more discrete layers. This can make for very poor drainage and predisposes turf to *Pythium* root rot. Wherever you see algae growing on the surface of soil or grass, you are likely to see *Pythium*.

What should you do? Don't overirrigate! Improve air circulation and drainage. Use slow-release fertilizers, avoid excessive watering, avoid

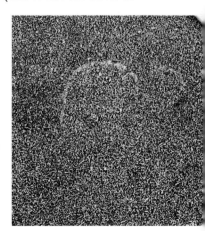

Pythium *root rot attacks areas that are perpetually wet.*

compaction, and top-dress with compost. Amend with composted poultry litter. The pathogen attacks the roots, so the grass may die, but using a fungicide makes no sense. The problem is largely cultural due to poor drainage. Fixing the drainage problem should eliminate problems with the fungus.

Summer patch is deceptive: You may see only a swirling area of browned-out grass or thinning. Bluegrasses, bents, rye, and fine fescues all get the disease. The infection occurs during cool, wet weather, but you don't see the symptoms until it gets hot and dry and the grass is stressed. Cool, wet summers are less likely to produce summer patch.

Look for wilting, frog eyes, swirls, or generally browned-out areas that occur in the

Summer patch is usually visible during the first hot, dry spell.

hottest part of the lawn. The spots may occur in the same place year after year. Roots will appear tan or brittle. Grass will experience a color change from wilted blue to reddish to tan to straw. The disease first reappears in areas where disease was active the year before; it is especially prevalent near sidewalks, buildings, and southern slopes.

Maintain a 5.8 to 6.0 pH in the root zone, raise the mowing height in hot weather, and avoid fluctuations in soil moisture from wet to dry. Try slow-release fertilizers rather than soluble ones, and core-aerate to improve layering. Look for ways to cool down areas routinely attacked by summer patch since damage is worse in soil that is 5 to 10 degrees warmer than surrounding areas. Using an irrigation system to briefly cool the crowns during the hottest part of the day is a good practice. The pathogen attacks the roots, so the grass is likely to die. Wait till the following year (around tax time) to use a fungicide—as a preventative before the infection period begins. Once you see the symptoms, the grass is already dead.

Aschochyta, a very visible leaf blight, occurs on most kinds of grass all year long during periods of high humidity. Look for needlelike dieback from leaf tips, with twisted straw-colored leaf tips giving an overall tan sheen to the turf stand. Fungus grows down from cut leaf tips very slowly, so the next mowing may nip it off. Avoid excessive irrigation and nitrogen applications. The fungus is unsightly, but generally, the turf will outgrow the problem.

Mushrooms

Generally, the mushrooms we visually encounter aren't bothering anything. But fairy rings are an exception. These are fronts of fungus actually infesting the soil, and they come, like hurricanes, in three grades:

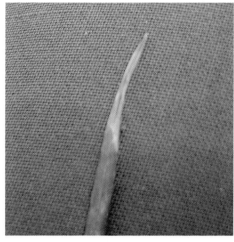

Aschochyta *can often be removed by mowing.*

Grade 1. These are the most important from the standpoint of your lawn. Organic matter is broken down at an extremely rapid rate, and all moisture is absorbed by the advancing fungus so that the grass dies. Treatment involves rewetting of mushroom-dried areas of soil through aeration or physically digging the infested soil out to a depth of 1 foot (told you to save those cores!). Soil infested by fairy ring actually has a musty, moldy smell.

Grade 2. Green arcs are familiar sights as fairy ring moves through the soil. Mechanical aeration helps, as does drenching the area with water. Fertilization

Grade 3 fairy ring can be a plain old mushroom or it can be a darker green ring.

can also be increased to mask the symptoms, but that may predispose the grass to other diseases.

Grade 3. These are isolated mushrooms, toadstools, and the like. Rake them out and be done!

Insects

In Chapter 6, you learned more than you ever wanted to know about insects in your landscape and how to tell the groups apart. In this chapter, we'll give you the cheapie version because, for most of the country, four major groups of insects are associated with extensive turf damage—two kinds of beetles, caterpillars, and chinch bugs.

White grubs devour turf roots.

Turf-Eating Beetles

Juveniles of scarab beetles (white grubs, in case you were wondering) chew off roots right near the surface, so the turf dehydrates, dies, and because the roots are gone, can be rolled up like a carpet. Scarab beetles include Japanese beetles, Oriental beetles, European chafers, Asiatic garden beetles, June beetles, and masked chafers.

The lifecycle starts with adult beetles mating in May and June. Adults are not especially susceptible to pesticides. Females deposit fertilized eggs in the turf, which then grow and develop over the course of the summer. You actually don't see the feeding damage on turf until the grubs have grown quite large, toward the end of summer, when they are eating a lot of the turf root system. At this point, you see wilting, discoloration, and possibly areas scratched up by raccoons and skunks looking for grubs to eat.

After these large grubs have fed through about the middle of September, they start to tunnel back down below the frost line to spend the winter, coming back up to the surface next April or so for a quick feed before the changeover to adulthood.

Action Thresholds for Turf Pests

Thresholds for damaging numbers of turf pests are as follows: European chafer five to seven per square foot, Oriental beetle eight to ten per square foot, Japanese beetles eight to ten per square foot, Asiatic garden beetles eighteen to twenty per square foot, green June beetles five per square foot, chinch bugs fifteen to twenty per square foot, and sod webworms ten per square foot. For blue-grass billbug adults, five to eight every five minutes of your observing them running across pavement (or dig a plastic cup into the turf area, level with the soil, and check it every couple of days for two to five trapped and angry billbug captives).

So when should you treat? The most sensible window for treating actively feeding grubs is between the beginning of August and the middle of September. Unless you have eight to ten grubs per square foot, your turf should be able to tolerate feeding by most scarab young without your trying to control them.

It is pointless to try to treat them in spring because they feed for so short a time that little damage is done, and the spring growth surge that cool-season grasses have generally covers up the damage very quickly. At this point, the grubs are so large that they do not respond well to most insecticide treatments anyway.

If you treat, and I hope that you don't unless absolutely necessary, several things will offer you a greater level of success. First, return clippings for at least two mowings after application. Since grubs move 4 to 8 inches deeper in the soil when conditions are hot and dry, water the top 2 inches of soil ($1/4$- to $1/2$-inch volume—use your rain gauge) twenty-four to thirty-six hours before treating so that grubs move back into the root zone, promoting better contact and efficacy. Water again after treatment to keep grubs in the root zone so they will have as much contact with your control as possible.

Billbugs, the Other Turf Beetle

Billbugs are actually weevils, a kind of beetle with a long, narrow snout. Juveniles (who look like legless versions of white grubs) tunnel inside grass shafts, causing the upper parts of the grass plant to yellow and die.

Turf next to driveways and sidewalks are the preferred sites for egg laying, mostly in areas of high thatch. Anything that encourages quick heating in spring—such as pine needles, mulch near paths, or low mowing—may

Billbugs can cause damage to turf although this one is no longer a threat!

contribute to billbug population problems. Suggested timing for control is April through mid-May. Billbugs also dine happily on *Zoysia*. Use control products that will remain in thatch, and water them only lightly.

Treat adults before soil surface temperatures hit 75 degrees F. (use a meat thermometer to check soil temperature) and young when temperatures exceed 75. You can also overseed with grasses containing a good guy fungus called an endophyte.

To monitor, do the tug test on the grass and look for sawdust-like bug poop. American, Adelphi, Eclipse, and Midnight Kentucky bluegrass all resist billbug damage.

Caterpillars in Turf

Although armyworms and cutworms can infest turf, our primary concern from year to year is the sod webworm. Brick red cocoons that may turn up during your garden diggings are the pupal cases of turf-infesting caterpillars. Caterpillar problems in turf are easily mistaken for other kinds of problems like drought or disease.

Damaging numbers of sod webworm are restricted to areas that get a full day of sunlight. Partial shade will also have sod webworm, but not enough to worry about. The worst risk of damage is mid-July to the end of September.

Endophyte-Enhanced Grass

Endophytes are good guy fungi that live inside grass seed. They produce compounds toxic to surface-feeding insects. Unfortunately the compounds are not moved into the grass's root system, so they have no effect on grubs. Only fescues and ryes are able to be purchased as endophyte-enhanced, so check the label.

Treating Caterpillars in the Lawn

For any caterpillar pest, treat late in the day and then avoid mowing one to two days after application. Caterpillars hang around at the surface, so don't water after treatment; otherwise, you'll push the treatment material beyond where they are likely to have maximum contact with it. Caterpillars are nocturnal, so delay putting your treatment out until early evening—it will have less time to be degraded by the sun.

Small populations late in the year usually don't need treatment, but make a note and look in the same place the following spring. **Leave your ants alone—they carry off as much as 90 percent of sod webworm eggs.** Overseed with endophyte-enhanced grasses in fall.

Sod webworms overwinter as large caterpillars, so if you see birds picking at the turf in early spring, this is probably what they are after (especially blackbirds, robins, and flickers). Sod webworm poop looks like small, green, mouse droppings.

Sod webworm adults are easily seen in summer.

An infestation of juveniles **rarely** kills turf. Fine fescue and perennial rye are at the greatest risk of death, but they are easily overseeded with endophyte-enhanced rye and fescue.

This pest is more common on newly established lawns, especially Kentucky bluegrass. When you see damage in mid- to late summer, you are likely to find small brown patches of closely cropped grass that look like disease. Mature "worms" are 3/4 inch long and are covered in black polka dots.

Chinch Bugs

These piercing, sucking insects feed on Kentucky bluegrass, perennial rye, bentgrass, and *Zoysia*. Grass turns yellow to red-brown and looks drought stressed, but water doesn't help. You are most likely to see damage in June with droughty conditions. Chinch bugs come out of overwintering sites when temperatures get up around 70 degrees F. Chinch bugs may overwinter in tall grasses near your lawn, so check out ornamental grasses or native plantings for their presence, as well. Often the greatest numbers of chinch bugs occur in weedy lawns with lots of bents, fescues, and thatch. Adults are only $1/5$ inch long, so get out your magnifying glass!

Chinch bugs do better on turf that is overfertilized and full of thatch. Adults are black and white with small triangular heads and tiny red eyes; they appear to have an X on their back where their wings fold. The young have a bright orange abdomen bisected by a broad white stripe and either a black or orange thorax and head.

If you just can't wait for nature to take its course, treat adult chinch bugs in April and May before egg-laying occurs in mid-May, and overseed with endophytes in the fall. The endophytes will usually whip the problem right

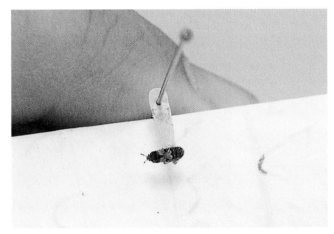

Chinch bug adults are relatively small.

Chinch bug larvae are brightly colored.

Monitoring for Turf Pests Other Than Grubs

Monitoring for sod webworms, armyworms, and chinch bugs involves a groovy and simple technique that even a child can have fun with. Mix about 1 ounce of lemon dish soap with 1 gallon of water. Measure out a 4-foot-square area of turf on the margin of the good turf area and the bad turf area. With a watering can, pour the solution of dish soap and water into the measured area. Pests should surface within eight to ten minutes. (When the soil is dry, irrigate the area before applying the soap solution.) Mowing your 4-foot-square area low may also be helpful to the eyeball. The soap doesn't hurt the insects, but it sure does annoy them! They'll come to the surface and shake their tiny fists at you, so you can count them. You may see chinch bugs more easily if you lay a white flannel cloth over the drenched area. They'll crawl into the nap and get stuck there, enabling you to more easily count them.

Chinch bugs can also be tracked using a coffee can with both ends removed, pounded into the ground and then filled with the lemon soap and water mixture. You'll get floaters in about ten minutes. Very satisfying if you have had a bad day!

into shape. Focus on areas where you always have outbreaks for any control programs, and use products that will remain in the thatch. Water in only lightly. Starlings are good indicators of chinch bug presence. You'll have more problems in full sun and with southern exposures.

Big-eyed bugs are very efficient predators of their cousin the chinch bug. In fact, they look like the chinch bugs, but their eyes are enormous—hence their name. If you wait long enough, big-eyed bugs will always get the better of the chinch bugs because they like similar habitats and will migrate to where there is plenty of prey. Still, turf damage may be visible before populations of big-eyed bugs are large enough to gain control of the chinch bugs.

"Pining" Away

Caring for Conifers and Broad-Leaf Evergreens

We love evergreens for many reasons. We love them for their holiday associations of life persisting through the winter and for the notion that the dead whisper to each other from the branches of yews. We love them for the architectural framework they provide in our gardens; evergreens are ideal for space definition—you can make garden "rooms," frame a dramatic scene, screen out your neighbor's tacky garbage receptacle, or create a dark background for spring-blooming trees and shrubs. And we love them because they offer a romantic, imaginative focal point in landscapes. Check out landscape paintings by the masters of art, as well as the most miserable of community center craft projects; many have a single conifer or two as the focal point.

This is normal fall browning on narrow-leaf evergreens.

What Is an Evergreen?

Evergreens retain the better part of their leaves throughout the year and are loosely divided into two categories: broad-leaf (*Rhododendron*, andromeda, boxwood, etc.) and narrow-leaf (pines, firs, spruces, etc.).

They normally lose foliage in autumn just like deciduous trees. Changes may be bizarre enough so that nervous owners become convinced the tree is getting ready to die. Most evergreens have foliage that lives from one to three years, so the amount of shedding that you see from year to year differs for different kinds of trees. Look for color changes and shedding to first be apparent on the inside areas of the branches. Individual bunches of pine needles will change color and be shed in autumn. Hemlocks and yews shed individual needles over a long period. Spruces and firs also produce needles that are retained for five to six years, and shedding may or may not be restricted to the oldest needles. Arborvitae shed their oldest branchlets in autumn.

Rhododendron, hollies, and mountain laurel all produce leaves individually. Holly and laurel only retain their leaves for one year. *Rhododendron* often retain their leaves for two years, but may shed them at one year, especially during dry periods like late summer and early spring. Hollies tend to shed leaves at about the same time as they put out new leaves in spring.

Another kicker is that in drought years, only sparse new foliage may be produced, which cannot adequately mask yellowing foliage from the previous year. Transplant shock will also cause sudden yellowing and

The Most Common Problem with Evergreens

The number one problem with conifers of any sort is yellow tips. Most often, this indicates too much moisture. So before you go any further in this chapter, check the soil, the planting depth, and the amount of moisture your conifer is getting because everything in this group is much less tolerant to waterlogging than are flowering plants!

needle drop, but this may not occur for up to two years after transplant. Evergreen needles often redden in response to cold; that color normally goes away once temperatures rise.

Narrow-Leaf Evergreens

Almost everyone has a pine, juniper, spruce, yew, or **something** with needles in their landscape. These "needles" are actually modified leaves, and this is where we derive the term *narrow-leaf evergreens*. The catch-all term *conifer*, which we also use to represent narrow-leaf evergreens, means cone bearing. In practical terms, the narrow-leaf evergreen gives us a windbreak and some insulation from extreme heat and cold. If you want to create a windbreak like the pioneers often did, plant a hedge of 8- to 15-foot-tall evergreens **perpendicular** to the direction of the prevailing wind. In other words, if the wind usually blows west to east, your conifers should march north to south. Such a wall will also deaden traffic or schoolyard noise pollution.

Insect Problems on Narrow-Leaf Evergreens

Pitch mass borer creates unsightly, but not especially harmful, insect damage. Areas on the trunk that have been mechanically injured are especially susceptible to attack. Avoid wounding or pruning in spring just before the adult moths fly or summer when moths are emerging. The single juvenile lives and feeds in the cambium, and large piles of pitch and frass accumulate around the feeding area until the caterpillar turns into a moth. Areas that have been previously attacked are subject to repopulation. The pest requires two to three years to complete its lifecycle. It is mainly a problem on five-needled pines.

    Eastern pine shoot borer adults emerge shortly after two-needled Scotch pines break bud. Juvenile damage is similar to the white pine weevil in that shepherd's crooks are formed, but in this case, side branches are also attacked.

It is mainly a problem on five-needled pines. Weakened shoots often droop or break, and there is needle loss. Mulching beneath the tree may help to reduce the numbers of this pest.

European pine shoot moth juveniles tunnel around in buds and new young shoots, causing brown, stunted needles, or needles die, giving the whole tree a reddish cast in cases of severe infestation. These pests mainly occur on Austrian pines and other two-needled pines. Light infestations sometimes actually make the tree look better—it looks bushier. The juveniles are small and reddish brown.

Nantucket pine tip moth juveniles are very small and tan; they tunnel around in the bases of needles or buds, causing damage similar to the European pine shoot moth. You may also see Eastern pine shoot borer, which we talked about above. These pests appear on two-needled pines.

Zimmerman pine moth tunnels under the bark of terminal shoots as a pink or greenish juvenile; injured twigs have a mixture of pitch and frass at the entry site. These pests are especially prevalent on Austrian pine.

Pales weevil adults hang out in leaf litter under the trees they infest. They are attracted to freshly cut pine stumps, as well as fresh pine bark and sawdust, particularly of Scotch pine. These pests eat pine bark and damage young trees in particular. The weevil is rusty black with brown spots.

White pine weevil lays eggs in the terminal leader and kills it, causing the characteristic shepherd's crook, which often results in stunted, deformed trees. The killed portion may also serve as an entry point for wood decaying fungi. White pine, Norway spruce, Scotch pine, and jack pine are readily attacked. Pitch pine, red pine, and red spruce are occasionally attacked.

The Differences Between Pines

Pines come with two, three, and five needles per cluster, bound by a membranous sheath at the base. Take a look!

* *Two needles:* Austrian, mugo (Swiss mountain), Scotch, Japanese black, Japanese red
* *Three needles:* pitch pine (This is seldom used in landscaping, so we're ignoring them in this chapter.)
* *Five needles:* eastern white, Swiss stone, limber, and Japanese white

The Differences Between Evergreens Other Than Pines

* Spruce has round needles; fir has flat needles.
* Spruce needles when pulled off the branch leave a small "thingie" attached; fir needles do not.
* Hemlock needles have two white lines down the back of the needle.
* *Chamecyparis* (a group in the cypress family) has white banded lines on the back of the scales; arborvitae (sometimes called red or white cedar) do not.

The best control is simply to prune them out. Cut just above the nearest living whorl of branches just as soon as you notice the infestation. Remove all but the largest living branch at that whorl so it can become the next terminal leader (sounds like a political revolution to me). Discard or destroy prunings offsite—the pest can continue developing inside.

Diseases of Narrow-Leaf Evergreens

Unfortunately, many diseases bear several different names, which makes it all that much more confusing to determine what your plant has.

Sphaeropsis (*Diplodia*) tip blight is most likely to be found on Austrian pine shoots in spring. The earliest symptom is resin that is pushed in small drops from newly expanded buds. The buds persist for a month or so in this manner and then die off. This disease in canker form is a problem on blue Atlas cedar suffering from salt and drought stress. You are also likely to see *Sphaeropsis* (*Diplodia*) tip blight on Japanese black pine shoots.

One of the most common evergreen diseases, it is readily recognized by black pepper dots beneath the sheath surrounding the base of the needles. You'll see it more with wet, rainy weather in spring and early summer. It infects wounds. Remove dead branches, cones, and debris promptly. Prune off infected branches just below the youngest live branch whorl. Only prune in dry, fair weather because tip blight can infect pruning cuts in wet weather. Do **not** plant new pines near infected trees. Mulch around the tree base to decrease compaction or digging damage—and **please** no overhead irrigation in spring!

Infections are greatest on fifteen- to twenty-five-year-old trees. Resin may be exuded, which causes brown needles to adhere to twigs after death. You may also see kinks in cankered twigs. *Sphaeropsis* infects trees in dense shade more readily and easily infects trees planted in soils that are extremely wet, dry, shallow, sandy, or nutrient deficient. *Sphaeropsis* also has an easier time infecting trees that are outside their natural geographic range (for example, Austrian pines in New York).

Cenangium **canker** girdles twigs over the winter. It shows up in spring as browned needles and twigs below the canker line on Japanese red pines. There may be rusty brown cups with a bright orange lining during damp weather.

Atropellis **canker** on Scotch pine, which is more prevalent in the Adirondack region, can girdle and kill branches up to 1 inch in diameter. Around the second week in May, you might see black cups emerging from bark cracks. You'll also see a blue-black stain on the wood beneath the cankers. Look for brown tissue under the bark, surrounded by a yellow, healthy area on cankered branches. *Atropellis* canker also affects Austrian pine with small, white, elliptical cankers at needle bases. Cankers can mimic *Sphaeropsis* (*Diplodia*) or frost damage. Crowded, moist conditions favor the disease.

Juniper tip blight is actually two different fungi that produce identical symptoms, but different controls at different times are employed, depending on which you have. Both diseases cause brown dieback of young needles and shoot tips. They also girdle shoots and produce black or gray fruiting bodies. The giveaway is that *Phomopsis* infections are still pale green in spring but turn brown by early summer; *Kabatina* infections are already brown by late winter. Treat *Kabatina* in fall and *Phomopsis* in spring.

Phomopsis *and* Kabatina *blight are common with overhead watering of junipers.*

To avoid the disease, avoid prolonged needle wetness from irrigation and avoid excess nitrogen. Plant your junipers where they have plenty of sun. Also don't plant 'Bar Harbor', 'Wichita Blue', and 'Blue Star' junipers, which are highly susceptible. Instead, plant resistant Russian arborvitae (*Microbiota decussata*), which has a similar form and quality to junipers.

Cytospora (*Leucostoma***)** is a canker that is the bane of many a gardener whose evergreens are unhappy in areas with hot, dry summers. The trouble is that the disease passes back and forth between spruces and firs, which in suburban landscapes are often planted in proximity to each other. Spruce branches die from the bottom up, so it looks like a large dead tree with a tiny live Christmas tree at the tip-top. Lower branches of spruce drop huge numbers of needles, which may turn purplish before they drop. You'll see it on old or stressed trees and more severely in sandy soil because of low moisture. No fungicides are effective against this disease; just reduce stress and avoid lawn mower injury. Prune off branches touching the ground.

In spring, look for light-green to reddish brown on needles on the lowest branches. You may see resin (whitish when it dries) exuding from a canker farther back on the branch from the needle drop. Prune out infected branches beyond the canker, water, and mulch well. Plant tall ornamental grasses around the base of the tree to mask the damage or death of lower branches.

Brown felt blight has a wide range of hosts, including spruces, firs, and junipers. This disease kills branches by plugging air holes in needles when the tree is blanketed

Leucostoma *canker is typical on older, drought-stressed blue spruce.*

by snow. Most fungal development occurs in spring at temperatures slightly above freezing. In windy areas, this blight is more common on the leeward side.

Pine pitch canker, a common disease in the southeast, is caused by *Fusarium* fungus. Death is usually from multiple branch infections. (Oddly enough, *Gladiola* and pines can cross-infect each other in Florida!) Resin-soaked areas encircle and girdle branches, causing dieback in autumn. In spring the dead needles are still hanging on. Insects are implicated in the spread, including tip moth, needle miner, and deodar weevil. Physical damage or twisting or ripping cones can also contribute to disease. High fertility and serious water stress also contribute to disease prevalence.

Seridium **canker** on cypress trees is one of those diseases that tend to occur on plants installed beyond their natural range or in monoculture landscape plantings, such as Leyland cypress in hedge rows. Prolonged drying around roots seems to increase the disease, so make sure your soil moisture profile is deep and even. Italian, Leyland, and Monterey cypresses are most susceptible. Foliage fades and dies most visibly in spring during rapid growth. Drops of resin are exuded, and pockets of pooled resin are seen as streaks in killed bark.

Seridium *canker is a likely culprit in dieback on Leyland cypress.*

Cankers on young trees are usually on the main stem. Cypress bark beetles and cypress bark moth are both implicated in disease spread.

Needle Cast Diseases of Narrow-Leaf Evergreens

Leaf spots of narrow-leaf evergreens are called needle cast fungi. Many bother our evergreens, usually due to excessive leaf wetness or stress. Below is a menu of malefactors that make your needles look messy:

Cyclaneusma **needle cast** is a problem for Scotch, mugo, and eastern white pine and is usually brought on by environmental stress. Needles begin to yellow in fall, with needle cast in late fall. Reduce leaf wetness! These events (yellowing and casting) on second-year foliage also occur in fall. *Cyclaneusma* starts as light-green spots, which then yellow and enlarge to cause yellow bands before the whole needle yellows. You'll see transverse brown bars on Scotch pine only. You may also see creamy white spore masses.

Rhabdocline needle cast affects only one important host, for the most part: Douglas fir. Branches turn brown in late summer. Needles develop dark brown bands and spots, and then fall off in winter. Increase air circulation around the tree's base. Prune off lower affected branches by late April.

Lophodermium needle cast affects pines (also firs, and spruces getting a bit too much shade). The fungus produces football-shaped black fruiting bodies that cause the needle surface to bulge like Uncle Henry after the Thanksgiving feed. It attacks the current season's growth; in fall, infected needles have red spots with yellow margins.

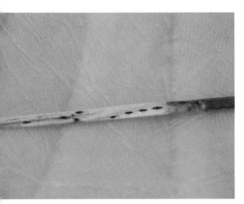

Lophodermium *needle cast has football-shaped black dots.*

In spring, needles turn red and then straw. Once the needle turns completely straw colored, black dots appear scattered up and down the needle, but not in a straight line.

Ploioderma needle cast occurs in two- or three-needled pines. It looks like *Lophodermium* and *Elytroderma*, but black fruiting bodies are confined to straw-colored lesions in the center of needles rather than along the whole needle. The tree will lose year-old needles, particularly on the lowest branches.

Swiss needle cast (*Phaeocryptopus***)** occurs mostly on Douglas fir and occasionally on true firs, hemlock, and pine. It infects year-old needles, but they are not cast till two to three years later. Needles turn yellow-green and then mottle with brown. This disease is more common with rainy summer weather.

Brown spot needle blight is found on Austrian, Japanese black, mugo, pitch, spruce, and eastern white pine. Killed needles drop during October and November. Spots are straw to light brown with a dark border. Warm, wet weather favors the disease and looks like *Dothistroma* needle blight.

Dothistroma needle blight affects thirty species of pine, including Austrian, Japanese black, and mugo pines.

Rhizosphaera needle cast causes defoliation on spruce, especially Colorado blue spruce, white spruce (Norway is fairly resistant), Austrian, Japanese black, mugo, and eastern white pine, as well as Douglas fir. Needles on low branches are affected first. *Rhizosphaera* spreads up or down, creating "holes" in branches, and is worse on trees less than 22 feet tall. Late-summer yellow mottling of first-year needles is common; needles eventually turn purple and brown. The brown is visible in winter, and needles drop next summer and

White Pine Decline

What is "white pine decline"? This phrase often describes trees with yellowing, banded, brown-tipped, or otherwise off-color needles. Shoot and needle lengths are shorter than normal, and there may be sparse tree canopy or sap exudates on branches, drooping needles in winter, and wrinkled bark on any area of the tree. The tree exhibits reduced growth and vigor, and eventually dies, usually from a combination of factors.

White pines do best in deep, well-drained, fertile, acidic soil, so the first thing to check is the pH and the drainage. They are also extremely sensitive to salt in the soil and to air pollution. If your pines are in the runoff bands from areas regularly salted in winter, you may have found your culprit. If you are in the Piedmont and coastal plains area, white pines tend to die between the ages of seven and twenty-five, often with a sudden collapse of the top part of the tree during the first round of stressful weather. The tree may or may not have had a single limb die the previous season. The following year, even less growth occurs, the needles turn light green, and a month or so later you're conducting the funeral.

Liming, mowing, disturbed or compacted soil (especially heavy soils), fertilization, and particularly a pH of 7 or above can cause your pines to stress or croak. Other contributors are extremes of temperature and moisture (drought). A thorough watering in late fall will help the trees go into winter well hydrated, as will mulching the base.

Look for evidence of bark beetles or borers, through clues such as resin on the trunk, pinholes, tunneling patterns under bark, or oval cavities filled with wood fiber under the bark. These pests will move on to healthy trees in a planting, so get rid of the sickly trees ASAP!

Check the roots of pines you suspect are in decline: If a cross-section of the root is brown and the outer layer slips off like a glove, you've got root injury.

fall. Spores develop in rows on needles and are spread by splashing. This disease is associated with low pH and its effects on fertility.

Isthmiella (Lirula) needle cast affects white spruce and fir. Dead needles remain attached until they have weathered several years. You'll see branch segments with dead needles alternating with segments with no needles.

Fir interior needle blight manifests in early fall when older needles turn brown but remain attached. Black fruiting bodies appear in infected needles that drop by spring.

Botrytis is an issue in Fraser fir. Don't allow weeds to grow too tall around them, and don't plant dense ornamentals too close together, or you will increase humidity and the likelihood for a *botrytis* outbreak.

Bifusella and Canavirgella blights can cause the tips of white pine to die in early summer, but these fungi do not turn them brown or reddish brown until early fall. Be careful not to confuse this with salt damage.

Mycosphaerella fungus affects Virginia and Scotch pine. In late August, yellow spots appear on the lower branches, especially on the north side. Needle tips turn brown, but the needle base stays green for a while longer before croaking completely.

Meria blight symptoms on larch are rather sudden, but *Meria* weakens the tree rather than kills it. When larch needles fall off, you'll just think it's frost damage! But you can tell the difference because frost-nipped needles actually stay on the tree while blighted ones fall off. You'll also see white dots along the lines on the lower leaf surface during wet weather. Sanitation is key!

Root Rots of Narrow-Leaf Evergreens

Root diseases of conifers are more common that you would think and, like inflammation in humans, can lead to devastating effects.

Phythophthora produces particular problems in younger Fraser firs. The disease is attracted to newly forming or wounded roots. You'll first see yellowing of plants with this rot, followed by complete browning of the foliage. If you carefully peel away a small section of bark, you can see reddish brown discoloration in the root collar, while similar tissue above remains green and healthy. Heavy soil is the culprit again, so if you must grow evergreens on this type soil, switch to spruce or pines (but not white pine!).

Armillaria root rot, those evil shoestrings, often invade trees weakened by some other agent of defoliation like drought or bark beetles, **but it can also infect vigorous trees!** The disease is hosted by all pines, spruces, firs, and Douglas firs. Large trees can often confine it to a few large roots for many years, but the tree becomes progressively prone to wind throw. The first symptoms are off-color foliage and stunted growth. Browning of needles

Japanese Black Pine Decline

Japanese black pine decline is actually a number of problems, all of which combine to take out the tree in early summer to early autumn, despite previous vigor.

Factor number one is the pine wood nematode (PWN). PWN is weird because it is a nematode vectored by an insect, the eastern sawyer beetle. PWN is seen in jack, Aleppo, Austrian, Japanese black, loblolly, lodgepole, long leaf, Monterey, mugo, pitch, ponderosa, red, Japanese red, sand, shortleaf, slash, Swiss stone, Virginia, eastern white, atlas cedar, deodar, balsam fir, eastern and European larch, and blue and white spruce.

Trees die so quickly that brown needles stay on the tree. In cedars some branches die while others stay green; larch needles yellow and then drop early. In very large trees, you may see branches start to die in autumn, and then again in spring. If the disease does not take a rapid course, older needles brown and die first. You may or may not see resin-soaked wood in the trunk. The nematode actually eliminates resin flow to wounds causing the tree's immune system to shut down. Cool, moist weather seems to prolong the time until death, perhaps by reducing stress to the tree.

Trees dying of PWN are also attacked by bark beetles carrying wood-decaying fungi like blue stain and other secondary invaders. The presence of bark beetles can often be detected by white resin or pitch tubes on the lower part of trunk or stumps. High temperatures, water stress, and attack by secondary pathogens favor the increase of nematode populations and the development of wilt.

Japanese black pine can succumb from any one or combination of the following factors: PWN; turpentine bark beetles, which vector blue stain fungus; and *Cenangium* canker. Again, cardinal signs of decline are foliage discoloration, which occurs midsummer to late fall, or late winter to spring, and resin tubes on the lower trunk. Trees infected in fall don't break bud the following spring. Trees may show symptoms as early as four to eight weeks after infection. Infected trees should be removed and estroyed by burning or burying to eliminate breeding sites. Reduce the number of stressed and dying trees or stumps that will attract insect vectors.

and death usually follow within two months. Examine a suspect tree for evidence by removing a bit of bark from the root collar area. Look for a dense white mat of fungal tissue growing between bark and wood. If you don't see the mat, or shoestrings, it's likely not *Armillaria*. In autumn you may see clumps of honey-colored mushrooms at the tree's base. No chemical treatments are available, so your job is to reduce stress on conifers, remove all old stumps, and avoid planting susceptible trees near infected areas since the shoestrings can travel up to 60 feet!

Procerum **root disease** is most common in eastern white pine but is also seen in other pines, Douglas fir, white fir, and Colorado blue spruce. Hot weather causes sudden death and decline. The first symptom is delayed bud break and stunted twig elongation, but those may be the only symptoms seen for several years.

Annosus **root rot** is primarily a problem in thinned pine plantations, but also occurs in many other conifers. It is a major cause of death in eastern red cedar. It produces shelf fungi at the root collar at or below the ground line (you might have to dig a bit to expose the area). Broken, infected roots are shredded and stringy. Bark beetles may be attracted to trees infected with the fungus. Slow growth and wind throw are common side effects. Evergreens growing on sandy soils are more susceptible.

Black stain (*Verticladiella***)** occurs in the west on conifers living in cool, wet sites. It causes death and staining of roots and lower stems of conifers. Once again, bark beetles are implicated. Height and needle length are decreased, the crown thins out, and stained arcs that have spread across several growth rings are visible in a cross-section of the trunk. Often this disease is seen in conjunction with blue stain fungus or *Armillaria*.

Arborvitaes

Arborvitaes, also known as red or white cedar, do not deal well with hot, dry conditions like we often have in urban and suburban areas. Unfortunately we use them almost exclusively in these areas as screening plants. In fact, the trees can become stressed out by heat and drought south of USDA zone 6 unless carefully sited and tended. In nature, arborvitaes are found in cool swamps or around streams or lakes. They are also often found on neutral to alkaline soils. This is another stressor since many eastern soils tend to be acidic. Arborvitaes are often damaged by winter drought, with tip burn becoming noticeable very quickly if a sudden cold snap occurs before a sufficient hardening-off period. For this reason, the trees should receive a deep watering just before cold sets in. Arborvitae roots are very shallow, so appropriate mulch will also help them conserve moisture. Browning may follow a warm,

Hemlocks

If you see yellow banding on hemlock, chances are you have a case of *Cryptomeria* scale. This scale has a transparent, waxy cover and produces two generations a year. It gets on hemlock and true fir, turning them a grayish green with heavy infestations. The elongate hemlock scale may be present, as well, but is hard to control with contact products. Control is aimed at late May to early June, but crawlers continue to emerge throughout the entire growing season. These scales are easy to recognize by their parallel sides. Waxy filaments can fool you into thinking you have adelgids rather than male elongate hemlock scales. This scale may be especially prevalent on fir, as well.

Hemlocks are also an excellent example of why you should avoid pruning in hot weather and drought. These poor trees are subject to serious scorching when temps head over 95 degrees F. Branches may even be killed back several inches under these conditions. Hemlocks are also more sensitive to prolonged drought than a lot of other narrow-leaf evergreen plants, with the worst damage occurring on southern exposures, rocky slopes, or compacted areas where roots are unable to penetrate deeply. As if the poor things hadn't suffered enough, they are also exceptionally sensitive to ozone pollution, which frequently accompanies drought and heat in metropolitan areas.

dry wind if the ground is still cold or frozen. This might easily happen near a road or large building, which reflects heat. Arborvitaes are **not** a good choice near any area where saltwater might be thrown up on the foliage.

Be warned, as well, that although they are located near rivers and streams in nature, problems with ornamental plantings are often associated with waterlogged soils. Arborvitaes are listed as being moderately tolerant of water-logged soil, but that waterlogging has to be of an intermediate nature, such as a sudden storm, rather than constant soaking like you would experience with improper irrigation rates.

Insects of Arborvitae

Mites can cause yellowing and specking of foliage. A tap test onto a sheet of white paper is a great way to monitor for them. Remember that if you plant your arborvitae in full sun against a white wall, there will be no habitat for predatory mites, which can nearly always keep spider mite populations in check. A semishaded situation, on the other hand, allows predatory mites to survive. When monitoring arborvitaes, look for shriveled tips of branchlets, which indicate excessive dryness or a heavy infestation of spider mites.

Arborvitae leafminer can do a lot of damage.

Bagworms can make your arborvitae look as though it wears some strange ornaments!

Arborvitae leafminers are serious pests that overwinter as juveniles in mined-out foliage, feeding again for a very short period before pupating three to five weeks. The adult moths emerge in late spring and then lay eggs during late June and early July. If you hold the foliage up to the light, you'll see that the mined area is translucent; you'll also see emergence holes.

Adults are tiny and silver gray. If you look closely, you'll see that the forewings have brown and black markings. Eggs are pink and scalelike. The juveniles are only about $1/8$ inch long. They are yellowish green or sometimes pinkish with a shiny black head. These caterpillars burrow into the leaf scales beginning in summer, with peak feeding injury in fall. Juveniles tunnel into the growing points and kill affected arborvitae branch tips. Mining starts from the tip and then moves toward the base. Foliage yellows and then browns as damage progresses. You can prune out heavily infested twigs or branches, but bag and discard prunings in a remote location. unfortunately, arborvitae leafminers tend to be attracted to plants in shady places.

An arborvitae can lose up to 80 percent of its foliage from leafminer attack and still survive. But repeated attacks and defoliation gradually weaken the tree to the point that it becomes susceptible to other stress-induced diseases and insects; a combo attack can finish it off.

Bagworms prefer arborvitae to all other trees. Bags can be removed by hand during winter. Because bagworms are cold sensitive, they are not a problem on arborvitaes in their more northerly range. You can use *Bacillus* *thuringiensis* (*Bt*) to control bagworms, provided the application is timed correctly.

Snow blight tends to occur on arborvitaes during a cold, snowy year, especially if they are being grown on a potassium-deficient site. The snow blight fungus causes foliage under snow to appear matted together and brown. Removing snow promptly reduces the incidence of snow blight.

Cercospora **needle blight** symptoms are first noticeable in summer as necrosis and foliage discoloration on lower branches of the stem. Deeper foliage is attacked first, and the disease progresses up the tree until only the outermost foliage is left green. Diseased shoots drop off in October and November. The disease is spread by water.

Didymascella (*Keithia*) **leaf blight** makes arborvitaes unsightly. Light-brown to tan spots form on the leaves, followed by a large dark-brown spot in the center. This spot will eventually drop out, leaving an unsightly pit. Symptoms show up first on year-old foliage in spring as bleached areas. The dark-brown spot will be obvious by late June. Severely diseased twigs often fall off in autumn. If they don't, they bleach to a silvery-gray with dark cavities. Snow cover may make the disease worse. Individual scales brown first, followed by whole shoots and progressive dieback.

Younger trees are more susceptible. Initially the disease is seen with much greater frequency on the lowest branches. It will not kill plants older than four years. Be aware that an older specimen tree or hedge may harbor a light infection, which can jump onto a seedling or young transplant.

Sphaeropsis (*Diplodia*) **blight** problems are associated with stressed trees in droughty sites where other vegetation—such as turf—is competing for water. Excessive nitrogen also contributes to *Diplodia* outbreak, so hold the fertilizer, please! *Diplodia* will ravage plants stressed by excessive pruning or those with wounds caused by the ever-popular weedwackeritis. The best way to recognize *Diplodia* is by the black pepper dots embedded in the leaf tissue and shorter-than-normal needles. If you have Austrian pine nearby, which is very susceptible to *Diplodia*, you might want to consider a different planting.

Seridium **canker** can also wreak havoc on Leyland cypress. If your arborvitae needles are dying back from the tip, it could be environmental stress like drought or cold injury, or a root problem, but it could be due to a fungus called *Seiridium*. Recently pruned or wounded trees are the most susceptible.

White stringy rot can set in when roots are wounded, such as during transplant or when planting annuals in a bed surrounding the arborvitae. The rot starts out as pink to reddish brown and then becomes white, pitted, and stringy, with black flecks at an advanced stage. It is only a weak pathogen.

Armillaria root rot (shoestring rot) usually hits trees that are already weakened from some other stress. You may see clusters of mushrooms at the base of the tree during autumn when moist conditions are present. The plant's age does not seem to matter. Trees may be more susceptible to wind throw, which can be problematic since healthy arborvitaes are also subject to wind throw due to their shallow root system. You may see yellowing, branch dieback, decayed roots, and lesions that partially or totally girdle the plant at the root collar.

Resin or swelling near the root collar may be present. The resin may form crusty lesions in the root collar area, and because the root system is affected, the plant may wither and die very quickly. Excavate a root and carefully remove some of the bark over a diseased area. You should see a mat of cream or tan fungal threads if you have this disease. You may see narrow black ridges on the surface of diseased roots.

Armillaria *infection also plagues evergreens.*

The fungus is most common in areas where oak trees grow, or were growing, and in fact, the fungus can persist for many years in dead roots. Therefore, your most frequent symptoms occur in transplants that are three to four years old—at the point of transplantation, the fungus infects wounded roots and grows for several years before girdling the plant. If only a small portion of the root collar and root system is infected, you may be able to save the plant by aeration and exposing the root collar to drying conditions.

Normal Fall Browning

Don't mistake normal fall browning for a disease or insect problem. Arborvitae sheds its oldest branchlets in autumn, and the plant may appear to have very serious interior browning. This is perfectly normal for this time of year.

Pestalotiopsis is a weak pathogen frequently found on arborvitae. Tips of branchlets turn brown or tan, and then black pepper dots form beneath the browned tissue. Usually this fungus is a secondary invader on the oldest leaves killed by a primary pathogen or insect. It is especially prominent on arborvitae damaged by cold or stressful environmental conditions. The fungus grows from the tips towards the bases of the branchlets and occasionally can cause a shoot blight where the young shoots wilt and turn brown. Mulching the plants may help to reduce environmental stress and therefore disease.

Pestalotiopsis *forms black dots in straw-colored tissue on arborvitae.*

Phomopsis blight is common in arborvitaes near junipers and typically involves tip blighting of new leaves since old leaves are resistant. Lesions start out as little yellow spots, while new shoots fade to light green and then turn reddish brown. A gray band may appear at the base of the dead part of the shoot. Killed shoots hang on the plant and weather to gray. Black dots develop in the gray band three to four weeks after infection. Infection can occur any time during the growing season. Shearing and fertilization both promote extended infection periods, as does prolonged leaf wetness with warm temperatures. Clip off infected shoots when you see them, and disinfect pruners before using them again. The golden foliage types of *Thuja orientalis* are particularly affected.

Canker causes no harm to the tree, so if you see a patch of abnormally smooth bark on the trunk of your arborvitae that you suspect is a canker, don't despair. Arborvitae occasionally gets *Valsa* canker, an opportunistic fungus that colonizes plants weakened by environmental stress, cultural problems, overfertilization, wounds, or other diseases. The cankers may be sunken and leak resin. You may also see black, gray, or white dots just beneath the surface of the sunken area. With a hand lens and a sharp knife, shave a thin layer of bark off the cankered area; you should see a circle of clustered dark dots, which are diagnostic for *Valsa* canker.

Brown root and butt rot infects roots of any age or enters the stem via basal wounds (watch those weed whackers!). The wood is stained yellow to red and then rapidly becomes crumbly. After the rot has progressed a little farther, infected wood turns dark-brown and cracks into cubical pieces, which smell like turpentine and aniseed. If a mushroom forms, it has a velvety head.

This rot may also be found in association with *Armillaria* root rot, which may provide an avenue of infection. Shallow, badly drained soil can also be a predisposing factor, or sites that are alternately waterlogged and then too dry.

Broad-Leaf Evergreens

This group of plants encompasses such beloved favorites as Mahonia, laurel, holly, azalea, *Rhododendron*, oleander, boxwood, and *Camellia*. Laurel suffers primarily from leaf spot brought on by environmental stresses and from being snacked on now and then by scales or caterpillars. Mahonia suffers from winter burn when planted in areas where it is only marginally hardy, and occasionally from leaf spot or rust. Oleander suffers from minor scale and caterpillar problems, and the occasional leaf spot. For the most part, all these problems are relatively small. The bigger issues are reserved for the rest of the common evergreens on our properties.

Insects on Holly

Hollies can be planted in spring or fall but prefer spring to avoid winter desiccation.

Got unhappy holly? It may have wet feet. Choose a site with good drainage unless you are planting *Ilex cassine*, *I. myrtifolia*, or *I. rotunda*. American holly likes moist soil but requires good drainage. Or try winterberry holly, which is deciduous and thrives in swampy conditions. You'll need a male plant nearby to produce berries, and often a specific male variety at that! American holly, meserve blue hollies, and China series hybrid hollies are all susceptible to black root rot if grown in wet or poorly drained conditions.

Leafminers create much worse visual damage in American hollies. Although the maggot can make mines in English holly leaves, the fly cannot complete its development in English holly. One leafminer is specific to English holly, but its mines are not as unsightly as the native holly leafminer. Native holly leafminers overwinter as juveniles in the mine within the holly leaf. Adults hatch and begin to fly as soon as a few new leaves form. Eggs are laid on the underside of soft new leaves, creating small green blisters. The juveniles (maggots) begin to tunnel in the leaf, at first making narrow mines that look brown from the upper surface, then broader mines in late fall, which become even larger throughout winter, culminating in a big old blotch in late winter.

If you carefully open a mine, you'll find a yellow maggot (oh, the thrill) inside with a brown head capsule. The tree may drop many of its leaves in response to mining, and you are left with an ugly stick until new leaf growth begins the following spring.

The best times to treat native holly leafminers are mid-May through the first two weeks of July. Soil treatments can be put down from mid-April to mid-May.

An adult female also wounds the leaf when she feeds by using her egg layer as a Ginsu knife. She pokes a hole; then she and the nearby males (who are sponging off her—get a job!) drink the sap. The round, deep scars left by this feeding may cause the leaf to curl or distort. A close relative to the holly leafminer mines the leaves of inkberry.

Holly leafminer damage is readily visible late in winter.

Holly berry gall midge lives inside the green fruit and has a fungal associate that prevents the berries from becoming red. So if your green holly berries refuse to turn red, you may have been visited by this pest. There is a difference in holly cultivar sensitivity, with early blooming varieties much more subject to attack. Affected berries also tend to be smaller than normal.

Pit-making scale, a yellow-green scale, causes injuries on twigs that are $^1/_8$ to $^1/_2$ inch in diameter. Feeding results in pits of various depths in the bark. The juvenile scales most susceptible to treatment are present in late June.

Mite damage on your hollies in spring and fall is probably the southern red mite, especially if the worst damage is in May and June. A cool summer can cause the populations to really build up, resulting in a disastrous population explosion the following spring. Foliage of infested leaves is gray-green, compared to normally bright green foliage. Usually by the time the damage is visually noticeable, the mite populations have already boomed and declined. Diagnosis should begin in late March or early April. Look at the underside of the leaf with a hand lens for eggs, or rub the underside of the leaf over a piece of white paper and then look for a reddish stain from the crushed eggs.

Weevil juveniles can do tremendous damage to roots of hollies, yews, and *Rhododendron*, especially on small plants. Adult feeding is unsightly, with lots of notching that remains on the leaves until they fall off. Use 6-inch-wide aluminum flashing buried 2 inches in the ground coated with lithium grease (I'm not kidding, I found some in a hardware store) on the top 2 inches to build a chemical-free exclusion barrier. It works well, provided you maintain the grease layer.

Environmental Leaf Problems of Holly

Most leaf problems in hollies are actually caused by environmental problems. "Spine spot" is caused by holly leaf spines puncturing adjacent leaves (sort of like being in a crowded elevator with a bunch of blow fish). If you have days of high winds when new leaves are young and tender, the old leaves will easily puncture the youngsters. The spots are tiny at first but then enlarge to become tan with a purple margin.

Like other broad-leaf evergreens, hollies are also quite subject to sunscald. These lesions are light-tan to gray and up to 1 inch in diameter with a well-defined margin. Scald usually results when hot, direct sun dries the tissue of succulent young leaves. This may occur when a larger plant or building is removed and sun can penetrate areas where it couldn't before. Secondary fungi often colonize scald areas.

Purple blotching, a genetic problem, looks unsightly but means nothing. Small, brown, corky, raised areas on the underside of the leaf indicate the holly is in waterlogged soil or is being excessively irrigated.

Marginal scorching of holly leaves may be caused by high salt content either in soil or on leaves. It can also be caused by having a holly in a dry, windy environment. In this case, you'll usually see wilt first.

Monitor for adult presence by wrapping the base of susceptible plants with burlap, which the adults like to hide in during the day. Find out if they are there early in the season before they start laying eggs. The juveniles look like a legless white grub. Heavy feeding may result in poor plants that have off-colored leaves. Check just below the mulch or soil line to see whether the juveniles may have girdled the plant.

Holly Diseases

Tar spot produces yellow spots on leaves in early summer, which then progress to a reddish brown as the season goes on. In autumn, these spots turn black and tarlike. The disease is most severe during prolonged wet periods along shore areas. Don't crowd your plants, and do prune to improve air circulation. Remove fallen, diseased leaves. Avoid copper-based fungicides—these may injure hollies growing in certain kinds of soils.

Canker, along with twig dieback, on hollies is usually caused by *Phomopsis*, *Botryosphaeria*, and *Nectria*. These three thugs enter through wounds on the bark, so keep the weed whackers away. Prune out cankered branches.

Botrytis may blight your blossoms with gray mold during a prolonged wet period. The mold can spread to adjacent leaves and twigs, resulting in significant dieback. This disease is usually gone after a few days of dry weather, but an outbreak at blossom time can impact berry production later in the season.

Sooty mold covering holly leaves is usually the result of aphids or scale.

Insects of Rhododendron and Azaleas

Culturally, *Rhododendron* prefer partial shade as an understory plant; the protection in winter of having other larger plants around them keeps them from sunscald and winter desiccation. *Rhododendron* are shallow rooted, so remember that they will draw most of their moisture from the top 6 inches of ground, which in winter may be frozen solid. *Rhododendron* continue to lose moisture through their large leaves all winter long; that can result in dried-out plants and damage, come spring. Mulching the roots is helpful in both winter and summer to conserve moisture and moderate temperatures or freeze-thaw conditions.

So what pH does a *Rhododendron* or azalea prefer? Although they will both grow outside this range, a pH of 4.5 to 6.0 is optimal. If your plants are surrounded by concrete,

Nutrient deficiency is often due to incorrect pH.

are limed regularly, or receive excessive runoff from concrete or limed areas, the pH may not be optimum and, as a result, the plant is stressed. Most often in this instance, you'll see bright green veins surrounded by yellow leaf tissue.

Rhododendron gall midge juveniles feed on the undersides of young leaves, attacking them as they emerge from bud scales and expand. Feeding begins on the margins, which begin to roll up due to a hormone secreted by the juve-

Holly Leaf Drop

Hollies naturally lose some of their leaves in fall. Excessive leaf drop the following spring may indicate a severe drought or serious overwatering the previous season. With a cold, windy winter, the holly may drop lots of leaves during winter and then refuse to renew its leaves the following spring. This indicates that the holly in question is not really winter hardy for that site.

niles. This rolling gives the juveniles somewhere to hide. Tissue develops reddish spots and blisters, which eventually become chlorotic (yellowed) and often necrotic (too much "otic" for even a rhody to handle).

Intense feeding may result in death of new growth or failure of outer tissue to grow while inner tissue keeps going, resulting in a twisted, cupped look. You can scout your bushes for these twisted leaves any time of year—they are much easier to see than the actual insect. All ages of plants are affected, but young plants may be hit particularly hard. The midge is a native pest of *Rhododendron* in the east (it's actually a kind of minute fly). Adults are short lived, so emergence is closely linked with the host plant's lifecycle. Peak emergence happens the last week in May at the zenith of *Rhododendron* bloom.

Rhododendron gall midges cause leaves to roll up.

Techniques to cope with gall midge problems include hand-picking twisted leaves as soon as they show damage. Prompt removal is necessary—a monitoring program is essential. Another suggested alternative is to use plastic sheeting to prevent juveniles from burrowing in the soil and the adults from emerging. This last technique is not great for the plant, however. Since the midge is a native pest, there are undoubtedly natural checks on their populations. The best solution is plant resistance. Gall midges feed preferentially on *R. catawbiense*, its hybrids, and on *R. maximum* and *R.*

ponticum. Evergreen azaleas, *R. carolinianum*, *R. obtusum*, and *R. yedoense* are mostly resistant. Carefully researched pedigrees can also help with plant selection.

Aphids cause distorted leaves that are twisted and puckered. Aphid damage of this sort is often accompanied by sooty mold growing on honeydew residues left by the aphids. Look for discarded aphid skins on the undersides of leaves. Sooty mold also accompanies heavy infestations of scales, which are very common on azaleas.

Azalea bark scale may make the plant look thin and poorly, with small white cottony dots on the bark. Luckily, cold temperatures kill off as much as half of overwintering azalea bark scale. These pests get on *Rhododendron*, too, as well as on Japanese andromeda, poplar, and hawthorn. They are very easy to confuse with mealybugs! Azalea bark scale looks more porcupine-like under a hand lens. Treatment should be targeted from June to mid-July. Look for pink eggs and pinkish crawlers. If the dots on your azalea are hard brown bumps, then Lecanium scale is a likely culprit.

Azalea leafminer caterpillar begins its damage by producing brown, blister-type mines and then later tightly rolls the leaf. Plants are thin and scraggly and may experience premature leaf drop. Juveniles pupate in leaf debris, so this is one time when you are justified in removing and destroying fallen leaves. If only a few leaves are affected, squeeze them to kill the juveniles within their mines. Ha!

***Rhododendron* leafminer** starts mining at the leaf edge and then takes an abrupt, almost 90-degree turn across the leaf. All the tissue from that point until you reach the tip below turns yellow, then brown, then dies. There are usually so few you can just remove and destroy affected leaves.

Lacebugs cause fine yellowish speckling of leaf tops. If you look at the underside of the leaf, you may be able to see pepper-sized dots—the waste products of lacebugs. Transplant your shrub to an area with slightly more shade so that predators can do their thing without getting fried. Increase your variety of flowering plantings, as well, to support larger groups of beneficials.

Mysterious white dots on azalea? Finally, an answer! After much speculation, the culprit appears to be Japanese mealybug. This creep gets on azalea, *Rhododendron*, crabapple, maple, yew, *Zelkova*, and *Camellia*. Look for them between May and June on the lower leaf surface. Settled crawlers inject a toxin while feeding, resulting in white flecking and plant damage. Several other bugs can cause similar damage, so it may be a complex of beasties.

Black vine weevil and caterpillars seriously chew up your *Rhododendron* leaves. The adult beetle notches the leaves. Climbing cutworms or loopers

Environmental Issues of Rhododendron and Azaleas

Yellowing of margins followed by browning indicates potential root problems. These problems are normally brought on by overwatering in heavy soils or the plant's being buried too deeply or smothered by excessive mulch. Early "wet feet" symptoms include yellowing and wilting of newly emerged growth. Overall yellowing, principally on older or lower leaves, can be brought on by nitrogen deficiency. Suspect this if under-decomposed mulch is used around plantings. Yellowing with darker green veins can be caused by high pH or an iron or manganese deficiency.

If the tip of the leaf turns brown, as described for either *Rhododendron* leafminer or leaf spot, but you also see brown rimming the outer edges of the leaf, the plant may have marginal leaf necrosis, for which there are many causes. Cold, coupled with winter desiccation, can cause these symptoms, as well as good old summertime drought, especially on newly established plants. Planting too deeply, girdling by weevils, and excessive salt also produce these symptoms. Damage from salt is especially common close to the house when foundation plantings have eaves protecting the soil around them from rain, which would otherwise help to leach salts.

If you have *Rhododendron* with very small leaves, make note that this symptom is common on plants enduring cultural and environmental stress. Although the leaves themselves may appear normal except for their size, closer inspection may reveal differences compared to previous years, or you may see subtle color differences. A good check on whether what you did last year is having a positive effect is to see whether this year's new leaves are bigger than the ones you dealt with last year.

take irregularly shaped hunks out of leaves (leaving much larger holes than the weevils that may extend the entire way to the midrib, or perhaps stripping the leaves completely). Like the weevils, they are night feeders—and can be picked off and destroyed if you have only a few plants and are willing to get out there with a flashlight after dark. If you see a caterpillar doing this kind of damage during the day, it's likely a sawfly youngster rather than a caterpillar. A strong jet of water is just the thing to knock them to the ground, where they become easy prey for the birdies. Caterpillars may also roll, web, curl, or distort leaves. Telltale chewing tells you whether webbing is the result of spiders or caterpillars.

Diseases of *Rhododendron* and Azaleas

Root rots and stem diseases are legitimate diseases that can occur on even the most pampered and well-placed *Rhododendron* (although they are more prevalent on plants that are ill sited or ill managed). Sure signs of root rot are wilted, downward rolled leaves, which turn yellow but remain attached to the plant. Smaller, more fibrous roots will rot first, culminating in involvement of the entire root system. This leads to a brown discoloration of the lower stems, as well as the root system.

Phytophthora is a common culprit, and all root rots are exacerbated by poor drainage. The only cure is to rogue the plant out and **not reuse** the same planting hole. Stem diseases usually affect only a specific part of the plant, in contrast to root rots, which affect the entire plant. *Phytophthora* and *Botryosphaeria*, the two rascals, cause reddish brown or black sunken cankers, which may girdle the stem. Prune out diseased areas to a wide margin below the cankered area, and destroy the prunings. Make sure to sterilize your pruning shears before you move on to the next victim.

Leaf spots are not always fungal in nature. Some *Rhododendron* suffer from physiological leaf spot, caused by cultural or environmental stress. The spots are usually dark purple and do not have concentric rings, halos, or tan spots in the center. Although the exact cause is not known, check the normal parameters such as pH, shade, and water. Fungal leaf spots will normally have a "bull's-eye" appearance or have several colors associated with the spot, such as a reddish outer ring with a silvery center. Another symptom of fungal infection is that the entire tip or most of one side becomes brown and

Environmental leaf spot can fool you into thinking you have a disease.

brittle and you may see tiny, black, pepper-sized dots in this brown area corresponding to the production of spores.

Bud blight causes flower buds to turn brown and fall off prematurely in spring. Black bristles may appear as the frustrating fungus produces spores. Remove infected buds, disinfect between prunings, and destroy infected parts. If buds turn brown but do not fall off, or flowers open only partially, cold injury in late fall through early spring may be to blame. Slice them open and look for brown inside to confirm. Death of the newly emerged growth followed by leaf distortion just below is likely a result of late spring frost.

Physician, Heal Thyself!

Speaking of last year, did you put the plant in last fall? If you did, and you planted it too deep (I'll plug my ears if you want to confess, la-la-la-la), the plant may look like it is suffering the results of poor drainage. Some of these signs include reduced top growth; smaller, yellow leaves; and the potential for root rot. The crown of the plant should be even with the soil, but beware that the whole plant can sink as the soil in the planting hole begins to settle, and the accumulation of or excessive mulch can also bury roots way too deep. Bear in mind, too, that broken branches left by humans, animals, or weather can contribute to unsightly dead spots in the canopy. Rather than assuming you have a disease, get up there on a ladder if necessary and take a good look at what's going on.

Brown blotches that originate mainly on the central part of top leaves and more often on southern and southwestern exposures may be the result of sunscald. Syringing the foliage with water during the hottest part of the afternoon may help until some shade can be provided for the plant.

You may see irregularly shaped, shiny brown areas or interveinal or marginal yellowing, often on only one side of the plant. This can indicate chemical injury through drift or runoff.

Azaleas with brown buds may have root damage, causing the buds to dry out and eventually drop off.

Rolled or Drooping Leaves

Leaves will roll and droop down due to cold weather. They return to their normal shape when temperatures get warmer. If leaves do this in summer, they may be reacting to drought or it may signify root rot. Dead leaves will remain attached to the plant, so make sure you know what you are dealing with—dig up a little area to expose the root system and check things out if you are not sure.

Petal blight, a warm weather fungus, becomes quite severe in May, especially in muggy, buggy, misty, rainy weather. Are the flowers of your mountain laurels, azaleas, elepidotes (large-leaf *Rhododendron*), and lepidotes (small-leaf *Rhododendron*, such as PJM and Carolina types that have brown scales on the backs of the leaves) rotting before your eyes? Petal blight could be the culprit. Symptoms are brown spots and an eventual swoon of the entire flower into a brown, slimy mass. By the time you see the disease, the spores are everywhere.

If you get petal blight every year, a first spray of a fungicide should be applied when the early evergreen azaleas are showing color, and then once a week for four weeks, especially if the weather is rainy. The fungicide should cover flowers and buds that are showing color—leaf coverage doesn't help since this fungus attacks only flowers. For those of you following a low-maintenance program, a better bet might be to rip out susceptible cultivars and replant early bloomers that escape harm by being up and about before the fungus is.

Azalea leaf (*Exobasidium*) gall is a strange fungal disease primarily of azaleas and their relatives. The dominant symptom is leaves that swell into a bladder shape. Rid yourself of the problem by picking off and destroying the gall. Don't plant your azaleas in heavy shade; do increase air circulation. Avoid wetting foliage when watering in spring. The most severe problems occur with overhead irrigation during leaf expansion and high humidity in spring. Hand-pick the galls.

Algae may lightly coat the leaves of *Rhododendron* grown in heavy shade where it is chronically damp. No treatment is necessary—algae do no damage. Nor do lichens, which are often found growing on the bark of unthrifty plants. Lichens have a papery, gray-green appearance. Plants in deep, deep shade also tend to get spindly.

Powdery mildew causes some of the strangest symptoms of all on *Rhododendron*. Plants in the shade or in areas of poor air circulation are more likely to suffer this disease. The entire leaf is off color and coated with gray or whitish materials; the leaf undersides may be covered with pepper dots later in the season. The leaves may have diffuse yellow spots on the surface and weirdly arranged brown or tannish discolorations on the lower surface. This fungus can cause purple discoloration along the leaf veins, purple ring spots, or other permutations of the classic fungal leaf. Again, this is a case where you should rake up and discard fallen leaves to get rid of disease.

Septoria **leaf spot** of azalea can cause buds not to open and bud color to change from deep to pale.

Boxwood

One of the most common and frustrating things we see with boxwood as a broad-leaf evergreen is a rapid decline with no obvious cause. Some of it is linked to winter. Boxwoods often suffer severe winter damage, and they do not tolerate salt or poor drainage. Many times boxwoods are used to line a path or drive that then have copious amounts of road salts or de-icing materials applied, which becomes runoff—right into the boxwood roots.

If your *Rhododendron* particularly suffer from drainage issues due to wet springs, we can safely assume that boxwoods suffer similarly. When you add these factors together, along with the tight growth pattern of the favored

Volutella *blight on boxwood can make your plants look terrible.*

cultivars, you have a scenario ripe for disease of foliage and roots. Most of the problems we see in this situation stem from a combination of *Volutella* blight on the foliage. Root rot is often caused by *Phytopthora*. Many of you may actually have irrigated your plants more as they began to turn light green, thinking they were suffering from drought. This would have made the problem even worse. The best way to overcome these two diseases is to prune back dead stems to healthy tissue (although this may result in the loss of the formal lines and symmetry you planted the boxwoods for to begin with) and to remove all dead material that has fallen into the center of the plant and underneath. Mulch beneath the plant.

An application of lime sulfur or a copper-based fungicide in spring before new growth starts and after all dead material has been removed may be helpful in reducing symptoms of *Volutella* blight. Protecting the boxwood from winter damage also reduces its susceptibility to *Volutella*. Planting boxwoods in raised beds in heavy soil locations helps reduce problems with root rot from *Phytophthora*. For existing plants that are afflicted, you must not overwater, and you should try to incorporate organic matter into the soil around the roots to improve drainage. In the south, boxwood nematodes can increase the potential for root rots.

Index

Meet the Author

Tamson Yeh, Ph.D., received her bachelor's degree from Wells College, and a master's degree and a Ph.D. from the University of Rhode Island. She has written for publications such as *Long Island Newsday, American Nurseryman,* and *Golfweek's SuperNEWS.* She is a popular speaker on a variety of horticultural topics and has worked for the Cornell Extension Service for ten years, currently in Suffolk County. She was last seen in the company of two long-suffering children and a whole lot of pets. If she's seen holding a soil probe, she should be considered armed and dangerous.